THE POLITICS OF

FIELDWORK

THE POLITICS OF FIELDWORK

Research in an American Concentration Camp

LANE RYO HIRABAYASHI

THE UNIVERSITY OF ARIZONA PRESS
TUCSON

The University of Arizona Press
© 1999 The Arizona Board of Regents
All rights reserved
☉ This book is printed on acid-free, archival-quality paper.
Manufactured in the United States of America
04   03   02   01   00   6   5   4   3   2

Library of Congress Cataloging-in-Publication Data

Hirabayashi, Lane Ryo.
The politics of fieldwork : research in an American
concentration camp / Lane Ryo Hirabayashi.
p. cm.
Includes bibliographic references and index.
ISBN 0-8165-1864-5 (acid-free paper)
ISBN 0-8165-2146-8 (pbk.: acid-free paper)
1. Japanese Americans—Evacuation and relocation,
1942–1945—Research. 2. World War, 1939–1945—Concentra-
tion camps—Arizona—Poston—Research. 3. Poston Relocation
Center (Poston, Ariz.)—Research. 4. Poston (Ariz.)—History—
Research.
I. Title.
D769.8.A6 H58 1999   98-25489
940.54'7273'0979172—ddc21   CIP

British Library Cataloguing-in-Publication Data
A catalogue record for this book is available from the British Library.

The drawings by Jitsuo Kurushima reproduced in this book are
courtesy of Fusako Kurushima and the Bancroft Library, University
of California, Berkeley.

To
Hisako Tsuchiyama Roberts,
Joanne V. Hirabayashi,
and
Sofia Caballero Alquizola

CONTENTS

FIGURES

PREFACE

Tamie Tsuchiyama and JERS

During World War II, more than 30 American anthropologists participated in empirical and applied research on over 110,000 Japanese Americans who were subject to mass removal and incarceration by the federal government. However, the experiences of Japanese and Japanese American field assistants while carrying out much of this research have received little critical attention. How did these field researchers collect data in American-style concentration camps? What kinds of constraints and pressures did they face? How did they respond to practical, ethical, and political challenges? As a way of addressing these questions I have examined the case of the late Dr. Tamie Tsuchiyama, drawing from a combination of personal letters; ethnographic fieldnotes, reports, and other archival sources from the 1940s; original interviews taken in the 1990s; and published secondary sources.

In 1941, Tsuchiyama was an advanced doctoral student in anthropology at the University of California at Berkeley. Hired in 1942 as a staff member for Berkeley's Japanese Evacuation and Resettlement Study, Tsuchiyama entered Poston (a.k.a. the Colorado River Relocation Center) near Parker, Arizona, to perform ethnographic fieldwork there. Tsuchiyama was the only professionally trained Japanese American woman to carry out full-time research in an American-style concentration camp. Her personal correspondence from 1942 to 1944 allows us to reconstruct her fieldwork methodology, as well as the pressures leading up to her ultimate resignation, in protest, from the JERS project in 1944.

The concept of "colonial science" facilitates the critical analysis of Tsuchiyama's role in the Poston phase of the JERS research project. More than fifty years after the fact, Tsuchiyama's story also exemplifies how women of color, of junior status within the academy, may be subject to exploitation when they study their own "people" on behalf of senior Euro-American scholars. In this same sense, consideration of the use of Japanese and Japanese American research assistants by Euro-American social scientists during World War II is rich with lessons regarding the ethics and politics of ethnographic fieldwork.

ACKNOWLEDGMENTS

Everything I write, including this book, is constructed slowly, with the help of many different individuals.

I would like to acknowledge, first and foremost, Mrs. Hisako Tsuchiyama Roberts, who endured my repeated interviews and inquiries about the Tsuchiyama family and her younger sister, Tamie, with patience and grace. Listening to and learning from her made this project eminently worthwhile.

I couldn't have started this study without the encouragement and support of Professor Evelyn Hu-DeHart, the dynamic director of the Center for Studies of Ethnicity and Race in America (CSERA), which in January 1996 became the Department of Ethnic Studies (DES) at the University of Colorado at Boulder. At her behest, all the DES staff have helped me at one time or another, but I am most indebted to Amy Le, who carried out the task of transcribing Tsuchiyama's letters with meticulous care.

Many others have assisted me throughout, giving me feedback, advice, and support that were especially important at key moments: Noriko (Nikki) Sawada de Flynn, Arthur A. Hansen, James A. Hirabayashi, Yuji Ichioka, Madhulika Khandelwal, Brian Niiya, Roger and Lani Sanjek, Lowell Tsuchiyama, and Karen Umemoto. In addition, John W. Bennett, Malcolm Collier, George M. Foster, Katherine French, Arthur Harris, Gordon Hewes, Iwao Ishino, Gwenn M. Jensen, Frances Kawano, Ben Kobashigawa, Mitch Kunitani, Setsuko Matsunaga Nishi , S. Frank Miyamoto, Florence Mohri, Sue S. Kato, Alexander H. Leighton, Herbert Passin, Tamotsu Shibutani, James Sakoda, David Sills, Rosamond B. Spicer, Lily Utsumi-Shaw, James S. Yamato, Hisaye Yamamoto-DeSoto, Hisako Yamashita, Miwako Yanamoto, and Toshio Yatsushiro provided comments and insights about both Tsuchiyama, specifically, and the Japanese American experience, in general, for which I am very grateful.

Nelson H. H. Graburn, Chester Hashizume, Luis Kemnitzer, Leonard Mason, and Jere Takahashi responded quickly and informatively to my queries about Tsuchiyama's education in Hawaii and on the U.S. mainland.

Yuji Ichioka helped me resolve a number of questions regarding the *Poston Bungei* and enabled me to contact artist Jitsuo Kurushima's family. Eddy Masato Kurushima, Fusako Kurushima, and Pauline Fujino generously shared details of Jitsuo Kurushima's life and work. Jeffrey M. Handleman did the initial translations of the Japanese language texts that accompany Kurushima's drawings. I would also like to thank Kumiko Takahara of the Department of East Asian Languages and Literatures at the University of Colorado at Boulder for her comments and translations from a "native speaker's" perspective; these are the translations I have used here.

Dr. Bonnie Hardwick, head of the Manuscripts Department at the Bancroft Library, University of California at Berkeley, facilitated my access to key files and proffered sound advice about permissions. All of us who use the Japanese American Evacuation and Resettlement Study collection owe a great deal to archivist Elizabeth Stevens, who recently supervised the reorganization and microfilming of this vast collection of materials. Their colleagues—the librarians and staff at the Bancroft Library—dealt with my ongoing requests for microfilm and copies with unfailing professional courtesy.

My extended family is always a source of help and encouragement. My mother-in-law, Sophia C. Alquizola, endured, with her characteristic hospitality, my many visits to the San Francisco Bay area while I worked on this book. Marilyn Alquizola, James A. Hirabayashi, and Joanne V. Hirabayashi helped enormously by reading early drafts of the manuscript and offering cogent suggestions. Because—like Tsuchiyama—my mother, Joanne Hirabayashi, did graduate work in anthropology, subsequently obtained a master of library science degree at the University of California, and then worked for decades as a professional librarian, she has been a source of insights that were critical in developing the interpretations of Tsuchiyama's career advanced here.

Through their careful queries and editorial work, the staff of the University of Arizona Press helped me to finalize my manuscript. I would especially like to acknowledge the contributions of Joanne O'Hare, Alan M. Schroder, Christine Szuter, Kathryn Conrad, Mary M. Hill, and Linda Gregonis.

Finally, I would like to convey my deep thanks and appreciation to Professor Don K. Nakanishi, director of UCLA's Asian American Studies Center. Don and his colleagues offered me the opportunity to be a fellow of the endowed chair in Japanese American and Asian American Studies at the center during the 1995–96 academic year. In turn, the time and resources that the position at UCLA offered were integral to my being able to complete this manuscript in a timely fashion.

Despite all these contributions, I am solely responsible for the data and interpretations presented here.

THE POLITICS OF
FIELDWORK

1

INTRODUCTION

The late Dr. Tamie Tsuchiyama left a large body of fieldnotes, data, reports, and letters all having to do with her research in Poston, Arizona, an American-style concentration camp for Japanese Americans during World War II. These materials were collected for a University of California research project known as the Japanese American Evacuation and Resettlement Study (JERS), which employed then–graduate student Tsuchiyama between 1942 and 1944.

Tsuchiyama's JERS materials are fascinating in part because they represent a puzzling tragedy: despite the tremendous amount of time and energy that Tsuchiyama spent in collecting research data, as well as the amount of suffering she experienced, these data were not really used by anyone, including herself. At the same time, Tsuchiyama's files are intriguing because in the hands of a careful researcher they can still be used to gain unique insights into the political dynamics of the Colorado River Relocation Center, as Poston was officially known.

In order to find out more about her, I began to research Tsuchiyama's background. I found that no published data of any kind were available about her life, either before or after JERS, or about her fieldwork plans or methods. In this sense, even though she was a professionally trained anthropologist, Tsuchiyama is undoubtedly one of the most enigmatic figures who did full-time fieldwork on mass incarceration during the war.

As I learned more about her, I came to realize that Tsuchiyama, a second-generation Japanese American (or Nisei) born in Hawaii, was an intellectual pioneer in her own right. But although her graduate studies in anthropology began with great promise, her story is ultimately a sad one because it involves an unfulfilled and incomplete research project and a promising professional career gone awry. After two years of intensive fieldwork at Poston and after developing a very promising research agenda on politics there, Tsuchiyama quit her post as the study's primary fieldworker at Poston and never wrote about the camp again. How and why this happened has heretofore been a mystery, and it is the central event around which this book and my inquiries pivot.

The Significance of Tamie Tsuchiyama

Reserved, intentionally plain, and almost painfully shy, Tamie Tsuchiyama had been raised as a virtuous Nisei daughter; she was not the kind of person who would trumpet her own considerable intellectual talents or achievements. Before she died in 1984, she asked her sister to scatter her ashes at sea. She specifically and emphatically requested that her obituary be kept to a few short sentences.

Only five feet tall, Tsuchiyama weighed well under one hundred pounds before the war and only about seventy-five pounds during the last decade of her life. According to Mrs. Rosamond B. Spicer, an anthropologist who lived for a year with her husband, Edward H. Spicer, and their two-year-old son at Poston, "I remember her as being attractive, and *very tiny*, much smaller than any of the other girls." Mrs. Spicer liked her and recalled that she once bought Tsuchiyama "a gift of warm pajamas" but miscalculated; they were far too large for Tsuchiyama's slight frame.

Given these overt qualities, it is impressive, even striking, to discover that there was another side to Tsuchiyama: an intensity, a tenacious intellectual focus and drive, as well as a tremendous strength of will. These qualities were generally hidden from view but were nonetheless resources that sustained Tsuchiyama throughout her difficult career. Specifically, Tsuchiyama's passion for anthropology and her strong sense of justice provided a dynamic counterpoint to her generally retiring and introverted personality. And when her outrage over injustice was sparked and fanned into flames, as happened on occasion, the results could and did surprise and even amaze Tsuchiyama's associates and friends.

Despite her considerable academic accomplishments during the 1930s and 1940s, Tsuchiyama's dream of and aspiration for a professional career in her beloved field of anthropology were never realized. Nonetheless, Tsuchiyama's story, untold and largely forgotten today, is worth revisiting for its own intrinsic merits. I have no doubt, however, that, beyond this, her story represents a significant dimension in the history of anthropology and the social sciences for a number of different reasons.

Tsuchiyama was the first Asian American to earn a doctoral degree in anthropology from the then unusually large and prestigious department at the University of California at Berkeley. She is certainly also one of the first, if not the first, Japanese or Asian American of either gender in the United States to have completed a doctoral-level program in anthropology.

While an advanced graduate student in anthropology (she was at the "ABD," or "all but dissertation," stage), Tsuchiyama spent two years living in and carrying out fieldwork in Poston. This achievement is all the more remarkable because Tsuchiyama was the only Japanese American woman during the war years with professional training in the social sciences to be hired full-time to work as a researcher in the War Relocation Authority camps; all the other Japanese Americans doing fieldwork at this level were men.

Perhaps as central as her own accomplishments is the fact that Tsuchiyama's experiences as a fieldworker remind us of the sometimes fragile social relationships upon which anthropological research is predicated. Tsuchiyama was employed by Professor Dorothy Swaine Thomas, a Euro-American scholar, to collect ethnographic data in Poston under difficult and occasionally dangerous conditions. When Tsuchiyama was no longer of use to Thomas, their relationship deteriorated and finally ended in 1944.

An Ethnographer's Epiphany

Anyone who has perused the file containing the 1942–1944 correspondence between Professor Dorothy Thomas, director of the University of California's Japanese American Evacuation and Resettlement Study (the largest nongovernmental research project focusing on the mass incarceration of over 110,000 persons of Japanese descent during World War II), and then–anthropology graduate student Tamie Tsuchiyama has noted the disagreement and bitterness that characterized their final exchange. It represents, in my view, an epiphany for Tsuchiyama, that is, a key moment representing a culmination of linked events that changed her life forever.

Specifically, on July 28, 1944, Thomas wrote to Tsuchiyama and expressed her concern and disappointment because the quality of Tsuchiyama's penultimate report was "distinctly below standard." While noting that her baseline for this evaluation was, in fact, Tsuchiyama's previous research, Thomas emphasized that "the interests of the [JERS] study quite clearly call for 'production.' I would define 'production' as a finished performance, utilizing all the wealth of detail that you must have at hand. I would naturally expect a report superior in both quality and quantity to the 40-odd pages that represent your total output over the last nine months." This much said, Thomas still offered Tsuchiyama a chance to redeem herself, although examination of correspondence that was simultaneously being exchanged between Thomas and another JERS staff member, Richard S. Nishimoto, about retrieving all of Tsuchiyama's data should she quit suggests that Thomas was not optimistic about the outcome. "If you are willing to face the implications of this situation with complete frankness and to do the professional job of which your earlier performance indicates you are capable," Thomas wrote, "I hope you will continue [to work for JERS]. May I hear from you about this by return mail?"

Tsuchiyama's reply, dated July 31, must have been fired off on the same day that she received Thomas's letter. Beginning with "Dear Dorothy" (as she had addressed Professor Thomas in her correspondence since late 1942), Tsuchiyama responded: "Since I am reluctant to make any promises which I may not be able to fulfill *to your satisfaction*, I am requesting for the last time to be released from the Study as of July 15, 1944, to pursue other activities which are more acceptable to me. From the very beginning we have not seen eye to eye on how the Japanese should be studied so I see no advantage to you in my continuing further" (emphasis in original).

Soon after Tsuchiyama wrote this letter, she resigned from JERS. As far as I can determine, she never had contact with Thomas or any of her former JERS colleagues again. And although she finished her Ph.D. in 1947, in less than one academic year of residence at Berkeley, Tsuchiyama's dissertation was not on Poston or any of the other camps; nor did she ever, during her lifetime, publish a single article based on the fieldwork she had carried out during World War II at considerable intellectual and personal cost.

Interrogating History, Interrogating Anthropology

At one level, then, I seek to provide insight into Tsuchiyama's life itself. As a pioneer in her own right whose intellectual formation, accomplishments, and professional demise (in anthropology, anyway) have been neglected if not erased, Tsuchiyama's story begs to be told.

Although her life and the events surrounding it are now largely a matter of history, Tsuchiyama's story raises a number of key issues that have contemporary relevance beyond their biographical subject. Most notably, when placed in context, Tsuchiyama's life and work have broader implications for our understanding of the roots and assumptions of anthropology, as well as in terms of the production of anthropological data and thus knowledge.

At another level, Tsuchiyama's biography illuminates previously unanswered questions about her research at and on Poston. Tsuchiyama's fieldnotes and reports offer a somewhat different "take" on that camp, specifically, and on the Japanese Americans who were subject to mass removal and mass incarceration, generally. This was because of her background as an American of Japanese ancestry from the then Territory of Hawaii as well as the way that personal and intellectual circumstances between 1942 and 1945 interacted with and ultimately affected her research efforts. In this fashion, biographical information about Tsuchiyama helps us to appreciate an epistemological feature of the qualitative social sciences: the intimate linkage between a given researcher's background and intellectual formation, on the one hand, and the setup and exigencies of a specific research project such as JERS, on the other. This linkage also has methodological implications that are imparted to the resulting data, whether consciously rendered or not, as I detail below.

Similarly, an understanding of Tsuchiyama's biography and experiences as a fieldworker for JERS also heightens the contemporary value of the data and reports that she wrote for the Japanese American Evacuation and Resettlement Study during World War II. As I have developed it here, then, Tsuchiyama's story thus offers a paradigm that I hope will aid scholars who choose to study and utilize JERS's (and similarly produced) research data from "inside" these American-style concentration camps.

Still other issues, some of which mainstream anthropologists might find annoying, can be raised via Tsuchiyama's story.

In a provocative article published in 1993, the anthropologist Roger Sanjek exhorted colleagues to acknowledge the "intellectual colonialism" that has often characterized the relationship between Euro-American ethnographers and the people of color who have actually collected the field data upon which the former's ethnographies are based. Basing his critique on a short but very disturbing history of field "assistants and their ethnographers," Sanjek raises a series of questions that anthropologists and historians of the discipline should inquire into more systematically. Who actually collected the data for a given project? How and why were these data collected, and at what costs to the researcher(s) of color? Specifically, what does it mean, both in terms of the data and in terms of the field itself, when anthropologists utilize the services of "local" field assistants in order to get access to and actually to collect the primary data for a study? In the end, who profits from these efforts, especially in the sense of having access to the rewards that the opportunity to analyze, write, and publish the data in a formal ethnography entail?

I agree with Sanjek's queries: all these matters are well worth exploring in an effort to construct a more accurate and complete history of anthropology that does not erase issues, in regard to fieldwork, of hegemony, that is, the ability of one group to dominate another through a "combination of political and ideological means." In terms of thinking about the Thomas and Tsuchiyama relationship and keeping Sanjek's queries in mind, my initial point of inquiry is, why would what began as a mutually agreed upon relationship between two fascinating women—a graduate student (Tsuchiyama), on the one hand, and a professor/mentor (Thomas), on the other—as well as such a promising professional beginning (Tsuchiyama's) come to such an acrimonious end? Was Thomas, who is now widely regarded as having had a strong proprietary interest in her employees' data, merely acting out her role as a "responsible" project director? JERS was, after all, one of the largest privately funded research projects of its day, and Thomas's appointment as director was hard won; thus Thomas may have wanted a great deal of control because she felt she was subject to the scrutiny of colleagues and funding agencies alike on an ongoing basis.

Was this why Thomas felt free, alternatively, to try to coax and then to force more data out of Tsuchiyama in what can be retrospectively characterized as a kind of "carrot-and-stick" approach to intellectual mentorship? Is it naive to expect that such a vertically structured relationship between two persons of such unequal status and power could have turned out any differently than it did in the end? Alternatively, was Thomas, as a product of her times, the kind of social scientist who regarded "persons of color" (i.e., Tsuchiyama) as mere instruments, "data gatherers" whose time, energy, resources, and connections were to be made available—by means of the implied promise of future rewards—for more senior Euro-American scholars to exploit? Was Tsuchiyama aware of this possibility, in terms of Thomas's views and intentions? Did both parties only become overtly aware of this possible dimension of the relationship toward the end? If they did, can we reconstruct their respective reactions and how the realization altered their strategies as project director and as ethnographic fieldworker within the context of the larger JERS project?

There are other key questions that should be raised from the beginning. How do gender and race fit into the overall equation? Beyond their age, class, and status differences, was Tsuchiyama exploited by Thomas and then marginalized because she was a woman, especially because, as institutional settings, both the academy and Poston (in terms of formal politics) were largely dominated by the efforts and aspirations of men? Or was Tsuchiyama not taken seriously because she was a Japanese or Asian American woman? These are intriguing questions, all the more so because, as we shall see, Thomas herself had expressed deep concern over her own exploitation and marginalization as a woman in regard to the ranking of her tenured faculty position at the University of California (she was initially appointed as an associate professor at the University of California rather than a full professor) and in terms of her (ultimately successful) struggle to become the sole director of JERS.

Tsuchiyama's career trajectory in the post–World War II era reinforces the importance of such questions because, despite her doctorate and her path-breaking professional efforts, Tsuchiyama herself was never able to obtain a position, formal or otherwise, in her beloved field of anthropology. Given that even as stellar a figure as the late Margaret Mead never held a formal tenured professorship (although this may have been partly her preference by the time she was in her sixties), perhaps it should not be surprising that Tsuchiyama should fail to win a full-time faculty position. Still, it is troublesome to learn that Tsuchiyama could have worked so hard and was apparently capable of brilliance but received so little in return for her dedication. Institutional racism between the 1900s and the 1950s typically curtailed Japanese Americans' career opportunities, no matter what their abilities and accomplishments were. Tsuchiyama's story thus provides a vantage point on the professional career trajectories of first- and second-generation men and women of Japanese descent in the United States before and immediately after World War II.

After considering Tsuchiyama's life and work, especially in the context of the JERS project, I will return to the issues delineated in this introduction. I argue that we can best explore these questions by linking them to what both Sanjek and French sociologist Pierre Bourdieu propose as hidden colonial dimensions that are all too often deleted from the official histories of the social sciences. In this sense, examination of the historical past of the discipline, via the story of Tamie Tsuchiyama, Dorothy Thomas, and the JERS project, is rich with insights—historical and contemporaneous—in terms of <u>rethinking the politics and ethics of fieldwork</u>, especially when senior scholars of one color deploy junior scholars of another color to collect research data under difficult and sometimes dangerous circumstances. Thus, although the people and places I write about here have changed or are gone, I will show how and why this story offers a distinctive vantage point on issues that are still pertinent to sociocultural anthropology and its sister disciplines such as sociology.

Tsuchiyama's Correspondence

Since I was born after the war, I have found archival materials an especially valuable window into the Japanese American experience of mass incarceration. As in an earlier book on the Colorado River Relocation Center, *Inside an American Concentration Camp: Japanese American Resistance at Poston*, I have included primary materials—namely, a select number of Tsuchiyama's letters from 1942 to 1944—in the text itself. This gives readers access to key archival data I have found as well as a basis to evaluate independently the strengths and weaknesses of my interpretations.

Methodologically speaking, while the Tsuchiyama letters offer a window into a unique research situation, they have important limitations. They must be screened, in part, through a biographical reconstruction of Tsuchiyama's life, education, and professional trajectory just as they must be seen vis-à-vis the Japanese American Evacuation and Resettlement Study project and its director, Dorothy S. Thomas. Thus, we must constantly bear in mind the kinds of biases that each party brought to the JERS project, as well as the kinds of assumptions and pressures that were generated by the project itself. These are all issues I discuss in this book, but, from the beginning, I would like to emphasize the remarkable nature of Tsuchiyama's letters at a number of different levels.

First, the letters are the closest we are going to be able to come to understanding <u>Tsuchiyama's field research methodology</u>. This is significant both because of the quantity of material that she left on Poston and because Tsuchiyama was the only professionally trained woman of Japanese ancestry who was hired to carry out full-time fieldwork in an American-style concentration camp. (Of course, many, perhaps hundreds of, Japanese American high school and college students were hired to gather, process, and type up data in camp for one of the three major research projects that were carried out independently during the war. Japanese American fieldworkers who had received actual social science training were few in number, were typically Nisei who were advanced undergraduate or graduate students, and were almost exclusively men.)

Second, Tsuchiyama's letters offer us many fascinating details about day-to-day life in the camps, especially when they are read in tandem with Tsuchiyama's extensive sociological journal and field reports.

Third, the letters offer us an actual voice; that is, they provide the fullest account available of the rigors of fieldwork for Tsuchiyama, in her own words and from her own point of view. Some letters are extremely candid, revealing the raw emotions engendered by the difficulties of her research. Readers should also recall that family and personal correspondence from the camps was overtly censored at first and then, in many cases, self-censored. Thus, even Tsuchiyama's family received almost no information concerning her research at Poston, and I am certain that few "on the outside" besides her academic mentors really knew what Tsuchiyama was doing between 1942 and 1944.

In sum, a decade after I first read them, Tsuchiyama's letters have become the wellspring of much of the book that follows. They have allowed me to get to know Tsuchiyama as a fledgling anthropologist and fieldworker and have provided key information that enabled me to put her life and experiences back on the record. The letters thus fill in many gaps about Tsuchiyama's orientations, methods, and research findings that would otherwise remain empty. Most importantly, as the letters indicate, many of Tsuchiyama's difficulties in the field, leading up to her resignation from JERS, had to do with profound ethical and political dilemmas. I show this by reconstructing her training and her fieldwork experiences at Poston between 1942 and 1944. Tsuchiyama's work for the JERS project during this period raises difficult questions concerning field research in insecure and sometimes dangerous situations, the production of knowledge in anthropology and the social sciences, and intellectual authorship—questions that social scientists have yet to fully resolve. Painful though it might be, awareness and discussion of the ethics and politics of ethnographic fieldwork, as well as the further consideration of professional standards, can be sharpened through the examination of historical cases such as the one I present here.

ROOTS

A Nisei Daughter from Hawaii

Tsuchiyama's parents, both from Hiroshima prefecture, were Issei, or first-generation immigrants. Originally from the village of Kawa-sa in the county of Ashina, Nakazo Tsuchiyama, Tamie's father, born in 1875, was the youngest son of several children. When his mother died, his father remarried, and soon Nakazo had a stepbrother. Since he now had a sibling who would be heir to their father's estate, Nakazo Tsuchiyama decided to seek opportunities abroad. The family believes that he came to Hawaii, perhaps with a distant cousin, and stayed on the islands for a while before deciding to return to Japan to get married.

Although many Issei sent back to Japan for their brides, it was also not uncommon for a man to return himself in order to get married. Nakazo Tsuchiyama's bride, Yumi Sakamoto, born in 1879, came from the village of Morota in the county of Mitsuki, about two hours' walk from Kawa-sa. After spending a couple of years in Japan, the pair returned to Hawaii, close to the town of Lihue on the island of Kauai. Mr. Tsuchiyama began farming in Nawiliwili, a small valley near Lihue, initially specializing in table vegetables. By 1920, however, following a shift in crops that had already been pursued by most of the family's neighbors, the Tsuchiyamas were growing rice exclusively.

According to official War Relocation Authority (WRA) records, which are correct on this matter, Tamie Tsuchiyama was a second-generation U.S. citizen of Japanese ancestry, born on May 8, 1915, on the island of Kauai, Territory of Hawaii. Tamie was the third child. She had an elder brother, Kazuo, who was eleven years old, and a sister, Hisako, who was two.

Tamie was a somewhat sickly child. Between the ages of two and four she became quite ill on at least two occasions and almost died both times. These early illnesses may have resulted in a severe kidney ailment that was only diagnosed later in Tsuchiyama's life. Her sister, Hisako, commented, "We all gave in to [Tamie] in later years, remembering that we had nearly lost her as a child." Beyond this, however, Hisako's memories are of a pleasant childhood for the Tsuchiyama children, playing at the edge of their father's fields.

Unfortunately for the family, Tamie's father passed away on January 18, 1920. Because of the relative youth of the three smallest children (Hisako was seven; Tamie was five; and the youngest son, Tsugio, was only eighteen months), Mrs. Yumi Tsuchiyama had to stay at home. There, she did the best she could to manage the rice farm. Fortunately, the Tsuchiyamas' neighbors had formed a cooperative work group, although hiring wage laborers was sometimes necessary. Mrs. Tsuchiyama would join them, and together, working as a team, they would make sure that everyone's fields were planted and harvested in a timely fashion. At sixteen, Kazuo, the *sōryō*, or eldest son, made a great sacrifice in order to fulfill family obligations: he quit school. Going to work as a clerk in a large store run by one of the local plantations in Lihue, Kazuo, along with his mother, did the best he could to help provide for the family. Beyond sustenance, the immediate goal was to get and keep the younger children in school. "*Oka-san*, our mother, was sold on education," Hisako Tsuchiyama explained to me, "and she would do anything to support us." Back in Japan, her family, the Sakamotos, had sent Yumi to school, much to the amusement and derision of some village residents. The shame entailed in the gossip and teasing eventually resulted in Yumi's being withdrawn from classes; nonetheless, the experience had left its mark, and Mrs. Tsuchiyama was determined that her younger children would continue their schooling at whatever cost.

Because of his sacrifices, Kazuo earned the respect of the community. Putting aside his own needs to assume responsibility for his mother and younger siblings resulted in an elevated status in the eyes of neighbors, an esteem that the younger Tsuchiyama sisters didn't achieve even with their accolades in school and, later on, in the university. Hisako Tsuchiyama emphasized that she admired the Nisei *sōryō* because, like her own brother, they had such a difficult time, but they were <u>filial (*oya koko*)</u>, dedicating their lives, even after their own marriages, to fulfilling the needs of their family. A *sōryō* had to do well enough to care for his elderly parents, bring up his own children successfully, and then retire in such a fashion so as not to be a burden on anyone in old age.

This situation also created a strong sense of obligation toward the family in Hisako, Tamie Tsuchiyama's elder sister. While Hisako, at the age of fifteen, was able to go to the U.S. mainland in 1928 in order to continue her education at Los Angeles High School, Los Angeles Junior College, and then UCLA, she had made a self-imposed commitment to return eventually to Hawaii and do her share for the family. She kept this promise even though, in the end, she had to make educational and career sacrifices in order to do so. She even turned down a full scholarship that would have allowed her to enroll in a doctoral program at Wellesley, a private college for women in Massachusetts.

Hisako described Tamie as a very enthusiastic child insofar as school was concerned. Tamie was so anxious to go to school that, even before she was old enough to enroll, she would demand to go along with Hisako to the Lihue Grammar School. Like all local children who did not initially speak English, Tami was first placed in a "receiving grade" instead of in kindergarten. There she gained enough of a command of English to be enrolled in regular classes. Because of this arrangement, a grammar school education took nine years, instead of eight, for many of these Nisei children, although they might be allowed to skip a grade if they were apt pupils.

Although the Tsuchiyama children never went to Japan before the war, the official WRA records indicate that Tamie was able to speak, read, and write Japanese. This was in part because of the family's Issei parents: all the Tsuchiyama siblings spoke Japanese at home as their first language. Contrary to what was recorded on the WRA's Form 126 (a census form), Tsuchiyama did in fact attend a local language school—the Lihue Japanese school, or *nihongakkō*—a couple of blocks away from her grammar school. For about eight years she studied Japanese for an additional hour each day after her regular classes before going home. Although attendance at this school might seem to suggest an anti-assimilationist stance on the part of Tsuchiyama's parents, this was not the case at all. In regard to religion, for example, the WRA records list Tsuchiyama's affiliation as "Christian or Protestant." While true, this cold statistic hides an interesting story that illustrates a profound dimension of the lives of many Nisei in Hawaii.

Tsuchiyama's mother decided to send the Tsuchiyama children to the Congregational Church in Hawaii. Her choice of denomination is especially significant, because the Congregational Church was essentially the church of the Puritans, and Mrs. Yumi Tsuchiyama intentionally exposed her children to it for this very reason. "This is your land, and this is your religion," she told them as she sent them off to church. This is all the more interesting because both of Tamie's parents retained their respective religious commitments. Mr. Tsuchiyama had been a Zen Buddhist. Mrs. Tsuchiyama would apologize to the children as she went off to services at another local temple, saying, "Please excuse me if I go to the Nishi Hongwanji; I was brought up this way, and it is all that I know." Fully consistent with this approach to her children's religious instruction, Mrs. Yumi Tsuchiyama went to the Japanese consular agent in Kauai and had the Japanese side of her children's dual citizenship status revoked in 1927. In her view, in terms of their nationality the Tsuchiyama children should be Americans.

Pragmatic decisions along these lines clearly shaped Tamie's identity during her early years. They also help us to understand the shock that Tsuchiyama experienced when she observed the federal government's policy of mass incarceration of Japanese Americans on the U.S. mainland as well as her surprise and, on occasion, her contempt when Japanese Americans at the camp at Poston overtly expressed seemingly anti-American sentiments.

In 1930, Tamie Tsuchiyama graduated from Lihue Grammar School and enrolled in Kauai High School. Her transcripts indicate that she pursued an academic track, studying algebra, geometry, and chemistry as well as French and Spanish.

Studying Anthropology

After she graduated in the spring of 1933, Tsuchiyama decided to work for a year before leaving Kauai for the island of Oahu. In the fall of 1934 she enrolled at the University of Hawaii (UH) at Manoa, near Honolulu. While she was still a lower division student, Tsuchiyama discovered her professional vocation: upon enrolling in an upper division anthropology course, Tsuchiyama did so brilliantly that her professor, Dr. Felix M. Keesing, was very surprised when he discovered that she wasn't an upperclassman. Finishing at the top of her class, Tamie became one of Keesing's prize students. Tsuchiyama duly served as one of his readers, and Keesing encouraged her to pursue anthropology further. Because Keesing was the only anthropology professor at the university at that time, Tsuchiyama had to go to the U.S. mainland in order to pursue further course work. Thus, in the summer of 1936, after finishing her freshman and sophomore years at UH, Tsuchiyama left the islands in order to join her older sister, Hisako, in Los Angeles. Tsuchiyama enrolled at UCLA,

Tamie Tsuchiyama as a junior at UCLA, 1937. (Photograph by Toyo Miyatake; courtesy of Archie Miyatake)

where she completed her junior year in 1936–37. Her sister, Hisako, remembers that their waking hours were devoted to their respective classes and teaching assistantship duties. Their life was austere.

The year that Tamie came to L.A., we were living up in the Pacific Palisades area. To go shopping, we would have to walk up through Topanga Canyon out to Santa Monica Boulevard, to a large market. Usually, we'd pick up some breast of lamb at five cents a pound. (We didn't buy the stew meat, because it was twelve cents a pound, and I liked lamb better anyhow.) Then we would ask for some vegetables to add to our stew. Well, they would take a large carry-out bag and fill it with all kinds of vegetables: potatoes, carrots, corn, lots of things. We'd ask, "How much?" and they would only charge us ten cents for the whole bag, even though it should have been much more.

Today, some sixty years later, Hisako remembers the kindness of these Japanese American store owners; she feels sure that somehow they knew that the Tsuchiyama sisters—"these two small Nisei girls"—were trying their best to work their way through the University of California and generously gave them fresh produce for so little money.

Although her finances were limited, Tsuchiyama's abilities were quickly recognized at UCLA. Doing as brilliantly there as she had at UH, Tsuchiyama was named an honor student in 1937. She was quickly appointed as a reader by the single anthropologist on the UCLA campus, Professor Ralph Beals. Beals had arrived at UCLA in 1936, and he was hired with the special charge of building an anthropology department on that campus. Like Keesing, Beals was the only professor of anthropology at his university during his first years there. Since Beals didn't actually get a department going until 1941, it was also impossible for Tsuchiyama to pursue an undergraduate degree in anthropology at UCLA.

Once again, and now at the age of twenty-one, Tsuchiyama decided to move, this time in order to enroll at the University of California at Berkeley for the fall semester of 1937. In contrast to UH and UCLA, Berkeley did have a large, well-recognized anthropology faculty, and the department did offer an undergraduate degree program in the field.

Arriving in Berkeley, Tamie obtained lodgings with a schoolteacher. Her space was an upstairs living room that had a couch for a bed, a breakfast room, and a wonderful view of the Bay Bridge, which connects San Francisco to Oakland. The place was within walking distance of the University of California, and Tamie rented it for fifteen dollars a month.

I asked Hisako if her sister's move and their separation created any sort of problem in terms of this very small, very young looking Nisei woman moving up north and living on her own. According to Hisako, Tamie was so highly motivated, so focused, and so intense that her goal (a degree in anthropology) made her able to put aside any doubts or obstacles. If the move would allow her to pursue her goal, she was ready and willing to go out to Berkeley—alone, if need be. Money, though, was a major consideration. Before she moved to Berkeley, Tamie's elder brother, Kazuo, who was still working and contributing to his family, had sent Tamie a stipend during her undergraduate years. He continued to do so when she was in graduate school without the knowledge of the rest of the family.

With her prodigious appetite for her studies, Tsuchiyama excelled. She was named a member of both the Phi Beta Kappa and Sigma Chi honor societies. Taking only one academic year to finish up her baccalaureate, Tsuchiyama received her bachelor of arts in anthropology with honors from the University of California on May 21, 1938. While her undergraduate concentration was in anthropology, Tsuchiyama also did twelve units each in English and Japanese, ten units in German, and nine units each in political science and psychology.

After obtaining her degree, Tsuchiyama applied and was admitted to graduate school in the Department of Anthropology at Berkeley in August 1938. For the next three years, she worked with some of the leading figures in the field who were then members of the Berkeley faculty, including Professors A. L. Kroeber, Robert H. Lowie, and Paul Radin. Tsuchiyama found mentors in both Lowie and Radin. She became quite close to Paul Radin, who employed her as one of his readers; she would also occasionally house-sit his residence when he and his family were out of town. Of all the Berkeley anthropology faculty, Radin took the greatest interest in Tsuchiyama's graduate career, but before the war he left to pursue other professional opportunities in North Carolina.

It is important to note here that her older sister, Hisako, tried to discourage Tamie's ambition to do graduate work in anthropology. This was not because of her intellectual abilities, which Hisako acknowledges were outstanding, but rather because of Hisako's perception that there were simply no opportunities for a second-generation Japanese American, either in external scholarships or funding but especially in viable job prospects, even with a Ph.D. from the University of California at Berkeley. In addition, because of the family's economic circumstances, Hisako encouraged Tamie to consider a more practical career. Because of their situation, Hisako notes that Tamie had obligations to the rest of the family, too, and that she should have taken these into consideration when making key career decisions. Hisako remembers, however, that Tamie would not be budged. Hisako told me that Tamie was bound and determined to study anthropology at the graduate level, and nothing anyone said could deter her from this goal. In the context of the Hawaii-based Japanese American family of the 1930s, such determination might be seen as self-absorbed and stubborn, if not selfish. Nonetheless, when Hisako informed Tamie about her decision to return to Hawaii, Tamie reportedly responded, "I don't care what you do, but I am going on and getting my Ph.D." Sixty years later, Hisako's commentary was that "little did Tamie realize that her decision, concerning graduate studies in the field of anthropology, was going to turn out to be such a tragedy."

Finally acceding to Tamie's wishes, the family continued to underwrite her studies, as there were no fellowships or grants available. Having returned to Hawaii in 1938 and now working as a teacher, Hisako told Kazuo that she would take charge of this responsibility. Hisako began to send Tamie the same sum of money that her brother had been sending to her, thirty-five dollars a month, an amount that in those days was more than enough to cover all basic expenses. Hisako continued to send money every month from 1938 until 1942, when Tamie, who by then was in camp, asked her to stop.

With such support, Tsuchiyama's studies continued unabated. She took a wide-ranging set of courses and received A's in the fourteen out of nineteen grades posted on her transcripts; the rest were B's. She was actually quite well versed in Polynesia as a culture area and had planned to prepare this as a subject for her doctoral exams. However, in the end she was unable to do so, because none of the Berkeley anthropology faculty had the requisite expertise to test her knowledge.

By May 1941 Tsuchiyama had passed her comprehensive (doctoral-level) exams. A. L. Kroeber, who has sometimes been characterized as a misogynist insofar as women in the field of anthropology were concerned, actually wrote to her family in Hawaii, saying that she had passed "with flying colors." Later that same month, however, Tamie's mother, Mrs. Yumi Sakamoto Tsuchiyama, passed away in Kauai. Because her mother had taken ill suddenly, and because they knew that Tamie was preparing for her exams, her siblings decided not to notify Tamie in order to spare her any worry. When their mother died just as suddenly, the children were shocked. They quickly sent a short letter to

Tamie, but she was not able to get back to Hawaii in time to attend her mother's funeral. Their mother's death was a devastating blow for all of the Tsuchiyama children.

On May 19, 1941, the day her mother died, Tamie Tsuchiyama had gone out to Golden Gate Park with friends to celebrate the end of finals. She had come back very late. Around two A.M. Tamie had gone to bed and was dozing when she heard, very clearly, a woman's voice calling to her, "Tami-yo." Later, when telling her sister about this, Tsuchiyama told Hisako that her mother was the only one who had ever called her "Tami-yo." The voice, their mother's voice, spoke to Tamie, saying, "Mother is waiting for you. Study hard and return as soon as you can." Then Tsuchiyama felt a hand reach out and stroke her hair. Tamie told her sister that the touch was so physical, so real, that she sat up in bed and put out both of her hands in order to touch the hand that was stroking her hair. There was nothing there.

Would Tsuchiyama ever think of her mother's death as a portent of things to come? Certainly, growing tensions between the United States and Japan, the attack on Pearl Harbor, and the U.S. entry into war were soon to turn her world upside down.

RECRUITMENT

From Los Angeles to Santa Anita

Following the Japanese attack on Pearl Harbor, Americans of Japanese ancestry on the Hawaiian Islands were subject to curfews and other restrictions but were not incarcerated en masse (with the exception of several thousand persons who were deemed a potential risk). Since Tamie Tsuchiyama had been born in Hawaii, and since her family still resided in Kauai, she noted in a letter to Dorothy Thomas that she could have applied to return home if she had wanted to. Her personal correspondence indicates that her family was deeply concerned about her, in part because of anti-Japanese sentiments on the U.S. mainland.

According to her sister, Hisako, since Tamie had almost finished her doctorate by the end of 1941, the family thought that she should seriously think about moving away from the West Coast, in part because Tsuchiyama's old mentor and friend, Dr. Paul Radin, had many connections in other parts of the United States, and the family felt confident that Radin would look after her and help her finish. In her correspondence, Tsuchiyama herself mentioned the possibility of seeking employment as a university-level instructor in Japanese.

Instead of returning home to Hawaii or going back east, Tsuchiyama left the University of California at Berkeley and went back to Los Angeles. (Her transcripts indicate that Tsuchiyama officially withdrew from the University of California on March 13, 1942, and that she was granted an honorary dismissal on April 13 that same year.) Although her sister, Hisako, had already returned to the islands, Tsuchiyama was able to stay with a good friend of both sisters from their UCLA days, Edith Kodama.

On April 20, 1942, Tsuchiyama wrote to anthropologist Robert H. Lowie informing him that, for the last five weeks, she had been in Los Angeles trying to help out in the Japanese American community there. Tsuchiyama's letter to Lowie reflected her empathy for these soon-to-be-impounded people; the letter also reflected a growing realization that current developments, set in motion by the involvement of the United States in the Second World War, might provide a unique context for the study of long-term acculturation patterns of people of Japanese descent on the mainland.

Tsuchiyama experienced some weeks of vacillation, largely regarding what goals to pursue, both in terms of employment options and what camp she would ultimately go to if she followed through on the idea of carrying out fieldwork in such a setting. Manzanar, Santa Anita, and Poston were all mentioned as possibilities in her correspondence. In April 1942, Lowie, who was by then Tsuchiyama's main mentor in Berkeley's anthropology department, linked her up to Dorothy Thomas. Thomas was a sociologist affiliated with the University of California's agricultural sciences division who, over the course of that spring, became the sole director of the University of California's Japanese American Evacuation and Relocation Study (JERS) project.

By May 1, 1942, Tsuchiyama had entered the Santa Anita Assembly Center, one of fifteen temporary points of assembly to which all persons of Japanese descent in the Los Angeles area were ordered to report before being assigned to one of ten more permanent American-style concentration camps. Tsuchiyama arranged to go to Santa Anita with the Kodama family. She appears to have actually lived with Edith and the Kodamas during this period and thus was assigned a lettered sequence of the same WRA family identification number as the Kodamas.

While at Santa Anita, Tsuchiyama began to integrate herself into the larger community and simultaneously to collect data. Her letters to Lowie during June and August 1942, three of which follow, indicate an overlap between these two activities.

The first field report that Tsuchiyama wrote was titled "A Preliminary Report on Japanese Evacuees at Santa Anita Assembly Center." Dated July 31, 1942, the report was typed, double spaced, and forty-six pages long. In it, Tsuchiyama covered the basic setup of the transformed race track, the layout of the horse stalls and barracks, the socioeconomic background of the residents, as well as the great ingenuity Japanese Americans demonstrated in adapting to the spartan conditions by building their own furniture, planting gardens, and so on. Food in the assembly center merits a full fifteen and a half pages. Tsuchiyama noted: "To the administration the food problem must be an extremely difficult one.

The food habits of the first and second generation as well as rural and urban dwellers are markedly distinct and to prepare a meal that will satisfy the needs of all of them is a Herculean task."

> Further: During the early states of our initiation[,] complaints concerning food were the most conspicuous. The more audacious ones wrote lengthy letters to the War Department, the F.B.I. and to army headquarters in San Francisco entreating them to intercede for [sic] their behalf. One individual was sent to Parker [the only assembly center set up in the state of Arizona] for being too articulate in his complaints and too determined in his efforts to improve mess halls.

Tsuchiyama also noted that although there were many difficulties in the beginning, the situation "improved tremendously . . . [and] even those who preferred at first to starve than stand in 'bread lines' are now brazenly marching in to receive their share of government food."

The rest of the first field report focuses on the traditional ethnographic category, life cycle. Tsuchiyama covers birth, education, recreation, juvenile delinquency, and "crimes." Gambling, "sex offenses," and abortion are all treated in the latter section, as are the abuses committed by the Nisei *yogores* (tough guys) in Santa Anita. "[O]ne of the commonest 'crimes' for teen-age boys is the formation of gangs to 'beat up' people who offend them. . . . One of the most spectacular 'beating-up' incidents occurred in the Blue Mess Hall on June 22 [1942] when twenty youngsters, mostly from Hawaii, fought with the cooks because they had refused to give a generous portion of meat to one of their members."

Commentary on marriage, medical services, death, and religion makes up the bulk of the rest of the report. Tsuchiyama included interesting information about organized religion in camp, beginning with the statement that a tremendous variety of denominations was represented at Santa Anita: Catholics, Federated Protestants, Episcopalians, Buddhists (primarily Shinshu, but with adherents of the Shingon, Jodo, Jodo Shin, Nichiren, and Zen sects as well), Seventh Day Adventists, and adherents of a "Holiness Association." In her observations of the Buddhist service, Tsuchiyama noted:

> The service itself has innumerable Christian touches just as Christianity in Japan has been thoroughly "Buddhisized." Thus one notices such foreign intrusions as hymns, responsive reading and choir singing which

one would look for in vain in an orthodox Japanese temple. Furthermore, the change in Buddhism appears to be more than just a matter of external form. . . . it occurred to me that in spirit American Buddhism has a less pessimistic tone than that of Japan, emphasis on love having replaced that on compassion. The services [in Japanese] for the older generation are more orthodox and consist simply of sermons and prayers conducted by Japanese priests.

Her comments on Buddhism at Santa Anita contain one of the few explicit passages that note the impact on the unique conditions of life in a totally segregated facility operated by the federal government.

The attendance at Buddhist services is relatively small—approximately five hundred or so as compared with several thousand in Protestant gatherings. This marked difference is partly accounted for by the fact that many Buddhists now residing in the center hesitate to attend services for fear of F.B.I. agents investigating them. . . . [A]t the outbreak of the war numerous Buddhists began attending Christian churches for they naively felt that by embracing an 'American' religion they might receive kindlier treatment at the hands of Whites.

Religious books and services were one of the few domains where Issei were permitted free use of the Japanese language; in the beginning, residents were not permitted access to certain forms of leisure that revolved around the Japanese language because of suspicion about their connotations of Japanese nationalism and/or militarism.

In her concluding section, Tsuchiyama focuses on "leadership" in Santa Anita, noting that representatives from neither the Japanese American Citizens League nor the community at large seemed very visible in camp. After speculating as to why, she observed that "the more likely reason is that there is extreme danger for any group, political or otherwise, to become too prominent."

Tsuchiyama's second field report from Santa Anita is dated October 3, 1942. It is typed, double spaced, and twenty-eight pages in length. The focus of the report is largely the attitudes of the various generations and intragenerational subgroups toward daily life at Santa Anita.

Tsuchiyama's discussion of Issei attitudes begins by noting their feelings of "complete resignation" when war broke out and rumors of possible mass incarceration were circulated. Beyond this, she identifies a more "conservative" Issei attitude entailing an identification with, if not an emotional attachment to, Japan. These are contrasted with beliefs of the more "realistic" Issei, who realized that their destiny, and especially the future of their children, lay in America.

Similar treatment, emphasizing a range of cultural and political stances, is given to the Nisei, or second generation, as well as the Kibei—essentially Nisei, born in America, who were sent back to Japan for education, often staying there through their teens. Some Kibei, for example, were assessed by Tsuchiyama as being "pro-Japan." Others, however, were liberals who "appreciated America and her democratic ideals infinitely more so than the Nisei who had taken democracy more or less for granted." Similarly, Tsuchiyama's analysis of the Nisei revolved around her division of them into four basic groups: the socialites, progressives, liberals, and "rowdies."

According to Tsuchiyama, the socialites were the upwardly mobile Nisei whose hopes for white-collar jobs and good marriages had been ruined by the war. They were a cliquish set, enjoying dances and bridge parties among themselves. Tsuchiyama characterized them as "fence-sitters waiting for the turn of events" that would indicate to them what the future would bring.

The progressives, on the other hand, appreciated "intellectual discussions, art, music, literature." They did not speak Japanese very well and were sometimes "astonished" at the "Old World traits" of some of Santa Anita's Issei residents. In terms of their loyalties, the progressives saw themselves as good Americans and had been eager to volunteer for duty in the Armed Forces until they were rendered 4-C, ineligible to serve, after the attack on Pearl Harbor.

The liberals were basically the left-leaning progressive Nisei who had been affiliated with groups like the Young Democrats before the war. Tsuchiyama notes that they were "well informed on political, social and economic affairs" and "appeared least race conscious of all Nisei types." She also notes that "all of the leading liberals at Santa Anita were Kibei." (It is worth noting here that Tsuchiyama herself and some of her colleagues, such as the Kunitanis, fit into this general category.)

The rowdies were young men, from age sixteen to their early thirties, who were alienated and prone to form gangs in camp. The rowdies were keen to fight and willing to take on peers and even authority figures. Tsuchiyama wrote:

They also delighted in cornering lone policemen—Japanese as well as Caucasian—and picking fights with them. The beating of policemen became so prevalent in camp that two days before the much publicized riot of August 4 all Nisei cops and all young Caucasians were removed and "toughies"—those who had been stabbed or shot at least once— substituted. After the riot I am informed that none of the Arcadia police-men dared to make their rounds alone during the day, and at night rode about in trucks rather than cover their beat on foot. During the riot, the rowdies were responsible for the beating of the "Korean spy" and the molesting of others suspected of informing.

Beyond this classification, the report focuses on responses to different aspects of life at Santa Anita: the National Defense Project, which was involved in making camouflage nets; Americanization; the JACL, or Japanese American Citizens League; Euro-Americans, with some particularly disturbing observa-tions about anti-Semitism among the Santa Anita residents; and "contact with the outside."

The final section of the report describes the political organization of the Japanese Americans at Santa Anita. As in other assembly centers, the Japanese American residents were encouraged to elect representatives, but meetings were to be held under a set of very strict guidelines: they could only meet in a special room (the Government House) with the permission of the authorities, meetings had to be conducted entirely in English, and a stenographer had to be present in order to transcribe all discussion that took place. Tsuchiyama's report notes that popular government, in which only a little more than half the residents participated, broke down quickly. In less than two weeks, the FBI raided the camp and arrested six individuals, charging them with holding a "secret" and therefore illegal meeting.

Tsuchiyama's Initial Fieldwork

As the child of immigrant Japanese, Tsuchiyama's interest in studying mass incarceration was partially based on her background in Hawaii and on the mainland. As well as speaking and studying the Japanese language as a child, she had had contact with Japanese Americans in both settings before the war. Although I do not suppose that she had read a great deal about Japanese Americans before 1940, as this was not among her areas of specialization within anthropology, there was not a great deal of literature available on this subject in any case. Beyond this, her background and personal experiences meshed with her academic work, especially her graduate training in anthropology, and with the outbreak of the war, the removal of Japanese Americans from California and the West Coast stimulated a range of questions in Tsuchiyama's mind. We can see from her letters to Professor Robert Lowie that both comparative differences between the Japanese Americans in Hawaii and those in California were at play in this regard, as well as theoretically pitched questions having to do with processes of adaptation and assimilation. In sum, apart from the crisis situation generated by the U.S. entry into the Second World War and by Executive Order 9066, Tsuchiyama's initial experience with fieldwork was not too different from that experienced by ordinary fieldworkers in that her background and training combined to spark her initial interest.

Tsuchi's initial interest

Tsuchiyama regarded her stay at Santa Anita, then, as kind of preliminary fieldwork venture entailing both her own personal interests and the possibility of obtaining full-time employment as a staff member of Dorothy Thomas's research project. Correspondence indicates that Tsuchiyama was already a part-time employee of the University of California and, as such, received $62.50 a month for her efforts in Santa Anita. Even though she was only a part-time researcher, Tsuchiyama could use this experience to sharpen her language skills, think over possible foci, and begin to fix on key concepts and even initial hypotheses that might help to guide data collection.

Interestingly enough, in her case, basic logistical matters that a fieldworker would ordinarily have to grapple with were already solved. Tsuchiyama did not have to deal with funding or with many of the ordinary physical arrangements at the fieldwork site such as housing, food, and so forth: the federal government provided for everything, although conditions were often poor in terms of facilities and even basic supplies in the beginning.

Tsuchiyama also carried out other basic steps that would seem familiar to fieldworkers, then and now. She began to make initial contacts and to build rapport. As far as I know, while the Euro-American authorities at Santa Anita were informed about her presence and her university affiliation, Tsuchiyama did not ask permission of the residents of Santa Anita to do ethnographic research on her compatriots. Perhaps because she worked on a semiclandestine basis, I have found only limited indications of the "presentation of self" issues that one often finds in ethnographies or in the memoirs of anthropologists, that is, a fieldworker's comments on how variables like age, stage in the domestic cycle, gender, class, nationality, and so on are managed, given that each of these have an impact on the fieldworker's access to people and information.

Another point of interest is Tsuchiyama's active engagement in participant observation at Santa Anita. Although she refers obliquely to this at first, Tsuchiyama agreed to work as a "girls' supervisor," overseeing some five hundred women who were part of the camp's camouflage net project. She would continue to consider this kind of engagement later on during her fieldwork at Poston, as is clear from her letter of December 1, 1942.

The camouflage net project at Santa Anita was generally regarded as a successful endeavor. One account, presented in a short study, reported that "in the summer of 1942, 800 camp inmates put together 22,000 nets, resulting in a savings to the government that more than offset the entire cost of feeding the camp population. The project employed only citizen volunteers who worked 44-hour weeks in eight-hour shifts, producing 250–260 large nets per day at their peak. The nets varied in size from 22' x 22' to 36' x 60'."

In June workers initiated what developed into a one-day strike. According to historian Brian Niiya, workers' grievances ranged from pressure tactics that had been initially used to fill the necessary quota of workers to poor labor conditions and exploitative wages. "Many workers were allergic to the hemp nets, and thick burlap dust and dye fumes irritated lungs, eyes and throats. Additionally, workers had to labor kneeling on the floor for eight-hour stretches under the hot sun. After their shifts, they then had to wait in long lines for meals. For this, they were paid $8 a month."

Readers will note that Tsuchiyama's descriptions of conditions and the subsequent strike in her letters to Lowie offer related insights and thus represent a unique commentary by a first-hand participant-observer of this controversy. In addition, her subsequent letters from the Poston camp indicate that this experience gave Tsuchiyama insights into labor problems at Santa Anita, as well as into the broad causes behind and the dynamics of the strikes as well as a riot that eventually erupted at the assembly center that August.

Beyond her comments in regard to the workers under her supervision, there really isn't any kind of commentary about the role expectations that fieldworkers often have to grapple with, at least when it is publicly known that they are anthropologists collecting information about society and culture.

As far as I am able to determine, her real pursuits were probably known to only a few at Santa Anita. This fact made her fieldwork situation different from the classical cases described in the literature and taught about in graduate programs. Secrecy also extended to her research at Poston, and it becomes clearer how damaging clandestine research can be—perhaps not so much in this case to those who were subject to it, although today this would be regarded as a rather serious ethical violation, but rather for the anthropologist who must hide and dissimulate her real enterprise.

This dimension of her fieldwork in camp is also significant because, according to her own correspondence, Tsuchiyama was visited by FBI agents while at Santa Anita. In all likelihood, such visits were noted by neighbors and might even have become the basis for suspicion. However, Tsuchiyama reports that an FBI agent merely wanted her to enlighten him about various Japanese religions, including Tenrikyu. In addition, Tsuchiyama claimed that, subsequently, Tenrikyu priestesses were released from Justice Department internment camps where they had been confined immediately after the Japanese attack at Pearl Harbor, although records on Tsuchiyama that I obtained through the Freedom of Information Act shed no further light on this topic.

At one level, the Japanese Americans (and one Issei, Richard S. Nishimoto) who participated in JERS, or any of the research projects that relied on internees to collect data, had to be careful about how their data collection activities might be perceived. It is clear from Tsuchiyama's letters to Lowie that FBI agents had the power to search the barracks, as well as to interrogate and remove any individual whom they suspected. Because the FBI did, in fact, exercise these powers, there was a great deal of concern about searches and seizures. Tsuchiyama's letters provide a number of examples of these phenomena in the Santa Anita camp and the kind of resentment that was incurred, including at least one incident where a crowd of Japanese Americans gathered and began to stone the Santa Anita Military Police.

Such incidents were accompanied at Santa Anita and elsewhere by persistent rumors about the presence of *inu* (literally, "dog," but here meaning spies of Japanese descent) in camp who were tipping off the authorities. We now know that the FBI did in fact receive intelligence along these lines that consisted of volunteered information; there is also evidence that agencies, including the FBI and the Office of Naval Intelligence (ONI), among others, actively placed "operatives" in the WRA camps, including Poston. Whether we will learn much more than this, unless participants step forward with their stories, is unclear. In the context of the situation and the times, then, it is not surprising that Tsuchiyama, like the other, official JERS fieldworkers, was already concerned about being labeled as an *inu* and did everything in her power to avoid such an accusation.

Second, Tsuchiyama's correspondence indicates her ongoing concern regarding the security and integrity of her fieldnotes. Interestingly enough, Tsuchiyama's fears in this regard were so frequently expressed that some of her colleagues, including Thomas and Nishimoto, regarded her actions as almost paranoid; Nishimoto commented on this in a somewhat condescending fashion in a number of his letters to Thomas. In fact, according to her letter of August 24, 1942, when Tsuchiyama arrived in Poston, her Santa Anita fieldnotes *were* confiscated by "police" officers. This experience, which made her feel as if her research could be impounded at any time for "security reasons," would certainly have been enough to spark deep and ongoing concerns about protecting her sources and the information she was obtaining.

This is something that every good fieldworker has to consider. In doing ethnography today, it is a widely accepted ethical imperative to put the safety (via anonymity or by other means) of one's informants before all other considerations. This was not as widespread a commitment before World War II, and in retrospect one admires Tsuchiyama's concerns and wishes that other researchers had been as scrupulous in their efforts to protect the privacy of the people who cooperated with researchers' requests for information. Unfortunately, Tsuchiyama's complicity from the beginning in a clandestine fieldwork situation raised contradictions that would not be so easy to manage over the long run.

Letters to Robert H. Lowie, 1942

> 1207 W. 36th Place
> Los Angeles, Calif.
> April 20, 1942

Dear Dr. Lowie,

I was extremely interested to hear that plans are being made in Berkeley for the scientific study of Japanese in reception centers and would appreciate greatly if you would inform Dr. Thomas that I shall be happy to cooperate in whatever way I can. She may be interested to know that for the past five weeks I have been helping in the orderly evacuation of Japanese from the Los Angeles area and have accumulated considerable data which may be of value to her. When I left Berkeley last month I had full intentions of accepting a job teaching Japanese in one of the Eastern universities but when I realized the plight of my people in Los Angeles I decided to make a study of them before and after confinement in "concentration camps" not so much to gather data for a monograph which I intend to write someday on the acculturation of the Japanese in Hawaii and California but to test a few personal theories I have harbored for some years. Dr. Thomas may also be interested to hear that some of my more enterprising friends have taken motion pictures with army permission of the earliest evacuees to Manzanar, the reception center in Owens Valley, with the hope of preserving them as documentary films. I am informed that for public consumption the authorities have requested that the more unfavorable portions be cut but as far as I know they have not been destroyed and may be available for research at a later date.

I do not know whether Dr. Thomas consulted authorities before making her "somewhat elaborate plans" but I doubt from personal experience whether they will permit a scientific investigation of the Japanese in reception centers in the immediate future at least. The favorable accounts of camp life in newspapers and over the radio in conjunction with frequent denials by the army of "certain rumors" concerning evacuation, which I know from personal experience to be true, lead me to believe that the authorities are not particularly desirous of acquainting the public with true conditions in these camps. This suspicion is further substantiated by the fact that the authorities will not permit any White person, with the exception of White wives, to take up residence in camp. This became evident when the Maryknoll Brothers, who have worked with the Japanese for many decades, and some 400 Caucasian teachers, who will lose their jobs with the evacuation of several thousand Japanese school children, applied for admission into these camps and were refused. All these things in conjunction with attempts in Congress to disenfranchise American-born Japanese have given rise to unhealthy explanations such as the desire of the authorities to segregate Japanese so that at the end of the war they may find justification in claiming that the Japanese are inassimilable and should be deported to Japan; that the authorities are afraid to allow Caucasian friends of the Japanese to reside in camp lest they expose true conditions to fair-minded citizens, etc. etc. All in all the stage is set for an extremely fascinating study of personality types. Particularly interesting to me at the moment is the reaction of unfortunate victims of interracial marriages. Since the army decrees that anyone with a drop of Japanese blood must observe curfew and be removed from the Pacific Coast we are encountering a number of ruptures in family life—many of which, to me, seem unnecessary. I am told that within the last few days the army has given sanction to the reunion of non-Japanese wives with their Japanese husbands in camp, but as far as I know no non-Japanese husband has been permitted to rejoin his wife.

Last week I interviewed Miss Mahn, Indian commissioner for the Colorado River Indian Reservation, and was accepted as social service worker among 38,000 Japanese to be concentrated on this reservation at an early date. I was originally scheduled to leave this morning for Parker, Arizona, but was informed at the last minute that the army has indefinitely postponed the staff's departure. Since the area in which I am residing at present must be evacuated by the 29th of this month, unless the army speeds up our project or unless I move to an unrestricted section of this city, I may have to go to Manzanar, Santa Anita, or any one of the other reception centers already in use. I do hope, however, that the Parker project will come through in time since my job as social service worker will give me access to certain type of sociological data without appearing too inquisitive to the authorities or the Japanese. If I am sent to another camp I hope they will permit me to conduct adult classes in English or [Americanization] studies. But wherever I go I am planning to make a detailed acculturation study and shall be happy to cooperate with Dr. Thomas. If she has formulated a definite program for research by now and I do not have to leave Los Angeles within the next week or two (army orders change so frequently that we can never be certain of the exact date of departure) I may be able to run up to Berkeley for a day or two to discuss plans with her if she so desires. Once I enter camp I presume it will be rather difficult for me to leave and furthermore I am duly warned that censorship will be extremely strict.

I hope that both you and Mrs. Lowie are well and that the war has not brought drastic alterations in your life. I would appreciate very much if you will give my regards to my fellow graduate students.

Sincerely yours,
[signed] Tamie Tsuchiyama
Santa Anita Assembly Center
Arcadia, California

June 24, 1942

Dear Dr. Lowie,

A number of factors prevented me from answering your letters of June 10 and 15 promptly. For one thing there has been much discontent for the last three weeks in camp and I deemed it unwise to communicate with you especially when I feel that my mail is being carefully scrutinized. The fact that many of my letters do not seem to reach their destination or arrive there at a very late date leads me to suspect that my letters are being censored. Also since June first I have been employed as girls' supervisor on the camouflage net project and the sit down strike of some 1200 workers last week left me with little time to write to you. Now that the project is functioning smoothly again I asked to be released today in order that I may devote full time to research but the director begged me to remain until he could find someone capable of managing some five hundred girls. From tomorrow I hope to go on a half-day schedule and within a few weeks to drop out completely from the project.

As you may have read in the San Francisco papers about 1200 workers employed on the camouflage net project—the only national defense project in the center—staged a two-day strike in protest against what they termed inhuman conditions. While making my round of nets I sensed a considerable degree of discontent for some time but did not anticipate a strike for at least two weeks. The strike began when a group of men working at the extreme western end of the grandstand walked out in protest against the bad food served in camp and the other hundred nets [sic] followed one by one. The immediate cause appeared to be unappetizing food offered at lunch—in fact the Los Angeles papers jocularly referred to it as a "protest against sauerkraut, a dish of German origin, and wiener sausages served at lunch"—but the underlying causes were long hours of monotonous work weaving burlap strips into nets in the hot afternoon sun, uncertainty of payment, coolie wages ($8.00 a month for 8 hours of work daily; i.e. 4 1/2 [cents] an hour), bad food (type of food we would have hesitated to feed hogs in pre-evacuation days), and last but not least annoyance at the idea that "prisoners of war" had to be "blackmailed" to work on a national defense program on a patriotic note. The battle cry of the workers seemed to be: if you must appeal to us as patriotic citizens to perform the dirtiest job in the center, give us the treatment accorded American citizens and we will wholeheartedly cooperate in finishing the quota set up by the U.S. Army. Public reaction to the strike was extremely varied but interesting in that it revealed the thinking of different groups of Japanese in camp. One of the most articulate councilmen demanded that the 1200 workers be blacklisted and sent to Parker Dam [on an old riverbed some sixteen miles south of Parker, Arizona], the "Devil's Island" of assembly centers, for chastisement; some called us "true Americans" for attempting to preserve the American standard of living. No matter how dreadful the strike must have appeared to the outside world at least it was instrumental in bringing about wholesale improvements in camp which two months of so-called "self-government" could not obtain for us. Apparently the administration is fearful of the consequences if it cannot produce the quota demanded by the U.S. Army and is willing to appease workers to some extent to receive greater cooperation.

With reference to your letter of June 15 asking me whether I would like to be transferred to Tule Lake I have given considerable attention but am still suffering from indecision. Climatically speaking Tule Lake probably would be the most desirable of all relocation centers. But from the viewpoint of a successful investigation I wonder whether it would not be more profitable for me to follow the Los Angeles group to Parker Dam, Arkansas, Wyoming, or any other relocation center to which they are sent. As I mentioned before, since March 10 I have been studying the Japanese in Los Angeles and neighboring areas and moved with them to Santa Anita. Since I have investigated them in their pre-evacuation and assembly center stages I feel that it might be wiser for me to continue residing with them in their relocation stage rather than going to Tule Lake where I have had little or no contact with the evacuees before removal to their final site. Also you may have known that there are marked regional differences among the Japanese in California—e.g., the Japanese in Los Angeles are much more Americanized than those in San Francisco. Furthermore most of the Nisei leaders now in evacuation camps are concentrated in Santa Anita or Manzanar. In other words Los Angeles offered greater social and economic advancement to Japanese than any other Pacific Coast city. Therefore it would be extremely interesting to study the adjustment these leaders will make in their relocation center since their attitude will largely determine the attitude of the majority of the Japanese-Americans after the war. Also from the memorandum sent me by Dr. Thomas I infer that four investigators are being sent by the University of California to Tule Lake. Since there will be at least three other students making the survey at Tule Lake I wondered whether it might not be more advisable for me to go to another relocation site in order that we may obtain greater perspective on the problems confronting the Japanese in different relocation centers. With the above in mind, I prefer to leave the decision to you and Dr. Thomas. If you both feel that I shall be of greater service to you at Tule Lake I am ready to leave for northern California whenever you wish; otherwise I should like to follow the Los Angeles group to whichever center the Army will send them.

With reference to your suggestions for acculturation study it is very difficult to procure data on Shintoism, Buddhism, and the Japanese language at the present time. Since F.B.I. agents in pre-evacuation days investigated practically every Shinto priest and language school teacher within their reach, people are still reticent about divulging information concerning Shinto sects or the Japanese language. In a lengthy conversation with one of the most influential Buddhist priests in camp I was recently informed that membership in Buddhist organizations dropped markedly at the outbreak of the war because most of the members felt that Buddhism was an Oriental religion and that they would probably receive kindlier treatment from Caucasians if they embraced Christianity, and "American" religion. This was confirmed by a noted Methodist minister who maintained that his church in Los Angeles was filled to capacity in December and January when most of the more spectacular F.B.I. raids occurred. I have little reason to doubt that secret meetings of the Tenrikyo sect (a modern Shinto sect very similar to Christian Science) take place in the center but fear of F.B.I. agents who make almost daily rounds of camp, prevent them from holding public meetings. You may probably be interested to know that one of the members of the Los Angeles Branch of the F.B.I. occasionally visits me to acquaint himself with Japanese culture and I was extremely happy to learn that soon after a lengthy conversation with him on Tenrikyo, all of the Tenrikyo priestesses interned on Terminal Island were released and sent to Santa Anita. Many of the American-born Japanese who felt that they were true Americans and were scornful of learning the Japanese language wish to study it now in camp but so far permission to hold Japanese classes has been denied. On the other hand, English classes and democracy training classes for the first generation and those who have recently returned from Japan are very popular. A few days ago a petition was circulated in camp to start a Japanese newspaper for the benefit of those who could not read English but I am informed that the request was denied by the administration. Curiously enough, the leader of this movement was removed this week from camp, but whether this was due to his agitation for a Japanese newspaper or because of his alleged Communistic leanings I have not yet been able to determine. Anyway, things are happening fast and furious at Santa Anita and anyone with an I.Q. of 75 or above who attempts to improve conditions in camp is on the suspect list and chances of his being sent to Parker Dam or some other "Devil's Island" is very great. Since army orders seldom give you more than half an hour to get ready, I have unpacked only my barest essentials and after finishing my laundry carefully repack them in my suitcases. The most familiar greeting at the mess line is: "All ready to leave for Parker Dam?"

If Dr. Thomas would like to have me send in a weekly report I shall be happy to do so but I cannot guarantee its reaching her. She can rest assured however that I am putting in from six to eight hours of research daily and have accumulated considerable data since May first when I set foot for the first time in [an] American "concentration camp."

Please give my regards to Mrs. Lowie and my fellow graduate students. At night when the floodlights from the twenty sentry's [sic] towers scour the camp and prevent me from falling asleep, I pretend that I'm back again on the sixth floor of the [the University of California's Doe] library stacks and attempt to recapture, if only for a fleeting second, the security that was once mine.

Very sincerely yours,
[signed] Tamie Tsuchiyama

Dist. 6, Barr. 33, Unit 4
Avenue T
Santa Anita Assembly Center
Arcadia, California
July 8, 1942

Dear Dr. Lowie,

This is just a short note to inform you that I am still located at Santa Anita. Due to a riot which occurred in the center on the day I was scheduled to leave for Arizona, all travel permits were automatically [canceled]. I hope that by next week the excitement will have sufficiently subsided to enable the authorities to grant my release. Martial law was imposed on the center immediately after the riot Tuesday afternoon and only lifted last night so I could not communicate with you earlier. I have just been informed that the post office will open in a few hours so I am dashing off this note in the hope that it will reach you before you send any letters to Poston.

Now that the official news of the riot has been released to the press I presume I may present my side of the story with impunity. Early Tuesday morning I noticed a great deal of excitement in my area (District 6) and upon inquiry was informed that a corps of 200 policemen imported from the outside had begun a house to house search for contraband in the stable area and District 7 and would arrive in our neighborhood within a few hours. Those who had managed to escape from the raided areas informed us that not only articles which everyone knew to be prohibited in the center, e.g., knives, liquor, electric stoves, foods that required cooking, etc., but also such supposedly harmless objects as scissors, nail files, buckets, tubs, *geta* or wooden clogs, saws, chisels, files, electric razors, knitting needles, crochet hooks, and even cash were being confiscated. Curious to see exactly how much truth was incorporated in these assertions I casually strolled over to District 5 when it was undergoing investigation and was mildly shocked to note some policemen breaking into houses in the absence of their occupants. In such cases I noticed that all suitcases and boxes that were locked were hauled out and thrown into the pile of contraband. I further made certain that all of the articles alleged to have been taken from District 7 and the stable area (with the exception of cash) were actually included in the pile of contraband. While surveying the loot I met two of my friends who indignantly told me that not only their diaries and manuscripts but books written in English had been seized by the police that morning. Among them were the Tolan reports and Tolstoy's works. Toward noon the air was tense with a feeling of resentment. Some muttered that the police had no right to confiscate cash, others that the police had no right to break into homes while their occupants were away at work inasmuch as no one had been notified that an inspection was to occur that day.

Suddenly about two-thirty or three in the afternoon I saw people running toward the Orange Mess Hall in our district and upon arrival discovered several policemen running for shelter into the building while hundreds followed hurling pebbles at them. Accounts as to how the riot started differ considerably but the most popular one is that a little boy attempted to cross the bridge separating District 6 from District 7 carrying a small bag and was stopped by guards who insisted on inspecting it. The little fellow challenged their right to stop him and when the police attempted to lay hands on him the crowd which had been inspecting the pile of contraband nearby broke loose and commenced to stone them. Within a few minutes several thousand gathered near the mess hall and the next instant I perceived two policemen with guns retreating before the surging crowd. I immediately rushed over to the main gate separating the Japanese section from the soldiers' quarters and discovered some twenty or thirty military police lined up on the other side of the fence. Behind them were truckloads of soldiers to prevent any form of violence by the mob. In the meantime the order to cease inspection had been given and all of the policemen fled to the police barracks for protection.

The beating of the Korean "F.B.I. informer" [see bibliographic essay] which was highlighted in the official news, occurred about an hour later in Government House while I was away at supper. I managed, however, to see his bruised body being carted to the center hospital for treatment. For several weeks I had heard threats of "beating up" all F.B.I. informers so I was not particularly surprised when the incident occurred. The victim was notorious in camp as "[a] Korean spy" and had made himself especially obnoxious to a certain group when he failed to resign from the police force when all other Japanese policemen did a few days previous to the riot. According to some of my policemen friends they resigned as a protest against the removal of Nisei lieutenants and captains while others maintained that they did not wish to take orders from the "Korean spy." The resentment of center residents at those who "tattle-taled" on them had become rather acute in the last few weeks and all those suspected of writing any sort of reports or were friendly with Caucasian officials in camp or with F.B.I. agents had been notified through devious means of their precarious situation. The beating of the "Korean spy" encouraged the disciplining of others suspected of "treachery" and various individuals on Tuesday night are reported to have had unwelcome visits. In some cases military police were stationed near their homes to protect them from the unruly elements.

From four o'clock on Tuesday afternoon to Friday evening martial law prevailed in camp and communication with the outside world was suspended. Soldiers on trucks with mounted guns patrolled the barracks to maintain order although the excitement had more or less subsided by Wednesday morning. On Friday a corps of 200 Army officers and military police made a resurvey of the raided areas to ascertain the truth of the allegations in Tuesday's riot. As a result of the army inspection an order was issued by Col. Karl R. Bendetsen assuring the people that all non-contraband seized by the police on Tuesday would be returned to the respective owners and that a list of contraband would be posted before inspection would be resumed.

I received a letter from Robert Spencer Tuesday morning (which I hope to answer today) requesting me to get a visitor's permit for him on August 15. I do not know whether the ban on visitors will be lifted by that time or not but as I expect to leave within a few days for Poston I am afraid I cannot comply with his request. Furthermore, only *very special* visitors are allowed within the camp, others being restricted to a thirty-minute chat in the visitors' house across a very wide table under the constant supervision of the Arcadia police. Under the circumstances even if visitors are permitted here by August 15th I see no advantage in Spencer making a trip from Berkeley solely to interview me. Everything that I calculated would pass the censor I have already mailed to you; other reports will have to remain in a nebulous stage until later. At present my chief worry is whether I can take out my field notes without too much trouble. Several disconcerting rumors of confiscation of all manuscripts and diaries before leaving Santa Anita have reached my attention but so far I have been unable to ascertain their truth. I do know, however, that these were taken from some of my friends in Tuesday's raid.

If Spencer is to be located at Gila and I manage to get to Poston, we may be able to get together occasionally for the exchange of ideas. I do hope, however, that his racial background will not unduly hinder his research. The Japanese in Santa Anita, at least, are becoming extremely "group conscious" and rather suspicious of any Caucasian who appears to be interested in them. Caucasians in camp generally fall into one of two categories: administrative officials or F.B.I. agents in masquerade. Conditions at Santa Anita may be highly exaggerated in comparison with other assembly centers or relocation areas so my generalizations may not apply to others. Santa Anita seems to be the "bad boy" of assembly centers—at least we don't hear of strikes, "secret meetings," and riots in other areas. In fact, we are getting on the nerves of the Army and latest reports claim that 10,000 of us will be shipped within in a few weeks to Lamar, Colorado, in place of the evacuees now located at the Pomona Assembly Center.

Unless something unexpected turns up I shall send you the section on political organization and attitudes within a few days. Until further notice please send all letters to Santa Anita.

Sincerely yours,
[signed] Tamie Tsuchiyama

An Ethnographer of Mass Incarceration

Having finally made up her mind to do long-term fieldwork for Thomas on the mass incarceration of Japanese Americans, Tsuchiyama decided to leave Santa Anita. The Japanese Americans who had been forcibly assembled there would all be moved again, within short order, to one of the ten more permanent War Relocation Authority (WRA) camps. According to a letter that she wrote to Robert H. Lowie, Tsuchiyama had also become dissatisfied because there were too many restrictions placed on her research at Santa Anita. Because of her decision to engage in scholarly research, Tsuchiyama, unlike her compatriots, was given the special opportunity to decide which camp she would go to.

As we have seen, as early as April 1942 Tsuchiyama was being courted by Thomas in regard to accepting a full-time staff research position with JERS. Correspondence between Thomas and Lowie indicates that this possibility was being constantly assessed in terms of Tsuchiyama's research work in and reports on the Santa Anita Assembly Center. By the time she went to Poston four months later, Tsuchiyama must have agreed to become the primary JERS fieldworker in that camp because she was, in fact, already on the JERS payroll. By August 12, 1942, however, only a day after she had arrived at Poston, Tsuchiyama had also been recruited by Dr. Alexander H. Leighton to work for the Bureau of Sociological Research (BSR) at Poston. A brief discussion of this situation will serve to clarify the nature of Tsuchiyama's affiliations and provide an introduction to the different research projects that were operating in this one camp, which was one of the largest of the ten facilities run by the WRA.

Beyond her disdain for constraints at Santa Anita and Dorothy Thomas's and perhaps Lowie's endorsement that she go to Poston in order to become the JERS project's principal fieldworker there, we do not know the other reasons why Tsuchiyama might have selected that particular camp. Perhaps she had also heard about the creation of the BSR at Poston.

The BSR was the brain child of the director of the Office of Indian Affairs (OIA), John Collier Sr., and anthropologist Alexander H. Leighton. Collier hired Dr. Leighton, a medical doctor and psychiatrist who had an ongoing interest in comparative cultural research, to set up and run the BSR, which was explicitly created in order to aid and advise the OIA bureaucrats who ran Poston from its creation in 1942 through the end of 1943. Thus, existence of the BSR, which was unique to Poston, may have initially attracted Tsuchiyama because it gathered a number of well-known anthropologists into a team-research situation. Given the exigencies of fieldwork in a setting like Poston, the promise of collegiality should not be underestimated.

It is also clear from her correspondence that when Tsuchiyama arrived in Poston on August 11, 1942, her status as an anthropological researcher for the JERS and BSR projects was fully and explicitly understood by both WRA and OIA officials, including Wade Head, chief director at Poston, Ralph Gelvin, Poston's assistant director and the superintendent of Poston III, and, of course, Tsuchiyama's academic colleagues and her one-time supervisors at the BSR, Dr. Alexander H. Leighton, and Dr. Edward H. Spicer. When she arrived, Tsuchiyama was immediately assigned quarters, by herself, in apartment 11 B, Block 31, of Poston's Unit I.

Tsuchiyama's initially tentative connections with the various research projects and their personnel provide an indication of how open-ended everything was in the beginning. Her relationships also illustrate the constant jockeying that characterized the association between the different researchers who carried out their studies in Poston between 1942 and 1945.

Various letters in the JERS files clearly document tension on the part of JERS sponsors like Berkeley professor Robert Lowie, who had been involved in the initial conceptualization of the research project but who then withdrew in order to assume other wartime responsibilities, regarding the idea of Tsuchiyama working for both BSR and JERS simultaneously, a sentiment that Thomas and BSR director Alexander H. Leighton apparently concurred with.

When he found out that she was actually employed by both projects, Leighton was willing to strike a compromise rather than lose her services completely. Accompanied by Poston's assistant director, Ralph Gelvin, Leighton asked project director Wade Head if it was at all possible for Tsuchiyama to hold research positions with BSR and JERS simultaneously and be paid for both. As an additional condition, Leighton insisted on being given carbon copies of any research reports that Tsuchiyama might write for JERS.

By August 26, Head had approved of this arrangement. Tsuchiyama was to be paid $19.00 a month by the BSR as well as her "usual compensation" from JERS. It is worth noting a few more facts about her salary. A March 1943 letter to her from Thomas's assistant, Morton Grodzins, indicates that Tsuchiyama's initial JERS salary had been quite small, starting at a mere $7.50 a month, as she began to make her transition to the Poston camp. Because of her good performance there, beginning in March 1943 she began to earn $62.50 a month. Once she received an offer of a year-long contract as a full-time JERS staff member, her salary rose to $120.00 a month. In short, compared to the $12.00 to $19.00 a month that most Japanese Americans earned in these camps, Tsuchiyama's monthly JERS research salary by 1943 represented a good deal of money. When Dorothy Thomas learned of her dual employment situation via the BSR, however, Tsuchiyama was summarily cut from the JERS payroll. Yet Tsuchiyama must have inspired the same feeling of confidence in her worth in Thomas as she had in Leighton, since Tsuchiyama was duly reinstated as a JERS staff researcher after the negotiations described above were completed.

Interestingly enough, after all these worries and negotiations, Tsuchiyama's dual research role only lasted three months. Although this might seem like a very short period, it is important to remember that the BSR might well have been one of the most exciting and dynamic field training schools then operating in the United States.

First of all, the BSR was run by two relatively young but already accomplished scholars, Drs. Alexander H. Leighton and Edward H. Spicer. Ancillary staff included scholars like Elizabeth Colson, who went on to have a long and productive academic career. Professionally trained scholars who interacted with the BSR staff included Solon T. Kimball, David H. French, and Conrad M. Arensberg, each of whom, like Colson, went on to become distinguished anthropologists.

Second, according to transcriptions of BSR staff meetings, Leighton, Spicer, Colson, and others gave lectures on an ongoing basis that were intended to instruct the Japanese American personnel in the art of fieldwork but also very clearly served as vehicles for preliminary analyses of and discussions and debates about the evolving situation in Poston. The BSR kept thorough records of these meetings, including almost verbatim transcripts, so we know that Tsuchiyama herself gave two extended lectures to her colleagues within a month after she arrived in Poston.

On September 12, 1942, for example, Tsuchiyama, listed as "Dr." Tsuchiyama, gave a lecture entitled "Cultural Background of Japanese Evacuees." Leighton and Spicer attended, along with eight other BSR staff members, including Toshio Yatsushiro, George Yamaguchi, Tom Sasaki, and Kenny Murase, each of whom pursued postbaccalaureate degrees and eventually became university professors. This lecture, transcribed along with questions and answers throughout the session, is almost forty double-spaced typed pages in length. Again, in anthropological fashion, Tsuchiyama covered classic topics such as material and nonmaterial culture, the latter including social organization (local groups and marriage and family) and individual life cycles (birth and baptism, education, recreation, juvenile delinquency and crime, death and burial). In sum, the data were taken from her previous reports, summarized above. On September 15, Tsuchiyama gave part two of her paper, focusing largely on religion, language, folklore, and economic and social status. Fifteen BSR members, staff, and guests attended. Over forty typed pages, the lecture transcript reveals that this was basically an expanded version of what she had previously written in Santa Anita.

Similarly, at Leighton's behest (and via the facilitation of sociology professor and JERS consultant Robert Redfield), accredited courses, sponsored by the University of Chicago, were also set up in Poston for the Nisei who wanted to carry out further studies in order to supplement their BSR training and prepare for possible application to graduate school in one of the social sciences. On this basis, Tsuchiyama co-taught a course entitled "Introduction to Anthropology" for the BSR.

One of the Nisei students in the class, now professor emeritus of anthropology Iwao Ishino, who taught for many years after the war in the Department of Anthropology at Michigan State University, recalled that

> Tamie, along with Elizabeth Colson, was team-teaching an introductory course in Anthropology for the benefit of about a dozen of us neophytes who were on the staff [of the BSR] as research assistants.
>
> It is interesting that in this group . . . five of us went on to get our doctoral degrees and remained in the academic world. Tamie, no doubt, had influenced us by the example she set. As for myself, I was amazed by her lecture on prehistory . . . covering the paleolithic, mesolithic and neolithic periods as if she were reciting the multiplication tables. . . .
>
> Certainly she was a shy and retiring person, but she was intelligent, sympathetic, and genuine. She, Elizabeth Colson, and Katherine Spencer remain in my mind as the three [most] promising women anthropologists I had the privilege of knowing in the World War Two period.

In such a setting and with such role models, as Ishino points out, it is not surprising that a number of the BSR's Japanese American staff went on to establish themselves in professional academic careers. Japanese American staff members who went on in the field of anthropology alone, for example, included Ishino himself, Toshio Yatsushiro, and the late Tom Sasaki. In addition, Yoshiharu Matsumoto and George Yamaguchi, who also served as BSR personnel, went on to earn doctoral degrees in the social sciences, and Ken Murase later obtained a graduate degree and became a professor of social work at San Francisco State University.

In short, brief though her BSR employment may have been, like the other

Nisei on staff Tsuchiyama absorbed a good deal of basic information about Poston, about the style of applied anthropology promulgated by Leighton and Spicer, and about the art of fieldwork, even though she was affiliated with the BSR for only three months.

Tsuchiyama mentioned in her correspondence that she ended up resigning from the BSR partly in order to be freer to pursue other options, which included, at that time, either moving to Topaz, a WRA camp in Utah, or abandoning research on the incarcerated Japanese Americans completely. Other letters indicate that, early on in her research, Tsuchiyama felt frustrated by her BSR colleagues' expectation that she direct data collection on the part of Japanese American research assistants. Finally, Tsuchiyama noted that she found it "extremely difficult to establish rapport with" Leighton because of his very strong commitment to certain approaches and perspectives within the field of anthropology. In all probability, Tsuchiyama was referring to Leighton's interest in applied anthropology, which had not been a subfield specialty at the University of California at Berkeley where Tsuchiyama had been trained.

For his own part, Alexander Leighton's fieldnotes capture his impression of Tsuchiyama as anxious and often conflicted because she wasn't progressing quickly enough in terms of her own fieldwork agenda. The next day Leighton also recorded the thoughts of his colleague Edward H. Spicer, who had similar concerns and felt that Tsuchiyama might be pushing herself to the point of an "emotional break." Indeed, these early letters reveal an ambivalence, on the part of Tsuchiyama, that is worth emphasizing. On the one hand, from the beginning Tsuchiyama seemed all too willing to have Lowie and then Thomas make major decisions that would affect her work and life. On the other hand, her letters document her desire to do fieldwork "as she pleased." Selected letters from Tsuchiyama's correspondence file, which follow, offer the basis for some additional conjectures.

First, we should remember that Tsuchiyama was clearly a self-directed person (in a subsequent letter, she even describes herself as a "loner" and a "misanthrope"). Her initial reports from Santa Anita suggest that, even though a neophyte fieldworker, she was a competent observer, able to gather a comprehensive set of data in a fairly limited amount of time and certainly under less than ideal circumstances, especially for a beginner.

What we know about Tsuchiyama's work with the BSR suggests that her position quickly generated tensions, perhaps especially because Tsuchiyama's own conception of and approach to fieldwork was not validated. She was immediately asked to carry out assignments, including teaching and directing the research of others (primarily college-age Nisei), which interfered with what she clearly felt was the anthropologist's charge to gather copious amounts of original data on a first-hand basis.

There is also the question of how Tsuchiyama's affiliation with the BSR affected her rapport with the larger Japanese American community of Poston, something that Tsuchiyama didn't discuss explicitly in her letters. Certainly a more clandestine affiliation with Dorothy Thomas's JERS project would have allowed Tsuchiyama to have more independence as a fieldworker. In these early letters, we see that right after leaving the BSR, Tsuchiyama gained a new level of understanding with Issei leaders in the camp, including her soon-to-be-JERS-colleague, Richard S. Nishimoto. By the end of the year, she had actually written to Thomas, asking if it would be all right for her to run for an elected office in Poston's Unit I, both because she was being asked to do so by her neighbors and probably because she felt that such a position would offer additional possibilities in terms of communication and information.

Finally, I suspect that the vast gulf between the status of the already distinguished Dr. Alexander Leighton—a medical doctor, psychiatrist, and published social scientist—and graduate student Tsuchiyama—a young, intelligent, but somewhat withdrawn, fledgling anthropologist who was trying desperately to make her mark as a professional—contributed to possible misunderstandings.

As a result of these tensions, Tamie Tsuchiyama left the BSR and began to work exclusively for Dorothy Thomas and the JERS project. Tsuchiyama held this position as the principal staff fieldworker for the JERS project in Poston between 1942 and July 1944.

In sum, by leaving Santa Anita and entering the complex research environment at Poston, Tsuchiyama relinquished a situation where she could conduct herself as an independent fieldworker. For better or for worse, BSR expectations were that Tsuchiyama become more of a manager for that project—a manager whose principal duties were to instruct younger Nisei field assistants about how to best collect ethnographic data and then to assess those data in regard to the larger foci and aims of the BSR's mandate, which was to collect data that would help the Euro-American staff at Poston make the most effective decisions as well as camp policy.

Work with Dorothy Thomas and JERS, however, would also undermine

Tsuchiyama's professional development, albeit in a somewhat different fashion, as we will see below.

Letters to Dorothy Thomas and Robert H. Lowie, 1942

Block 31, 11-B
Poston, Arizona
August 24, 1942

Dear Dr. Thomas,

I had intended to write you immediately after arrival in Poston, Arizona, on August 11 but the circumstances were such that I was compelled to wait a week or two before I could inform you of my status here. I came to Poston with the definite understanding that I would work as an anthropologist for the Bureau of Sociological Research and that I could continue your research here. Upon arrival I was informed by Dr. Leighton that there was a W.R.A. ruling that no one in a relocation center could obtain income from the outside and he intimated that in all probability I would be compelled to give up your research. However, he as well as Mr. Gelvin, the assistant center director, were in favor of my continuing your research and wrote immediately to Mr. Wade Head, the director of Poston, who was then in San Francisco for a W.R.A. conference to find out whether it was permissible for me to hold two jobs at one time and be compensated for both. Mr. Head telephoned Dr. Leighton last Thursday that the outcome seemed favorable. He returned from San Francisco last night but so far I have received no definite answer as to whether I may continue your work here or not.

Dr. Leighton is very much concerned with my problem because he realizes that if I had known that I could not work for you in Poston I would not have accepted the job in the Bureau of Sociological Research. I regret immensely now that I had not stuck with the interesting Los Angeles group in Santa Anita and followed them from the pre-evacuation to relocation center stage as I had originally planned. I have been trying to ascertain the reason for my coming to Poston for the last few days and the only plausible answer I can find is that I was thoroughly disgusted with the restrictions placed on all research on Santa Anita and was ready to fall into any scheme that appeared to offer greater freedom.

Your letter dated August 12 containing my July check arrived a few days ago. In it you state that you offered to release me to the Bureau if Dr. Leighton felt that the responsibilities would be too great and that he accepted your offer. From the above I infer that I am no longer connected with your project. However, I feel that my work in Santa Anita was rather inadequate primarily due to the hostile attitude toward all research by the administration. Therefore to atone for it I propose to send you fortnightly or monthly reports from Poston gratis—i.e. if you still wish to hear from me. Dr. Leighton sees no difficulty in my performing two jobs at one time since the research will be along similar lines. Besides we have a large number of secretaries to take charge of the clerical side of the work. Furthermore Poston is a unique community in that it is the only relocation center (if I am not mistaken) under the jurisdiction of the Indian Commission. People here, I surmise, enjoy greater freedom than in any of the relocation centers under the direct management of the W.R.A. The population of Poston is primarily drawn from the rural areas of California and Arizona—Imperial Valley, Salinas, Coachella Valley, Orange County, Bakersfield, etc.—and a few hundred from the Boyle Heights area of Los Angeles (a Japanese section), so it would be extremely interesting to ascertain the degree of [Americaniza- tion] of these rural areas which are generally reputed to be rather Old Worldish. Under a sympathetic and "benevolent" type of administration as we have here I would hazard the guess that the Japanese in Poston will be able to duplicate to a great extent than anywhere else their pre- evacuation mode of life.

I shall attempt to send you the rest of the notes on Santa Anita by the end of this week. I had intended to mail you the section on politics and attitudes as soon as I reached Poston, where I had been assured there was no censorship of mail, but upon arrival I discovered that many of my notes had been confiscated during the baggage inspection by the police. Before an evacuee leaves for a relocation center his baggage is taken to police headquarters four hours before departure and thoroughly inspected for contraband, and the victim has no knowledge of what has been confiscated until he reaches his destination. I managed to carry out my diary in my purse so from it I have been able to reconstruct as accurately as possible the life at Santa Anita. My intentions in sending you a report by the 15th were good but having been accustomed to a temperature of 50 to 85 degrees at Santa Anita, the sudden change to 125 degrees in the Arizona desert in addition to a regularly recurring dust storm was too much for me and it has taken me about ten days to feel alive again. Dr. Leighton and Dr. Spicer, the head of the sociology section of the Bureau, tell me however that in another five or six weeks the weather will become tolerable and that we will feel like working again.

Sincerely yours,
[signed] Tamie Tsuchiyama

Block 31, 11-B
Poston, Arizona
Aug. 26, 1942

Dear Dr. Lowie,
I have just been informed by Dr. Leighton that Mr. Wade Head, center manager, has approved my request to continue your research at Poston while working as anthropologist for the Bureau of Sociological Research. Under the present plan I shall be paid $19.00 a month for my work with the Bureau and may receive the usual compensation from you. The only difference from Santa Anita is that I have been requested by Dr. Leighton to make a carbon copy of all reports sent to you for the Bureau.

I would appreciate very much if you will consult Dr. Thomas as soon as she returns from her vacation and let me know whether you would like to have me continue your research under these conditions. Dr. Leighton has kindly offered to write a letter to Dr. Thomas to clarify the situation.

Sincerely yours,
[signed] Tamie Tsuchiyama

Block 31, 11 B
Poston, Arizona
Sept. 17, 1942

Dear Dr. Thomas,
I was very happy to learn from you and Dr. Lowie that I have been reinstated and that I may start sending you reports from Poston. The remaining sections on Santa Anita are almost completed and should be in your hands within a few days.

We have been extremely busy the past few weeks interviewing pro-
spective research assistants for the Bureau. At present we have about
eleven or twelve undergraduates and college graduates working for us
in the three camps. Kenny Murase and Bob Sakai, both good friends of
Tamotsu Shibutani and James Sakoda, your research assistants at Tule
Lake, may work for me provided they can obtain their release from their
present jobs. In fact they are so enthusiastic about my research that they
are willing to volunteer their services on a part-time basis if they are
unable to break away from their present connections. Since Dr. Leighton
prefers to have me sit in the office along with Dr. Spicer and direct the
activities of the assistants rather than go into the field myself, I am
orienting the research in such a fashion that the data you desire will be
collected by them and analyzed by me before you receive them. Because
of the dearth of adequate assistants we have been able only to cover a
restricted phase of culture but with the increasing number of interesting
prospects I am certain the research will be more well-rounded. I am
planning this weekend to go through the Sociological Journal which
contains all reports brought in by the assistants since the Bureau was
founded in late June and attempt to reconstruct Poston life before my
arrival in the middle of August. I know that we have full data on political
organizations, the housing situation, survey of food conditions and religious organizations, but I doubt if any serious attempt has been made
to study other phases of camp life. Of course this will be supplemented
by the data I have gathered myself. I shall do my best to follow the
Shibutani-Najima-Shibutani outline; the sore spots will be rectified as
soon as my assistants' reports pour in. If you have no objections I shall
not send you weekly field notes for the next two weeks but will utilize
that time to make a preliminary report of Poston.

Sincerely yours,
[signed] Tamie Tsuchiyama

Nov. 2, 1942

Dear Dr. Thomas,
This is just a short note to explain my silence of almost a month and
to acquaint you with the progress of my research here. Somewhere in
the early part of October I recall mailing you a letter promising to send

a preliminary report on Poston within two weeks. At that time I was engaged in perusing all of the data gathered by the Bureau since its inception in June which I hoped to utilize along with my notes in writing the preliminary report. I also believed at that time that with twelve to fifteen research assistants working for us we would be able to secure a well-rounded picture of the camp. Unfortunately many things have happened since then to impede the progress of our research. For one thing the four most promising students—among them Kenny Murase— have left us to continue their studies in the East or to work in the sugar beet fields of Utah. Also the fact that our files are confidential and inaccessible to any group including the administration has aroused the curiosity of some of the people of Poston and many of us have been branded *Inu*, or F.B.I. informers and individually notified of the public's dislike for such behavior. Since many of the former JACL leaders and other "suspicious" characters were being beaten up by gangs at this time some were frightened enough to resign from the Bureau or used this excuse to leave us. The fact that Dr. Leighton is in naval service and must wear a regulation naval uniform has also tended somewhat to increase the distrust of the Japanese people toward us as a group. Many of my friends caution me never to be seen with him in public, while others persist in asking, "Why do you insist on working for a naval intelligence officer when you can get any job in camp? If you have a sincere interest in helping the Japanese why don't you give a few courses in adult education or teach in the public school system?" At present we have only four assistants in camp one, none in camp two (the entire staff resigned last week), and four in camp three. The tragic part of it is that the best ones have abandoned us and we are left with a few untrained and not too imaginative ones whom we can easily dispense with. Most of them are sophomores or juniors in college and I suspect more interested in receiving college credits than in actual research. I do not know whether I wrote you or not the last time that Dr. Leighton in an effort to train research scientists induced the University of Chicago to permit us to give extension courses in anthropology and psychobiology with the three departmental heads as instructors. I was assigned to teach the introductory anthropology course three hours a week but after much arguing managed to liberate myself from a third time-consuming task. I felt that my work with you and the research phase of the Bureau took up a full day's work and I had no extra time to spend on teaching. Furthermore since I was the only one of the three to have entree into the Japanese community in the face of anti-administration or anti-White attitude prevailing in camp my time was too precious to expend on something which they had instituted and which they were better qualified to perform. It was finally decided that I substitute for Dr. Spicer when he was ill or otherwise engaged or when my special fields were to be discussed. Thus last week I delivered three lectures on physical anthropology for him while he was visiting his family on the Papago Reservation.

The poor quality of the research staff in addition to my onerous office duties have prevented me from much actual field work aside from attending the regular meetings of the Temporary Community Council and the Issei Advisory Board, certain recreational activities, and keeping a record of prevailing sentiments in camp. The only systematic study I have started so far is the detailed investigation of my own block to see how a block actually functions. At present I am engrossed in the demarcation of the various cliques existing there.

So far I have full notes only on the following;

1. *Background Data:* Age groupings; marital status; geographical, occupational, and religious background of evacuees, etc.

2. *Political Organizations:* Civic Planning Board, the Temporary Community Council and the beginnings of the Permanent Community Council; the Issei Advisory Board; Block Managers' Organization (including records of block council meetings in my block); political cliques, etc.

3. Religious Setup in Poston.

4. The Housing Situation and its effect on family organization.

5. The educational setup in the three camps. (In addition to the formal structure it includes themes written by various classes containing attitudes of students [toward] evacuation, camp life, their future, etc.)

6. *Economic Organization:* Attitude of the evacuees toward cotton picking in Parker Valley; data on sugar beet workers in Nebraska, Colorado and Utah; and some incomplete notes on the economic setup in Poston.

7. Two food surveys conducted in camp one.

I have not yet made a satisfactory adjustment to Poston life. Since I knew hardly any one at the time of arrival there was no one to "soften" my initiation and as a result I built up a terrific wall of dislike for Poston which I am valiantly attempting to break down at the present time. My boss, Dr. Leighton, appears to be a brilliant and sincere fellow but because of his great enthusiasm for a certain brand of applied anthropology to which I do not subscribe I find it extremely difficult to establish rapport with him. This seems to be the general attitude as far as the senior staff is concerned. For the past few weeks I have been greatly troubled with the feeling of "being lost" in the Japanese community so yesterday I finally screwed up sufficient courage to ask for a month's furlough from the Bureau to do field work as I pleased. This means that I shall not have to be obligated to attend lectures and classes conducted in the Bureau or to be tied down to a desk to glance over second hand data. If I can show at the end of the month that I can handle the work of two or three assistants by myself I may yet convince him into demoting me to the rank of research assistant.

Mich Kunitani dropped in at the office a few days ago to inform me that [JERS fieldworker Rich Watanabe (a pseudonym)] had written him that the entire Tule Lake staff was "sick and tired of the Japs" and was planning to resign and go to Chicago. I hope this is only a transitory stage and that they will continue working for you, especially since Mich tells me that they are doing excellent work there. I often wish that you could send down two or three others to work with me so we could cover Poston adequately for your purposes. The Kunitanis and I often talk of you and hope that you will come soon to see us. Mich and I are also hoping that you might be able to take us to Gila when you visit your staff there to give us a broader perspective on research here.

At the moment cotton picking in Parker Valley and the Community Trust Fund are burning questions so I intend to sample the sentiments in camp in the next few days. This means I do not know how soon I can finish the preliminary report although I shall do my best to send it to you as soon as possible.

Sincerely yours,
[signed] Tamie Tsuchiyama

Block 31, 11 B
Poston, Arizona
Dec. 1, 1942

Dear Dorothy,

This is just a short note to inform you of my present status in Poston. As you may recall when I came to say good-bye to you Thursday morning I told you that all workers except those employed in the mess halls and other vitally essential jobs had been forbidden by the Emergency Council (the city council had resigned the evening before) to return to work for the duration of the strike and that all non-conformists would be treated as "dogs." Furthermore, one of the three proposals accepted by the administration in the settling of the strike was that "Poston residents be given the right to select and appoint all evacuee personnel in the administrative and important positions." As a result of this when the strike ended Tuesday evening, Nov. 24, workers discovered that they had automatically lost their jobs and that they had a free hand in selecting whatever jobs they desired and for which they were qualified. Taking advantage of the situation I informed Dr. Leighton that I did not wish to be re-employed immediately with the rest of the research assistants since I was still very indefinite as to my future plans and abhorred the idea of requesting a release shortly after being hired. I also inquired whether he would have any objections to my taking a less time-consuming job—say, like conducting a seminar in the Adult Education Department—and working only for you in case I had difficulty in securing my transfer or if I preferred to remain in Poston indefinitely. He answered that he had no objections but that he had the definite understanding that you needed me badly at Topaz.

My problem stated baldly is this: The future of Poston and to some extent that of other relocation centers will be largely determined by the succession of events in the next three or four months. For some unknown reason—perhaps to my apparent approval of the strike (I went to picket the police station every day with my fellow block residents primarily to save my neck but also out of intense curiosity)—I have gained the confidence of certain Japanese leaders who once suspected me of being an F.B.I. agent and I find it extremely easy to talk to them. The Issei in the block (the Nisei have always liked me) have come to recognize me as an individual and not another block resident and have been pressing me to accept responsible positions. The other night I was the first one to be nominated block representative to the City Planning Board and last night I was again nominated quad candidate for the Honor Court to investigate all people accused of unseemly conduct. I managed to evade both responsibilities b[ut] you can see from this that I am beginning to be accepted by the community. Since so many "history-making" events are occurring one after another I feel in a certain sense that I am needed here more than at Topaz at the present time. Furthermore the Bureau of Sociological Research is in no position to get much dope and I consider it a sort of "duty" to record as much as possible for future research. However, I am leaving everything up to you—if you still feel that I should go to Topaz as soon as possible I shall contact Mr. Head and have him write to Mr. Fryer; otherwise I should like to sit around and watch Poston for another two or three months. As far as Leighton is concerned I know he will not make any trouble for us. I heard via Spicer that he is willing to keep me in Poston at any price since he feels that I am the only one here who can possibly secure the type of data he desires. He realizes that he cannot approach me personally for information but thinks he might be able to use Spicer or someone else as contact man.

I wish you would let me know as quickly as possible what you want me to do. If I'm going to Topaz I think I'll spend the next few weeks making a thorough report on Poston while keeping up with current events. For this I wish you will send me the revised outline for writing up preliminary reports that you mentioned you were bringing down with you in your last letter. If I'm to remain in Poston I'll have to apply for a job within the next two weeks so I won't appear suspicious to the community. And another thing—do you have any objections to my running for the city council? I'm afraid that when the City Planning Board retires in a few weeks and the city council is to be elected in all probability I shall be nominated for Nisei councilman from my block and I can't keep on refusing a public office if I'm to keep up the front that I have the welfare of the public at heart. Besides this is the only way to get the lowdown on politics in camp. Everything has become very secretive after the strike so unless you happen to be within the intimate circle it is extremely difficult to get any reliable information.

By next week I hope to send you the data I have gathered on the strike. For the past four days I have been comparing notes with a Stanford graduate whom I've known for several years in Los Angeles on inside dope on the strike.

Mich and Ann are thoroughly disgusted with the Japs and are planning to go East as soon as their request to leave camp is granted.

Sincerely yours,
[signed] Tamie Tsuchiyama

Tuesday, Dec. 15, 1942

Dear Dorothy,

I was sorry to hear from Morton that you were in bed with the flu but am glad to hear in today's letter that you are much better.

I have been working like mad for the last three weeks but am not quite ready to send you that report on the strike yet. So many things have been happening here since the strike that it's a full day's work trying to keep abreast of things. I have finally finished analyzing the voluminous notes I gathered in the last four weeks and have typed off some thirty odd pages but I'm still on Thursday, the second day of the strike, so I'm afraid you'll have to wait a few days more. If Leighton wouldn't knock on my door so frequently to find out how much I know (everything is 50-50 as far as I'm concerned—if he isn't going to let me see what happened on the administrative side during the strike I see no reason why I can't remain mum on the Japanese side) I'll probably progress faster. I'll try my darndest to get it off to you by this Saturday even if I have to take a vacation from field work until I complete it. My report covers the period from two or three months previous to the strike which laid the foundations for it, to the election of the representatives to the new City Council which occurred today.

My present plan is to take a vacation from any type of work in Poston during December and January so I can get up to date on my research. As soon as I complete the report on the strike I am intending to write up the reaction of the people to the Spanish consul's visit last week as well as the attitude toward the proposed reclassification of Nisei for the draft which is receiving much attention this week. After that I shall start the preliminary report on Poston using the outline you sent me as a guide. I can't state definitely when it will be ready since its completion depends entirely on the state of activity in camp. If no more flare-ups occur for some time I believe it [can] be accomplished by the end of January. Would you rather have me send you sections as I finish (e.g., political organizations as distinguished from religion) or would you rather have the report in its entirety?

Sincerely yours,
[signed] Tamie Tsuchiyama

RESEARCH SETTING

The Japanese American Evacuation and Resettlement Study

Examination of the JERS project must begin with consideration of its director, Dorothy Swaine Thomas. It is also essential to introduce a conceptual tool long employed by anthropologists in their ethnographic research: the distinction between the "ideal" at a normative level (especially in terms of statements about what "should be" or what "ought to be") as opposed to the "real," which the anthropologist can gauge in terms of actual practices.

Dorothy Thomas was trained as a sociologist and demographer. She did her undergraduate work at Barnard College and was exposed to sociology, economics, social statistics, political science, and anthropology there. In 1922 Thomas attended the London School of Economics and began to pursue advanced statistics and a doctoral dissertation focusing on the social aspects of the business cycle, which she completed in 1924. From there she worked for the Federal Reserve Bank and in 1925 obtained a research fellowship from the Social Science Research Council (SSRC). She met the famous sociologist (later her husband) William Isaac (W. I.) Thomas during this period and worked with him on a book focusing on the "child in America." Subsequently, she joined the Teachers College at Columbia and in the 1930s also worked at Yale's famed Institute of Human Relations.

What is critical here is the fact that Thomas had extensive exposure to interdisciplinary team research in the social sciences, and this was quite unusual. It wouldn't be an exaggeration to say that she was a pioneer in this approach, and she worked at the key institutions (the SSRC, Columbia, and Yale) during periods when interdisciplinary team research was being formulated. Thomas also had world-class exposure—via her husband, co-worker, and distinguished sociologist, W. I. Thomas—to the importance and uses of qualitative data. One reflection of such interests is his classic co-authored work, *The Polish*

Peasant in Europe and America (1958), in which W. I. Thomas was one of the first social scientists to utilize extensively personal documents; Thomas made both substantive and methodological contributions in this regard.

In terms of the structure of the scientific field that framed her endeavors, we need to remember that by 1942 Dorothy Thomas was a midcareer professional in a male-run, male-oriented setting: the academy. Sociology, Thomas's primary emphasis, wasn't yet an established discipline. In 1942, because many of her Berkeley colleagues (including co-founder Charles Aiken) who originally helped to frame the JERS project had to move on to other wartime duties, Thomas inherited the mantle of JERS director; even then she had to battle the academy in order to secure her position. For example, in one of her letters to Nishimoto, Thomas complained that—even though she was JERS director and even though she had previously been an associate professor at Yale University—she had to "take on" a number of senior scholars at Berkeley, including A. L. Kroeber, in order to win the lofty appointment of full professor. Although she eventually won appointment at this level, we should note that Thomas's position was berthed in Berkeley's division of agricultural economics, perhaps also because sociology was not yet an established department at that University of California campus.

Regarding the genesis of the JERS project, Thomas explains in *The Spoilage* that an early and limited plan to study evacuation and resettlement was drawn up by her and Professor Charles Aikin, then of the Department of Political Science at Berkeley. As the complexities of mass incarceration became clearer, this small project was greatly expanded, and faculty members with other relevant disciplinary training were added. In retrospect, it is quite interesting to compare Thomas's post hoc accounts published in 1946 and in 1952 with those written in the early 1940s. In 1952, for example, in contrasting JERS with her "Swedish research" carried out during the 1930s with colleagues Gunnar and Alva Myrdal, Thomas noted that JERS "extended far beyond the range of my experience, could draw upon no systematically accumulated fund of knowledge, and [had] few realistic models . . . or techniques by which to guide procedures or check conclusions."

Thomas describes the tremendous logistic challenges facing the staff of the project and lists the plethora of techniques and indices that JERS staff utilized. Ultimately, Thomas characterized data collection as revolving around what anthropologists sometimes refer to as a "vacuum cleaner" approach to ethnography, that is, Thomas had the JERS staff collect anything and everything—who could tell what would be valuable in the end?

In retrospect, in 1952, regarding the Japanese American and Euro-American fieldworkers assigned to specific WRA camp sites, Thomas emphasized the project's *empiricist* bent, that is, that data collection was carried out with few if any presuppositions in a classic empirical and "realist" fashion. Thomas assumed that any subsequent framework that would be used for analysis would be developed out of the very ethnographic materials that were gathered by JERS staff fieldworkers. If we go back, however, to Thomas's "memorandum to field collaborators" of August 27, 1942, we can both confirm and refute aspects of her 1952 post hoc account of the JERS project.

First, from the beginning, because the discipline of anthropology was an integral part of this interdisciplinary team research project, it is true that Thomas *did* advocate a very open-ended approach to doing fieldwork in the camps. In her 1942 instructions to staff fieldworkers, Thomas stressed that fieldnotes were to be written up daily in an effort to produce a sociohistorical record of data "record[ed] on the spot and at the time the events are occurring." In addition to daily fieldnotes, Thomas demanded that fieldworkers begin an immediate organization of data into "preliminary reports on the structure of the community." Third, fieldworkers were to generate a summary every week, giving special attention to the evolving nature of the categories used to structure JERS data collection and data analysis. But this instruction in and of itself indicates that there *were* some foundational assumptions that were made, in other words, that the JERS study was *not* radically empirical or inductive. Thomas *did* employ a conceptual framework to which fieldworkers were supposed to attend, and the evidence that she did is in her own memo.

In the same 1942 memorandum, Thomas states: "The situation in which you are involved and about which you are making records is an *enforced mass migration.*" Right from the beginning, then, we can see that a definite conceptual distancing was at the basis of the entire JERS enterprise: a sterile euphemism was given pride of place, reflecting a deep commitment to academic research (necessitating disciplined noninvolvement) as opposed to critical analysis or intervention.

Beyond this, while noting that little that was known about *voluntary* migration was relevant to the present situation, Thomas proposed three guiding concepts that could serve to orient fieldworkers in terms of data collection.

These were (1) "culture conflict," conceptualized in terms of a Japanese versus American dichotomy; (2) social and personal disorganization; and (3) a subsequent process of reorganization. Readers familiar with "classic" models of "race relations" will see a familiar pattern in terms of the trinity of conflict, disorganization, reorganization. Dorothy Thomas's conceptual framework resonates with Robert E. Park's "race relations cycle." Park's son-in-law and University of Chicago sociologist Robert Redfield was a consultant to the WRA. Redfield also advised Dorothy Thomas and even provided JERS staff with office space at the University of Chicago when JERS opened up a branch of the project to study post–loyalty questionnaire relocation to that city. In fact, many informal "old boy"/"old girl" ties linked major players in the social sciences into networks of mutual aid and support during the war years and after. As the anthropologist Roger Sanjek emphasizes, these are some of the facts that desperately need to be placed in anthropology textbooks as part of the historical record of the social science disciplines.

Other subtleties are entailed in Thomas's presuppositions. The working concepts I've identified above were deeply influenced by stock demographic variables. Specifically, in her official publications Thomas would propose that differences such as rural versus urban, Issei versus Nisei versus Kibei, Buddhist versus Christian, relative age, gender, and family, occupational, and social status would all have a determining impact on how the cycle of culture conflict, disorganization, and reorganization would be played out.

Without going into further detail here, I propose that each of the focal concepts and the associated variables tended to generate preconstructed and essentialized units of analysis whose "meanings" became supercharged when tied to the foundational equation "American: Japanese:: loyal: disloyal." Thus, as anyone who has worked through Thomas's publications on mass incarceration such as *The Spoilage* and *The Salvage* knows, the variables Nisei, Christian, urban, young, "middle class–oriented" are contrasted with Issei/Kibei, Buddhist, rural, older, working class in order to "explain," on a post hoc basis, what "kinds" of Japanese Americans were willing and able to leave camp before the end of the war versus those Japanese Americans who chose to remain inside. In a tautological fashion, then, one can note how the so-called variables, integral to the social demographer's conceptual tool kit, became fixed into naturalized categories that were then used to account for individual and collective perspectives and actions.

When we turn from the conceptual and ethical framework of the JERS project, both explicit and tacit, there is still another dimension of the project to confront.

In this day and age, it is imperative that ethnographers prepare to enter the field by reading and coming to grips with the American Anthropological Association's code of ethics. This is a good attempt to formalize the dilemmas, priorities, and obligations an anthropologist is likely to face in terms of competing demands in the field, in academe, and beyond.

Formalized ethical codes are a relatively recent, certainly postwar development. Thus, it is noteworthy that Dorothy Thomas formulated both guidelines and standards that were circulated to all the JERS project's fieldworkers. In their preface to *The Spoilage*, Thomas and Nishimoto noted: "Constant efforts had to be made to guard against betrayal of informants [here, a synonym for Japanese Americans who provided JERS fieldworkers with data] and against divulging information even to friendly governmental agencies."

Although ethical standards concerning confidentiality formed an explicit dimension of JERS methodology, archival records indicate that things were not always so clear-cut in terms of the field setting and day-to-day practices of JERS fieldworkers. Most of these fieldworkers, whether of Japanese or European descent, were young. Even if they were advanced-level graduate students, most were relatively inexperienced and had little actual field training. On this basis, many of the JERS staff members sought out and appreciated contact with other social scientists, whether these were JERS colleagues, fieldworkers attached to other projects (such as the WRA's "community analysis section"), or WRA-appointed personnel, some of whom also carried out research as part and parcel of their staff duties.

In sum, in practice there appears to have been a great deal of leeway in regard to how stringently JERS fieldworkers adhered to their ethical charge. Perhaps because Dorothy Thomas herself put constant pressure on them to collect copious amounts of data, a climate developed where daily production, rather than ethical niceties, became the order of the day. It is not surprising, then, that the JERS correspondence files and journals alike indicate that pragmatic working relationships were often established between JERS staff and other non-JERS personnel who carried out research in camp and that a good deal of information changed hands. The latter was not, however, solely a JERS phenomenon. Research workers in the WRA camps, regardless of their affiliation, found it to their mutual advantage to gather additional material and to cross-check their findings, through a frequent, albeit informal exchange of observations and data.

Poston

Built on the western edge of Arizona, near the town of Parker, Poston was located on the Colorado River Indian Reservation. Like the Gila River, Arizona, camp, which was also located on a reservation, Poston was divided into multiple units—three in the latter case. Also, Poston was unique because it was the only one of the ten more permanent camps to be managed between 1942 and the end of 1943 by the then Office of Indian Affairs, directed by John Collier, Sr. Under this arrangement, OIA was directly responsible for setting up and running this camp, although it did so under the same general guidelines specified for the other camps by the WRA.

What was daily life like for Tamie Tsuchiyama and her compatriots in the Colorado River Relocation Center, as Poston was officially known? Archived materials from the 1940s remain an underutilized resource for developing a broader understanding of experiences and views from within the camp. The accompanying drawings of Poston were done by the Issei artist Mr. Jitsuo Kurushima (1905–1991) and first appeared in a 1945 issue of the *Poston Bungei,* a poetry and literary journal published in Japanese by Issei in Poston. Kurushima's work provides an excellent example of the integrity and humor depicted in the vernacular forms of artistic production in the camps.

DRAWINGS BY JITSUO KURUSHIMA

Kurushima's opening sketch shows initial arrival at Poston. Baggage is being unloaded from a truck. While a mother waits, tending to her children, another couple appears to be examining their possessions. The man's mouth is open, his jaw dropped, as if he were in shock at the sight of his surroundings. Another man is stuffing a bag with straw—this was the only kind of mattress provided in the beginning. Yet another man is shown sweeping the porch of the barracks, which were quite roughly constructed. The barracks typically needed a thorough cleaning to begin with, they were only provisionally furnished when the camp initially opened, and they required a great deal of care and repair in order to be made livable throughout the war years. Interestingly enough, the sketch of the buildings does not appear to resemble the actual layout of Poston's residential areas, so this drawing is probably of an

intake area near Poston's warehouses as opposed to the barracks themselves. "Welcome to Poston," indeed! This would also help account for the man's look of total amazement, as he and his wife hunker down to reclaim their baggage from the truck.

Kurushima's second drawing illustrates the strong winds that frequently whipped the dust across the desert plain where the camp was located, depositing fine sand into every conceivable nook and cranny of the barracks. The caption, in Japanese characters, reads, "Uh-oh. No looking allowed!" This is in reference, certainly, to the young woman's thigh, which is dangerously exposed as her skirt and coat are blown up by the wind. The man to the left is covering his face, either to protect his eyes from dust, or to avoid taking advantage of the situation, or perhaps both.

Kurushima's next drawing hilariously illustrates urban residents' great surprise and alarm in regard to the Parker valley area's rattlers and scorpions. The caption in Japanese has the young couple exclaiming "Uwaa!" and "Yaa!" (Note the young man's homemade *geta*, or wooden sandals, one of which has fallen from his foot as he jumps back to avoid the local fauna.) The caption to the right exclaims: "What we've got here; strange creatures!"

The daily routine, quickly established, of having to wait in line for everything was an omnipresent and inevitable part of camp life. One of two drawings on this topic shows the line in front of the barracks mess hall. A woman in the center of the picture yawns, as if to express her boredom. The woman on the left is carrying a tray from the mess hall, perhaps for a sick sibling or parent. While the kitchen staff rings the triangle, adults, parents, mothers

with babies, and youths line up as they did every day, three times a day, awaiting their turn for their chow. The mass approach to mess disrupted family life. Older children often preferred to eat with their pals rather than their families, and some parents lost control, as the ability to keep in touch (and also to reinforce family solidarity and discipline) during meals was eroded. The caption in Japanese reads, "Mess hall line."

In the following drawing, Kurushima depicts Poston residents waiting in line in order to pick up their meager paychecks. The caption in Japanese reads, "A long waiting line, for a $16.00 monthly paycheck, under a scorching sun." The monetary reference here is to the fact that most of the men and women who worked in the camps only earned between $12.00 and $19.00 a month. (Note the personification of the sun, which is done with Asian features.

The face on the sun is squinting, an intense caricature, as if to depict the fact that daytime temperatures in the summer months could reach 120 degrees in the shade.) Most folks in the line wear hats; a few women carry umbrellas to shade them from the sun. A man in overalls, just left of center in the foreground, mops the sweat from his face with a handkerchief. In the background we see a canteen. People could spend their meager earnings on small snacks, sundries, and supplies, but larger items had to be sent for via mail-order catalogs.

The established routines, described above, were challenged early on during the famed Poston strike of November 18–24, 1942. Kurushima's sixth drawing

is the most remarkable one of the set, especially in terms of how it corresponds to on-the-spot descriptions of the events of November 18–24.

First, there are numerous accounts of the many speakers (one of whom is shown in the background), as well as the bonfires at night. The speaker appears to be standing on one of the stages that were built for popular programs and events at Poston and were juxtaposed to one of the Poston police stations, which is in fact historically accurate. From the 18th to the 24th, Japanese music blared and all ordinary work routines stopped as Japanese Americans resolved to go on strike until the administration met their demands for a greater level of self-government (as first-generation Issei were unable to run for any elected office), as well as for better conditions at all levels of the camp.

Second, Tsuchiyama herself commented on the way that some Unit I residents drew block banners that, from a distance, resembled the Japanese battle flag, basically in order to tease Euro-American personnel with suggestions of popular solidarity based on an affiliation with Japan. (Incidentally, Richard S. Nishimoto once noted that, had pro-Japanese nationalist sentiments actually been the case, residents would have simply run up the battle flag instead of making facsimiles.) The facsimile is captured in Kurushima's rendering of the banner to the left.

Third, residents did indeed fabricate signs in English and in Japanese appealing for solidarity and unanimity in regard to their collective demands for rights, dignity, and self-governance, which, after all, had been promised by the WRA. The characters on the banner on the left proclaim "United in cooperation," echoing the sign in English.

Fourth, although residents did not literally hang a dog or dogs, as the artist implies, they definitely did put up illustrations of hanging dogs and hang actual bones during the strike period. The allusion is to *inu* (literally "dog" but meaning "traitor" and "spy"). The images were intended to suggest the possible fate of any Japanese American resident of Poston who dared to inform on his or her compatriots. This was, in fact, the actual trigger of the Poston strike: the arrest and detention of two men who were accused of beating a reputed *inu*.

Three additional drawings hark back to day-to-day life in Poston during calmer days after the strike. A montage captures a range of daily activities, including, in the top row, left, singing (in this case, a verse that goes, "Mountains and rivers, plains and trees. Where are they in this wilderness?") and, to the right, a performance (perhaps a classical recitation of *shigin*) in Japanese. In the second row, women carry out their toiletries at the barracks latrine (the sign says, "Women"). In the sketch to the right, women are also shown in the barracks laundry room, one hard at work washing but a group of four sharing a convivial moment. The Japanese caption to the right reads, "Live broadcast of gossip."

Issei men are the focus of the two drawings on the bottom row. Beyond the fact that an MP or guard (because of the holster under the armpit, as well as the jodhpurs and high boots) appears to be surprised by the dapper gentleman in front of him, the larger meaning of the drawing to the left is unclear

to me. The image on the right is of two men playing *go* (a board game, frequently described as a Japanese version of checkers). Although seemingly simple, through its command of postures and expressions the drawing effectively captures the intensity and absorption with which the older men passed their time in camp playing such board games.

Crafts became a very popular pastime for those with the tools and abilities. An older man, probably an Issei, is shown working with local ironwood. His

tools are very basic and include an ax, a saw, a knife or file, a wooden mallet, and a chisel. The tree stumps represent a popular Japanese art form known as *kobu*. *Kobu* entailed finding pleasing patterns or actual images in wood and then bringing these out through careful selection, cutting, carving, and polishing processes, often largely by hand. Part of the art of *kobu* was to alter the piece as little as possible, beyond cutting a bit in order to highlight an image and perhaps polishing the piece to a lustrous finish. The caption in Japanese reads, "Ironwood work." (See the Appendix, page 184, for a fascinating comment, offered by an Issei advisor, regarding the cultural significance of ironwood work in the Poston setting.)

On the other hand, in the following drawing a younger man, probably a Nisei, with special magnifying glasses perched upon his nose, is shown in a more modern shop. He has at hand a range of motorized tools such as polishers, a grinder, a saw or drill press of some kind, a blowtorch, pliers, and so forth. Like the Issei man, the younger man's posture and gaze suggest his intense concentration. Above his head hovers a plethora of images of possible creations, perhaps for a young woman whom he would like to impress with his hand-crafted adornments. The caption at the upper right reads, "Stone polishing."

The last drawing depicts departure. Friends, families, and compatriots who had lived, worked, and struggled together through so much would now be separated as the three units were finally closed between the end of September and the end of November 1945. Toward the rear of a convoy, in the back of a large truck, a family unit—husband, wife, and children—prepares to leave Poston (probably en route to Parker, Arizona, which was the nearest connecting train terminal). Hands wave good-bye, rub aside tears, and touch friends' hands one last time. The poetic caption that Kurushima composed reads, "In sadness is a faint hope that we might meet again someday. Farewell. Farewell."

Prior to the camp's closure at the end of World War II, two broad categories of people left Poston. One group was made up of persons who had decided to answer "no" to questions on the WRA's loyalty questionnaire issued in early 1943: either question number twenty-seven (pertaining to an Issei's willingness to foreswear loyalty to the Japanese emperor) or question number twenty-eight (pertaining to a Nisei man's willingness to serve in the armed forces of the United States). Those who answered "no" were classified as disloyal by the WRA and, beginning in mid-1943, removed as segregants to the WRA camp at Tule Lake, California, on the Oregon border, for the duration of the war. Those who were deemed to be loyal and who could find employment or education east of California might be relocated into the larger society between 1943 and 1945. As a precondition, however, the WRA made those who chose to leave camp before the end of the war sign an oath that they would avoid congregating with other persons of Japanese descent on the outside and make a good-faith effort to assimilate and be accepted by their fellow Americans.

Suffice it to say that, in any case, departure entailed facing and dealing with difficult challenges. In fact, it took much of the decade of the 1950s for Japanese Americans to reestablish themselves financially and otherwise.

Tsuchiyama as a Fieldworker for JERS

First, it is clear from her personal correspondence that during the twenty months she worked at Poston for JERS Tsuchiyama labored under very stressful field conditions at a personal as well as at a professional level. To begin with, the temperatures typical of the Arizona summers, which might reach 120 degrees in the shade, made life extremely uncomfortable for Tsuchiyama. Her sister, Hisako, once received a letter that was marked by small circular stains. "Don't worry," Tsuchiyama had commented parenthetically, "these marks are not tear drops." They were, in fact, drops of sweat that fell from her face and arms as she was writing. Tsuchiyama's hypersensitivity to the Arizona summer heat was so great that it left her unable to sleep well for days. On at least a couple of occasions, it even put her into Poston's Unit I hospital.

Elements of Tsuchiyama's personality added to the rigors of the physical climate and conditions. First, though clearly willing to carry out research as a member of a group, we have already seen that Tsuchiyama was a fairly self-contained researcher and scholar. She once wrote Dorothy Thomas that she "did her best work alone." From time to time Tsuchiyama even played up this quality in her correspondence, once calling herself a "lone wolf" who was not really able to work harmoniously with others.

Second, in spite of her relative inexperience as a fieldworker, Tsuchiyama set extremely high standards in regard to the quality and quantity of her fieldnotes and reports. Remember that, prior to 1941, her doctoral project had revolved around a library-based dissertation. As far as I have been able to determine, even though she had been an undergraduate anthropology major and was an advanced doctoral student, Tsuchiyama had never actually carried out fieldwork before on her own or even with others as a member of a team. As a result, her correspondence indicates that Tsuchiyama sometimes felt professionally inadequate, which is actually a rather common experience among fieldworkers—even experienced fieldworkers, let alone neophytes. Her tendency toward perfectionism was not aided by the fact that Thomas, while basically encouraging her, also put constant pressure on Tsuchiyama to produce and consistently mail her tangible research results, both relevant data as well as focused topical reports.

For her part, Dorothy Thomas did offer feedback at three levels. First, in her capacity as project director, Thomas organized two JERS staff conferences—meetings that were held over a couple of days, away from any of the camps. The first was held in Chicago in 1943, and the second was in Salt Lake City the following year. Extant notes from these two conferences indicate that both were similar to the BSR seminars. During these sessions staff members shared their research findings from their particular camp. Preliminary comparative analyses were developed in open-ended discussions, and plans for future research were outlined.

Second, one of Dorothy Thomas's favorite methodological techniques for cross-checking data was to send copies of reports written by one fieldworker in a given camp to another fieldworker from the same camp or sometimes to a colleague at a different research site. As I will detail below, on one occasion Thomas was actually able to arrange for Nishimoto and Tsuchiyama to visit Rosalie Hankey (later Rosalie Hankey Wax), a graduate student from the Department of Anthropology at the University of California at Berkeley and a JERS fieldworker who was assigned at that time to the WRA camp at Gila River in south-central Arizona.

This practice had both short-term and long-term outcomes. First, fieldworkers were pitted against each other, often writing Thomas to defend themselves or to attack the observations generated by a competing fieldworker. Second, Thomas eventually asked fieldworkers to completely rewrite materials that had actually been generated by someone else. James Sakoda brought this to my attention by pointing out the numerous times that Dorothy Thomas tried to have someone edit Charles (Charlie) Kikuchi's diaries and also the fact that Thomas and Nishimoto's book, *The Spoilage*, is actually largely based on Rosalie Hankey's fieldnotes.

Third, at an individual level, Thomas tried to encourage Tsuchiyama by reminding her that if she kept up her good work, Tsuchiyama would be in an excellent position to contribute significant publications to the record. Alternatively, however, Thomas also offered subtle reminders that she, Dorothy Thomas, was in a position as a senior professor to "make or break" the careers of the young scholars who were working for her.

As an example of her encouragement, on January 25, 1943, Thomas wrote, "Well, this is very fine material you are sending us, and we look forward to receiving more of it." Similarly, in a letter to Tsuchiyama dated July 14, 1943, Thomas responded in a fairly supportive fashion to Tsuchiyama's comment of July 12 that an enclosed field report might well be her "last contribution" to the study (i.e., JERS). Thomas wrote:

> I am concerned with your leaving Poston not only because that would be a severe loss to the study. I am sure it would not be possible to find a person to replace you or to even approximate a duplication of your work. But more fundamental than your importance to this study is the importance of your work. I firmly believe that your publications on Japanese Americans at Poston will constitute distinguished sociological and anthropological monographs. As a factor in the understanding of the Japanese minority group in America, they will be important.

Thomas, though, chose to end the paragraph with the following comment: "and they will also be important as a firm basis for your future career." Then, she closed her letter with the following advice:

> I know you understand these things, and I hope you will not allow the psychological and physical hardships of relocation center living to keep you from continuing your work. As I told you at Phoenix, I think you should leave the camp at intervals to refresh yourself and to plan new work. But I firmly believe it would be a mistake for you to cease working entirely at this point. I hope you will think this matter through very carefully. Above all, don't do anything in a fit of depression, and let me know from time to time exactly what your plans are.

Beyond this, there is a great deal of evidence that Tsuchiyama experienced special stresses and strains that, not surprisingly, revolved around trying to carry out fieldwork in a setting that was typically rumor-filled and uncertain. Uncertainty, in turn, generated tension and frustration. On occasion, the situation in Poston became overtly dangerous, and Japanese Americans who chose to voice unpopular perspectives and sentiments were sometimes attacked by their compatriots, which in some cases resulted in serious beatings.

As mentioned above, in terms of her own day-to-day stresses as a field-worker, Tsuchiyama's letters express a great deal of concern over the seizure of her fieldnotes by federal intelligence agents. To her credit, in order to protect the privacy and confidentiality of her research data, Tsuchiyama devised a number of techniques to thwart the interception of her notes and reports when she mailed them to Thomas, who was in residence at the University of California at Berkeley. (Incidentally, in a letter dated January 7, 1943, Thomas tried to reassure Tsuchiyama that no one appeared to be intercepting her mail. On the exact same date, however, Thomas wrote to Professor Robert Lowie, Tsuchiyama's mentor at Berkeley. Noting that sixty Nisei had had to be removed from the Manzanar, California, WRA camp because of death threats, Thomas commented: "evidently very serious things can and do happen, so Tamie is not quite as crazy as we thought she was.")

At the same time that she did everything in her power to forestall seizure and improper use of her research, Tsuchiyama worried that any Japanese American doing research in the camps could easily be branded as an *inu,* or spy, working on behalf of the WRA or even the federal government. In the polarized setting of the camps, such an accusation was to be avoided at all costs. It was very clear to everyone, early on, that some Poston residents were so frustrated by the climate of fear created by occasional FBI sweeps through the camp that they were willing to act on the basis of rumors. The famed Poston strike of November 1942, for example, was triggered by the arrest and detention of two men who were accused of beating a suspected *inu* badly enough to put him into the hospital. Finally, it is of critical importance to delineate and situate Tsuchiyama's sometimes open contempt both for Poston and for anyone who was seemingly too "pro-Japan" or even too "Japanese," both in terms of her personal background in Hawaii and in terms of the excesses that mass incarceration generated among mainland Japanese Americans.

As a Nisei, born and raised in Hawaii, Tsuchiyama expressed her dislike for Poston pretty much throughout her personal correspondence, now held in the JERS collection. One form that this took early on was Tsuchiyama's expressions of alienation from the harsh environment of the dusty and dry Arizona desert where Poston was located. Later, on July 29, 1943, she openly and contemptuously referred to Poston as a jail.

Her criticisms of individuals at Poston, whom she felt to be "pro-Axis elements," were also openly expressed in her personal correspondence. In retrospect, we can assume that this attitude may have been a product of her background as a second-generation American of Japanese descent, born in Hawaii and educated in the assimilationist climate of the school system on the islands between the wars. Such inclinations positioned Tsuchiyama, personally and politically, with a group of "ultraliberals" at Poston. This group was comprised primarily of second-generation Japanese Americans who were generally pro-American yet otherwise progressive in the sense that they were more cosmopolitan and international in perspective than their peers. Like Tsuchiyama, persons of this persuasion tended to leave camp, one way or another, before the end of the war. Many actually chose to "resettle" in urban areas in the Midwest or back east; such individuals were able to do so as early as 1943 if they passed inspection as loyal Americans and if they signed an oath swearing not to congregate with other Japanese Americans after they were released from camp, among other things.

In this sense, it is possible that for all her education and despite her basic empathy, Tsuchiyama lacked an intimate, insider's perspective on the life experiences of the Issei, Nisei, and Kibei on the U.S. mainland. Without such a perspective, she may not have been able to fully understand how prejudice and discrimination in the United States had actually intensified the cultural conservatism, parochialism, and seemingly reactionary political stance of pro-Axis elements at Poston. Without the benefit of such an interpretation, fieldwork on political developments, intrigues, and processes at Poston must have been emotionally and psychologically taxing for Tsuchiyama, to say the least.

Two subsequent letters from Thomas to Tsuchiyama, one in early August (August 4, to be exact) 1943 and then again in late September (the 22d) support this interpretation. Deeply concerned about Tsuchiyama's "state of mind," Thomas heartily approved Tsuchiyama's proposed plan: to leave Poston for some months in order to get away from the pressures in camp and to work full-time on writing up the fieldnotes and field reports that Tsuchiyama had been promising but had been unable to deliver. Thomas wrote: "It is perfectly agreeable to me for you to leave Poston now. Cleveland sounds like a good choice. My feeling is that you should not try to do as much investigation on the relocation aspects when you get there. The important thing is to write up your report on Poston, and if you can get decent living quarters, Cleveland is as good a place as any other to work in."

To be sure, management of stress and the need for short- and long-term relaxation and escape are typical dimensions of extended periods of ethnographic fieldwork. These are intensified if and when the ethnographer is removed from the usual diversions that she or he might otherwise pursue if carrying out research at or near home. What is more unusual in the JERS case is that trying to carry out fieldwork in a clandestine fashion generated additional stress for the on-site researchers. In Tsuchiyama's case the pressures were so intense that they necessitated periods of total removal from the camp setting—a fact that surely would have excited suspicions of its own. Certainly, people did leave Poston and the other WRA camps, from as early as 1943, on a temporary agricultural leave or if they could find a job in the Midwest or back east and if they could pass security clearance investigations. Thomas approved, even though it must have been logistically awkward, because this was the only way that she thought she could get Tsuchiyama to write up her notes. This decision on the part of both women, however, was a step toward the end of their professional and personal relationship.

The letters reproduced in this and the following chapter were written by Tamie Tsuchiyama between January and March 1943. I have selected these letters largely because they shed light on how Tsuchiyama carried out her fieldwork during her first critical year in Poston. In addition, I have also selected a few of the many letters that shed light on day-to-day events at Poston, particularly the climate of paranoia, given FBI activities in the camp, as well as a fascinating letter concerning the impact of Japanese language radio broadcasts, which were apparently being picked up on shortwave radio sets, a very small number of which had apparently been hidden in the barracks.

The letters show that even in Poston, Tsuchiyama could actually be a very productive fieldworker when conditions were right. In spite of the rigors of the overall situation in which she was trying to carry out anthropological fieldwork, Tsuchiyama actually produced a good deal of research. First and foremost, she authored a total of six completed topical field reports. She amassed a large "sociological journal" that included her own fieldnotes and clippings from her one-time Issei assistant Richard S. Nishimoto's diary and notes. She also collected materials for her journal from official WRA sources, from the camp's newspaper, the *Poston Chronicle*, from mainstream newspapers, and so on. She sustained a lively correspondence with a variety of colleagues and friends, and in fact her letters provide the best and possibly only available indication of her life, thoughts, and general state of mind from the early to mid-1940s.

Renewing an Acquaintance: Ties to Richard Nishimoto

Tsuchiyama's letters to Thomas reveal that Tsuchiyama had met Richard Shigeaki Nishimoto both in San Francisco and in Los Angeles prior to the war.

Tamie Tsuchiyama's elder sister, Hisako, was best friends with Kay Kawagoi, whom she had met while both were students at Los Angeles High School in 1929 and 1930. Kay had later married Richard Nishimoto's younger brother, Ken, and this couple actually wound up in another of the WRA camps in Arizona: Gila River. This was the basis upon which Tsuchiyama met Nishimoto socially before the war, although the exact nature of the relationship is never actually addressed in her correspondence. One of the few times that Tsuchiyama mentioned their prewar relationship at all, she wrote to Dorothy Thomas that the Nishimoto family originally knew her and continued to think of her largely as "Hisako's kid sister."

Once Tsuchiyama had arrived at Poston and begun working there, Nishimoto was clearly aware of her presence. There is also evidence that, in the beginning, Nishimoto was quite suspicious of Tsuchiyama's motives and intentions, and that he intended to keep a close watch over her activities. In fieldnotes dated December 29, 1942, anthropologist Edward H. Spicer recorded a somewhat strange conversation that he had had with Nishimoto during which the latter indicated to Spicer that he "came into the Bureau [BSR] for the express purpose of neutralizing Tamie Tsuchiyama, so that she would not hurt the Issei, if she happened to be an F.B.I. agent or something similar. [Nishimoto said to Spicer:] 'Look what I did. Dr. Leighton tried to help her when she was cracking up. Then you tried to help her. I came along and I keep her from going to pieces. And now she is neutralized. Swell, huh?' "

On the other hand, as early as December 1942 Tsuchiyama wrote to

Thomas that she had made a major inroad by gaining the confidence of Poston leaders who had originally suspected her of being a spy for the FBI. A month later, Tsuchiyama reported to Thomas that she was obtaining excellent data, largely because she had gained the confidence of the "real" political leaders in Poston who were operating behind the scenes but who were willing to reveal their thoughts and share their actions with her. In this same letter, Tsuchiyama specifically stated that she had gained the confidence of Richard Nishimoto, whom she describes as one of the most powerful community leaders at Poston. Interestingly enough, Tsuchiyama also noted in one of her letters that Nishimoto had confessed that he had been very suspicious of Tsuchiyama at first. Apparently, because of Tsuchiyama's knowledge of the Japanese language and her level of education, Nishimoto initially perceived her as his "most potentially dangerous enemy" in camp.

In short, after Tsuchiyama had reacquainted herself with Nishimoto, she soon came to believe that he could be an invaluable "key informant" who could better help her carry out her JERS fieldwork assignment at Poston. This appears to have been largely because of Nishimoto's status as an Issei and his early positions as a work crew boss and then block manager, both of which garnered him a reputation as a community leader and broker. Soon enough Nishimoto became a full-fledged political leader who engaged in power politics and who used his knowledge and influence, ultimately, as head of the block managers of Unit I in order to wrest control for himself and his group. He was largely successful in this regard and was widely consulted for advice between 1943 and 1945 by Japanese Americans, Euro-American bureaucrats, and social science researchers alike.

Once he got over his initial mistrust of her, Nishimoto appears to have been very sympathetic to and interested in Tsuchiyama's ethnographic project. That she was given copies of Nishimoto's own reports and field diary, which she often cut up and filed by topic in her own sociological journal, indicates that he was willing to help her materially as well.

To Tsuchiyama, then, being able to tap the knowledge, insights, and contacts of such an individual must have seemed like a godsend, at least in the beginning.

Letters from the Field, January–March 1943

Block 31, 11 B
Poston, Arizona
January 3, 1943

Dear Dorothy,

Please let me know as soon as possible whether you received my chronological account of the Poston strike or not since I am planning to withhold the mailing of my more confidential reports on the visit of the Spanish consul, the JACL resolution on selective draft and my analysis of the strike until I receive definite assurance of my papers reaching you. At the time I mailed my first report Spicer was greatly concerned with the active interest of the local F.B.I. and the administration in the research being done by the Bureau and by me and advised me to take every precaution possible. I took advantage of the Christmas rush to send you the report of the strike under two separate covers (the more "subversive" sections in an ordinary envelope) but am warned not to take another chance until I hear from you. The swell data I am receiving from the *real* political leaders in camp who are at present operating under cover are given in strictest confidence and will cease as soon as the F.B.I. intercept my mail and utilize it for purposes other than research.

Since the strike I have gained the confidence of X [Richard S. Nishimoto], one of the two most powerful political figures in camp (who incidentally informed me a few days ago that he had been trailing me for the past three months since he considered me the potentially most dangerous enemy in camp because of my academic background coupled with my knowledge of the Japanese) who supplies me with all the political intrigues behind the scenes so that I am at present in a better position to analyze camp politics. Frequently he gives me advance notices of certain movements on foot so that I shall more fully appreciate them when they appear in the open. The recording of the struggle for power between the administration and the evacuees, between certain political factions, and between the Issei and the Nisei, leaves me little time to study other phases of camp life not to mention the writing of the preliminary report. At the rate I'm going I'll probably need a two week vacation in Granada or Jerome after camp life resumes a more normal tone.

Sincerely yours,
[signed] Tamie

Jan. 11, 1943

Dear Dorothy,

I would appreciate very much if you will notify me immediately after you receive my report on the Spanish consul. My fear of the F.B.I. intercepting my mail may seem awfully childish and exaggerated to you but if you have been grilled by them as many times as I have or seen so many of your acquaintances "mistreated" by them shortly before evacuation you will perhaps understand. At one time in Santa Anita all of my mail going to Hawaii were treated chemically to see that nothing was being passed up. With conditions so shaky in Poston I would not be surprised to receive a "routine check-up" one of these days. Since I am making a carbon copy of all the dope I send you it is unnecessary for you to return any of my reports. In case anything happens to me X has promised to deliver all of my field notes to you so you may rest assured that you will get them eventually.

Two days ago it is reported that the F.B.I. came into Camp 2 to investigate one of the most influential Issei political leaders there. Apparently they or some of the administrative officials feel that his mere removal will restore peace and quiet to Camp 2. If they make another faux pas and take him away I'm afraid there is going to be a free-for-all fight in the three camps this time with much bloodshed. Since he is the restraining influence on the "actionist" group there his removal will mean the unleashing of much violence. Camp 3 is closely tied up with Camp 2 politically so will come to its aid and Camp 1 will be morally obligated to join the movement. We are waiting with trepidation to see what they will do—the evacuees are not ready to stage another riot yet. As far as Camp 1 is concerned the limelight is focused at present on the struggle for power between the Central Executive Committee [CEC] and the Issei Advisory Board [IAB]. The I.A.B. held a closed meeting last week and passed a vote of non-confidence over the C.E.C. and asked them either to resign gracefully or be pushed out forcefully. The C.E.C. this week decided to fight it out so much mud-slinging is in force at present. I hope the administration will be wise enough to adopt a hands-off policy this time and permit the evacuees to fight it out themselves.

I am typing up the report on the aftermath of the strike this week which will I hope give you a clearer picture of the C.E.C., the Labor Relations Board, and the Honor court as well as the new Nisei Council and the Issei Advisory Board. I suggest that you withhold comments on my Spanish consul report until you read this report.

As far as Topaz is concerned I would like to remain in Poston indefinitely. I have made swell friends here after the strike and am collecting the type of data which I know will be closed to me at Topaz. Besides I hate the notion of going thru another nightmare for the next 4 or 5 months while attempting to adjust myself to new camp conditions. I doubt if I shall be able to get as close to my subjects as I am doing now at Poston in any other relocation center. As Spicer remarks enviously, "Your field set-up is as ideal as any anthropologist can dream of." Furthermore, I am a lone wolf and cannot work harmoniously with others. I do my best work when I'm left alone. You must do a lot of talking to get me to go to Topaz if you *really* want me to go after my tantrum above. [Margin note: "I suggest that you read the analysis before you tackle the report."]

Sincerely yours,
[signed] Tamie

January 15, 1943

Dear Dorothy,

Two of my most reliable informants rushed into my office a few minutes ago and requested me to write to you to remove my reports on the strike and the Spanish consul's visit from the general files and place them in a separate section since they had read in the papers last night that a Senate committee had been appointed to make a study of relocation centers. They feared that since your study is so well-known there might be a possibility of the government impounding your files. I assured them that the reports were in safe hands but they begged me to write you—hence this note.

. . . The data on political intrigues which I have been gathering for the last two months cannot be duplicated anywhere so I hope you will treat them as strictly confidential matter. I am almost through typing the report on the aftermath of the strike which brings the section on political organizations up to date. The report on politics of pre-strike days will probably not be ready until the beginning of February. Incidentally I received X's help in answering your questions on the strike and have compiled a Who's Who of political figures in camp which will probably be of great interest to you since much of the mud-slinging going on at present dates back as much as twenty years. The prejudices and resentment harbored by the Japanese in California since the Exclusion Act of 1924 are coming out in the open now. My analysis of the strike will have to wait for another month or so since I find that the one I made right after the strike is very superficial after talking to several influential political figures. I did not fully comprehend the exact composition of camp at that time. I am at the stage now where I can predict with almost 95% accuracy what the reaction to certain things will be by certain groups in camp.

The frequent visits of F.B.I. agents in camp as well as the voting down of the camouflage project in Camps 2 and 3 are causing many people to become jittery. They feel that should Camp 1 also refuse to accept it there will be swift retaliation on the part of the government, most likely in the form of a big F.B.I. raid on possible "saboteurs." The situation is certainly shaky in Poston but exciting for us research assistants. Spicer and I frequently wonder whether we have unconsciously become foreign correspondents overnight and go solely in quest of sensational news or whether the conditions we think exist in camp *really* exist.

Spicer asked me to give his regards to W. I. the next time I wrote to you.

Sincerely yours,
[signed] Tamie

January 21, 1943

Dear Dorothy,

Thanks for your morale-building letter of January 8th. When I get into the dumps again I'll haul out your letter and pretend I'm "vital" to the study. One of these days if I try hard enough I may actually delude myself into believing it. . . .

Hastily,
[signed] Tamie

Block 31, 11 B
Poston, Arizona
Feb. 1, 1943

Dear Dorothy,

Last Thursday I mailed you three large envelopes containing notes on the aftermath of the strike, the history of the Central Executive Committee, some statistical data on the background of evacuees and a report on the Firebreak Gang written by Richard Nishimoto, informant X in my reports. He had originally intended it for the Bureau of Sociological Research but since he resigned from it about the same time I did because of disagreement with its policies he gave it to me as a Christmas present. I consider it a rather good report because of the sentiments and attitudes incorporated in it (especially toward the administration) as well as giving us background data leading up to the November strike. He informs me that this is the first report he has written since he left Stanford some thirteen years ago and is apologetic of his English. Since I had neither the time nor the paper to make you a copy of the report I mailed you the original in the hope that if you were sufficiently interested you could make a copy and send back the original. I have often thought of getting some sort of secretarial help so I can send you more data regularly but so far have been unable to find anyone, male or female, who can be entrusted with the confidential data included in some of my reports.

On Saturday I was approached by Kennedy, Employment Chief, Sears of the WRA Industry Department, and Reynolds, contractor of the Camouflage Project, to work as foreman for a month or so until the project got on its feet. Apparently I am the only one in Camp I with a supervisor's experience in it and they want me to start the thing rolling for them. They are well aware of the fact that I do not want to work more than a month and that my interests in the project are purely from a research angle but they still want me even though for a few weeks. I had a lengthy conversation concerning this with Spicer and X yesterday and they encouraged me to accept the job since it is the only way through which I can gather a lot of dope on Nisei attitudes which I cannot obtain elsewhere. Furthermore many of the administrative policies at present are being formed in the Employment Office so this will give me an opportunity to sit in on closed conferences, etc. I also wish to detect reverberations caused by the change in draft classification. The camouflage project was voted down last week in a poll taken of all three camps combined but was passed in a revote in the Temporary Community Council of Camp I on Friday so as far as we are concerned, the project will probably start by the end of this week. Since we are adhering to a five 8-hour a day week I shall have Saturday and Sunday to catch up on camp activities while keeping a detailed daily account of the project to be analyzed at the end of the month. If you disagree with my plans for the next four weeks please let me know immediately so that I can get out of the project before I get myself thoroughly involved in it. Reynolds promised me definitely that I may withdraw at any time if you disapprove of my plans. . . .

On Saturday at 10:00 P.M. the long anticipated event occurred—Tachibana, the restraining influence on the violent Kibei faction in Camp II was taken out by the F.B.I. and as a consequence Saburo Kido, national JACL president, was beaten and hospitalized in Camp I. I am informed by an authoritative source that eight Kibei responsible for the beating of Kido were caught and removed to Yuma but so far I have been unable to receive confirmation on anything because communication between the two camps was cut off yesterday. Political leaders in the other two camps are greatly concerned with the removal of Tachibana—I only hope this incident will not lead to open violence again especially with the Senate Investigation Committee about to pop in at any minute.

Regarding the conference in Salt Lake City in late March I certainly would like to participate. Do you want me to apply for a permit here or are you attending to all of them?

Please let me know as soon as possible if you have any objections to my working on the camouflage project for a month.

Sincerely,
[signed] Tamie

Block 31, 11 B
Poston, Arizona
March 4, 1943

Dear Dorothy,

On Feb. 24th I mailed you two batches of unanalyzed notes on the pre-strike political structure of Poston. Since the two brief articles by Spicer and the Public Relations Committee of the T.C.C. will give you a bird's eye view of the political setup I decided not to make a thorough historical analysis at this time but to wait until permanent government goes into effect within a month—i.e. the Constitution is scheduled to be ratified by the blocks within a month if there is no flareup in the next few days. Included in the notes were odds and ends on political organization such as the proposed code of offenses and minutes of the T.C.C. and I.A.B. meetings collected by Spicer and me while I was still connected to the Bureau.

I contacted Mr. Head shortly after I received your letter requesting his permission to go to Salt Lake City and he willingly gave his consent. Should you decide to postpone the conference please notify [me] immediately since my leave covers the original period from March 30 to April 8.

I decided not to work in the camouflage factory because it was too time-consuming and furthermore I could get all the relevant data from Mich, Jimmie Yamada and Kennedy of the Employment Dept. and by conversing with workers. I have attended all of the meetings of camouflage workers and have made several trips to the factory to get an insight into attitudes and actual working conditions. In this way I've obtained some interesting data which I hope to work up for you by the end of next week. At the moment Kennedy is making a vain attempt to shove labor union methods down the throats of workers but being unfamiliar with labor unions the workers seem rather indifferent. Head, by the way, is a damned conservative and extremely wary of union methods being initiated in camp. As far as the evacuees are concerned the opposition to the factory at the moment is not based on grounds of disloyalty to the Japanese government but on unequal distribution of wages. The T.C.C. last week approved a 65–35 distribution—65% of the monthly earnings going to the worker and 35% going to the trust fund. Their attitude is: If you insist on receiving good pay, why don't you build a block for yourselves near the factory and eat and sleep away from us? Why should you be getting 70 to 100 bucks while the mess hall workers receive only 16 bucks? . . .

I see in the papers that twelve more have been taken out of Tule Lake for "obstructing" registration. That brings the total to thirty-four, doesn't it? The people here were pretty sore when the news leaked out that Head had made the statement that all those who answered "No" to questions 27 and 28 would be sent to internment camps. Question 27, incidentally, read: "Are you willing to serve in the armed forces of the U.S. on combat duty, wherever ordered?" (This question was omitted in the case of aliens here.) Some of the evacuees wanted to make an issue of it but the political leaders told them to bide their time. As far as underground activities are concerned at present it appears that we are returning to pre-strike conditions. The rift between the administration and the evacuee camp is becoming wider and wider and the T.C.C. is losing its power. As soon as the pro-administrative Nisei leave camp for greener pastures outside within the next two or three months the break will have been completed and we might just as well call Poston an "internment camp." I have always maintained that the administration here is probably the best obtainable but they certainly are dumb or refuse to recognize the real situation. They take for granted that the most articulate Nisei, like Mich and Ann, are in the majority and fail to realize that the real composition of camp is entirely different. It has got to the point where many block managers refuse to transmit administrative instructions to block residents—they simply throw the notices into the waste basket when they arrive. The rift between administrative cliques is also becoming more pronounced. For instance the WRA faction had to employ a man called Hunter who was once slated to take Collier's job to act as liaison man between the WRA faction and the Indian Service clique in Poston. Another indication of administrative instability: Jimmie Yamada, executive aide to Kennedy, told me last week that the Employment Dept. received a requisition from Evans, Unit I administrator, for two "consultants" to go from block to block to find out who were opposing administrative policies in each block. If this isn't downright snooping, I'd like to know what it is. Well, things are pretty smooth on the surface here but underground forces are actively at work. X predicts an open break with the administration similar to the

November strike within two months, but I'm not so sure about that. His predictions are usually reliable though. Anyway, things are at a tension here and I'm planning to stick around for a while yet. My plans in early February were to dash out to Chicago as quickly as possible to preserve my sanity but as soon as my leave clearance is granted my feeling of being cooped up in a goldfish bowl may fade away. If I can be assured that my status as research worker will guarantee that no stigma of disloyalty to the U.S. government will be attached to me after the war for remaining in a relocation center for the duration of the "pro-Axis" elements, I may consider staying here indefinitely. X and other political leaders want me to remain in Poston to gather data to write up a history of the Japanese in California after the war. They feel with my academic background and my apparent understanding and sympathy for Issei feelings I'm the logical Nisei to write the history of our people since no adequate work has been done so far. Of course, this will mean a lifetime job but it sounds intriguing. They promise that they will give me as much background material as they personally can and will help me in obtaining good, reliable informants. Within two or three months I might be able to catch up on my work for you so that I can allocate half of my time to your work and the other half to collecting background material. Under the circumstances do you consider it [a] "legitimate excuse" to remain here for the duration? Mich and Ann tell me that it isn't worth it—that Nisei of my temperament and convictions rightfully belong on the outside to further the Nisei cause. I'm not so certain of that. I want to see a good book on the history of Japanese in California written from the Japanese point of view and since I know of no one who is at present attempting such a task I thought in my small way I might be able to do my bit toward such a goal. Anyway, I'll thrash this out with you in Salt Lake City in the near future.

Re the $50 honorarium for X I heartily recommend it. He has been most helpful in my work and the gesture may help in minimizing some of his antagonism toward U.C. U.C. to him is synonymous with Dr. Barrows whom he disliked thoroughly. Furthermore, he is a Stanford man and I consider it a great joke to have U.C. give him an honorarium. I do know that he has been carefully saving his money toward buying anthropological and sociological books and the fifty dollars would help tremendously toward this end. Incidentally, he is making a thorough study of his block which is composed almost entirely of Los Angeles people from Boyle Heights, so that I shall have a basis for comparison with my block which is predominantly settled by Salinas people.

Sincerely yours,
[signed] Tamie

P.S. X's address is: Mr. Richard S. Nishimoto, Block 42-2C, Poston, Arizona

Block 31, 11 B
Poston, Arizona
March 26, 1943

Dear Dorothy,

Just a short note to let you know that I'm still alive and in Poston. The camouflage report which I promised for last week is still unfinished because of several interruptions. The day after Bob left for Gila I woke up with paralysis of my left arm, felt uncomfortable but went about my work as usual. That night the whole upper half of my body began to ache and became so unbearable that I went for an examination to the hospital and the doctor suggested that I remain in bed for the next few days since he suspected it was pleurisy. I'm OK now except for occasional deep coughs that reverberate throughout my body. The notes on camouflage and manpower shortage are all organized so I'll try to have them ready for you before I leave for Gila Tuesday morning. I finally persuaded "Princess Ataloa" to give me a permit to visit Bob and Charlie. Trips to Gila are on a quota basis so that not more than 6 from Camp 1 or 12 from all of Poston are permitted to go there in a week. If I followed the regular procedure my turn would not have come until June or July since there is already a long waiting list but I played on Ataloa's sympathy for Cal and managed to secure an emergency permit for three days.

Bob visited me on Wednesday, the 17th, and we had quite a profitable conversation as far as I was concerned. He, on his part, secured some interesting corroboration on his informants from X, I think. It appears from his conversation that pressure groups in Gila are much more well-organized and operate more openly than in Poston. X further maintains that the leaders Bob mentioned were leaders in their communities in pre-evacuation days and not recent leaders as in Poston. They also seem to be more colorful personalities than those here. In connection with this I should mention that one of Bob's chief guinea pigs, Ogasawara, was seen in our camp last week looking up X with Kuroiwa, present head of the anti-administration clique in Camp II, now that Tachibana has been locked up in Lordsburg. X missed him since he was attending the regular meeting of block managers at that time but seemed to think that Kuroiwa might have imported him from Gila to help him because of the acute shortage of real leaders here or that Ogasawara was planning to transfer here because of domestic trouble in Gila. . . .

With reference to the camouflage project, things have been running more or less smoothly except for the mass meeting held on Wednesday night, the 24th, at which time all workers promised to refuse to accept their pay checks the following day since they felt the non-productive workers (i.e. the reefers, handymen, warehousemen, and all other non-weavers) were not receiving as much as they should. The Executive committee of the project was commissioned to take it up with the authorities but I don't know whether an agreement has been reached yet. Since the original contract stipulates that non-weavers would receive a certain percentage of that earned by weavers I don't quite see how they could demand more at this time. In Camp II according to one of my informants yesterday due to labor shortage they have been able to secure only 77 workers instead of the 300 or so required to run the factory at full capacity and if another five drop out in the next few days the factory will have to be shut down. I think I mentioned before that many of the net workers are quitting their jobs to go out to farm to evade the draft. At first many Nisei went into the factory thinking that they would be deferred since it was an army project but after Lt. Bolton made the statement that none of the jobs in the center was classified as vital defense work and that all Nisei would be eventually subjected to drafting they decided that perhaps farm work was a better bet.

Before I forget, Miss Colson of the Bureau of Sociological Research is planning to go to San Francisco in about three weeks to see you (i.e., as soon as Spicer returns from Minidoka where he is preparing the administration and the evacuees for the arrival of the WRA Caucasian analyst). I thought I'd let you know so that you needn't go out of your way to be nice to the Bureau since they have not been too cooperative to your representative in Poston. I admit they have been superficially nice in the hopes of squeezing something out of me since they feel I cover the other half of Poston which they do not touch but they certainly have not been too anxious to acquaint me with the administrative side of camp. Since I can get as much of the administrative dope from Kennedy, Haas, Gary, Findley and other friends in the administration as I can out of the Bureau I am planning to work at home from now on so that I won't have to be bothered with them. My roommate has finally left for Illinois so I have an [apartment] all to myself. The block manager has assured me that I may keep it as long as I wish. I like Spicer very much as a person but I'm sick and tired of being used by the Bureau to gain certain ends. They can have their own personal jealousies and ambitions among the senior staff without dragging me into it. This includes Embree and all other WRA analysts. Did I mention to you that he offered me a research job in the Chicago WRA office when he was over the last time?

As far as your advice via Spencer, "Remember X is married," is concerned you have no worry. I've known X for about eight years in San Francisco and Los Angeles, and his wife has known my sister for a much longer time. They think of me as "Hisako's kid sister."

Regarding the honorarium of fifty dollars, X burst into my office the other day and said: "California sent me a check for fifty dollars. How come?" When I explained to him he laughed: "California must be having the same difficulty as the Bureau in getting dope in the relocation centers to pay for junk like that." Since he rarely writes to anyone he asked me to thank you for it and to tell you that he appreciates it particularly since it came from a rival institution. . . .

[signed] Tamie

> Block 31, 11 B
> Poston, Arizona
> March 27, 1943

Dear Dorothy,

Bob sent me a short excerpt from a Tule Lake report yesterday concerning the "possible influence of Japanese radio broadcasts on the reaction of people here" and informed me that you were anxious to see what I could collect in Poston. I have already touched upon this subject in several instances in my reports—e.g. the report on the Spanish consul, page 6; and that on Alien Registration, page 6—and have the following on file which I had intended to incorporate eventually in a study of change in sentiments from Dec. 7, 1941 to say the summer of 1943.

According to my Issei friends Japanese radio broadcasts may be heard at 2:00 A.M. in Poston either through the long wave band (in which case it must be stronger than five tubes) or through the short wave system. There seems little doubt that there are several short wave radios in existence in Poston. The point of origin for these broadcasts is claimed to be Kiska or submarines emerging in the dark of night to broadcast off the Pacific Coast.

As far as Poston is concerned these "broadcasts" have a great effect on the relocation program. During all of October and November of last year when the sugar beet harvesters were going out in droves the broadcasts continuously advised the people in the centers not to go out. At that time they claimed that the war would soon be over—probably about May or August of 1943—and that there was no necessity for relocating themselves. Shortly after November 15, 1942 these broadcasts became very specific and warned the people under no circumstances to leave the centers during the following two weeks. Interestingly enough this critical period coincided with a rumored attack on Hawaii sometime in early December.

This aversion to going out is directly traceable to the famous speech Premier Tojo made on Dec. 9, 1941 which had a profound effect on the Japanese in America. The substance of his speech was: "I am very sorry for you but this had to take place as you may well realize. I expect you will have to go through many hardships but please endure the ordeal even if you have to sustain yourselves on wild roots and leaves. We will see to it that you will be amply compensated at the end of the war. Please do not concern yourselves with the post-war period." According to my Issei informants this speech gave the Japanese in California a renewed determination to carry on. Japan had not forgotten them. Even today whenever the occasion arises, his speech is quoted at great length to bring some obstreperous individual into line.

More recently—to be exact on Dec. 24, 1942—it was reported by someone who had presumably tuned in at Rowher, Arkansas, that Aoki, chairman of the Kikakuin or Planning Board, had announced that the

Japanese government had just completed a tentative plan for the coloni-
zation of Japanese Subjects in America after the war which had been
approved by the Cabinet. This was interpreted to be a reassurance to
the people in the relocation centers that they had not been forgotten—
that Japan would take care of them in the post-war period. This "rumor"
which originated in Rowher has been common knowledge in Poston
since January.

These so-called "broadcasts" have given rise to the [following] widespread attitudes in Poston:

"The Japanese government is going to take care of us after the war.
Why should we bother to get relocated now?"

"I'm not going out. Japanese broadcasts have repeatedly warned us
not to go. Their advice is good enough for me."

"Japanese broadcasts tell us not to go out of these centers. There
must be some good reason back of them."

These broadcasts have other far-reaching implications. Thus the
Housing Department is at present encountering some difficulty because
of them in reshuffling apartments to insure more equalization of room-
space. Now that May is almost upon us many Issei become irritated
when the Housing Department suggests their moving elsewhere. They
complain: "Why shuffle around apartments at this time? The war will
be over soon." Their deep conviction that Japan will win and will compensate them for their sufferings frequently results in attributing great significance to some rather trivial event. Thus the failure on the part of
the administration to allot a clothing allowance to an evacuee might
well bear international complications. For example, the other day I
overheard an Issei who had failed to receive his clothing allowance for
the month of October retort: "If they don't want to give it to me now
it doesn't matter. After the war I'll ask the Japanese government to take
care of that for me. I have my plans all made." A similar event occurred
at the last block managers' meeting on March 23 when an elderly Issei
attacked Evans at the close of the meeting with a volley of incomprehen-
sible pidgin English. Since Evans appeared not to understand him one
of the block managers offered to interpret for him. It turned out that
the Issei had failed to receive his January pay and was greatly indignant
about it. He had worked so hard and had not been compensated. He
threatened: "If you don't pay now, you'll have to pay the price when

the peace treaty is signed." Tragically enough, all this is uttered in utmost seriousness. This attitude that Japan will avenge any mistreatment of her subjects finds further outlet in statements such as these:

"If the M.P.'s should kill one Japanese, the Japanese government will retaliate by killing five Americans interned in Japanese concentration camps." (This was uttered during the November strike.)

"I tell those *ketos* that if anything happens to me those Americans interned in Japan will be placed on the firing line and they shut up." (This boast is attributed to Nagai, chairman of the C.E.G.)

Attitudes Concerning War News

Usually after an American broadcast announcing a great naval victory in the southwest Pacific people say: "Oh, oh, tomorrow we'll see 'Twenty Jap Ships Sunk' again." Whenever the headlines scream "20 Jap Ships Sunk" the reaction is: "Something must have happened to the U.S. Navy."

Nowadays when the Issei open their newspapers they glance first at obscure items in the back pages or at the bottom of the front page. They no longer place any credibility in the main articles of the day. Their comment to announcements of Allied losses in the Pacific is: "All those news are at least three months old. The Japanese radio broadcast them long ago." This attitude was most prevalent at the time of the announcement of the sinking of the Lexington. They claimed: "That was announced by Japan three months ago. The Lexington is gone, the Saratoga's gone, the Ranger is gone, the Yorktown is gone, the Wasp is gone, the Enterprise is gone—they haven't got any carriers left." Others continued: "They still haven't announced that they lost everything at Pearl Harbor. I wonder how long they are going to keep it secret." (This feeling was widespread until Dec. 7, 1942, when a lengthy article on the extent of the disaster appeared in the *Los Angeles Times*. Even then some skeptics were maintaining that the real extent of damages had not been revealed.)

From the time of the announcement of a great naval victory at Bismarck Sea to the time they conceded some success to the Japanese Navy, people were going about saying that according to the Japanese radio broadcast their loss was negligible and that the convoy had safely reached its destination. Contrary to the American press, the Japanese version claimed 73 flying fortresses shot down. Since these so-called "Japanese radio broadcasts" give news which in three or four months are usually verified by the U.S. press the people here have come to attach great credulity to them. Because of so many seeming contradictions in announcements made by the OWI they generally question the authenticity of war reports in local newspapers. Thus when MacArthur pleaded for more planes and Curtin claimed danger of imminent attack on Australia shortly after the announcement of a great Allied victory at Guadalcanal and the Bismarck Sea, people were snorting: "If the Japanese were completely wiped out, why should MacArthur plead for more planes and why should Australia be afraid of an invasion?" It just didn't make sense to them.

In any study of rumors in the relocation centers we must not overlook the great role of inter-center correspondence in disseminating rumors. Important events that occur in one center are usually common knowledge in other centers within a week. To give you an example of interchange of rumors between centers I shall cite the case of a letter received by a resident in Unit II from a Hawaiian evacuee now located at Rowher. According to him on his way to California his ship had been stopped by a Japanese submarine. Its captain boarded the American vessel and assembling the evacuees made a stirring speech advising them to remain quietly in the relocation centers because Japan would soon rescue them from their plight. Meanwhile the American captain stood at one end of the deck trembling all over. When the speech was completed, the Japanese officer clambered down, gave a salute to the Keto captain, and the submarine sank out of sight. People in Poston have swallowed this story completely and are pointing to it as another indication that Japan will take care of them in the post-war period.

One type of rumor very popular at Poston is the supposed attack on American soil by the Japanese which the U.S. government refuses to divulge for fear of lowering morale on the home front. Thus toward the end of June there was a rumor that Terminal Island had been bombed on June 15th and that everything had been completely demolished. Terminal Islanders in Poston exclaimed: "Gee that's swell. That's what they get for shoving us out like that." There was a rumor afloat in July that Hawaii had been severely crippled simultaneously with Dutch

Harbor. Again toward Christmas time of last year it was reported that Hawaii had once more been attacked.

Another fruitful source of rumors is the innumerable speculations as to the probable close of the war. When I first moved into Santa Anita people were planning to celebrate their fourth of July on Brighton Beach. When I arrived in Poston people were talking of "going home for Christmas." Around October of last year it was rumored that they were circulating a petition in Los Angeles for a negotiated peace with Japan and that a number of people were signing it. Subscribers to the rumor were [exclaiming]: "People on the outside must be weary of the war already." The newest rumor regarding this subject emerged about a week ago when the Japanese radio is reported to have broadcast on the evening of March 19 that Russia was negotiating for a separate peace with Germany and that the war would end in a month.

I have a great collection of rumors of this sort but have been saving them to write a systematic report on the change in sentiments for a certain length of period. If you wish I can start sending them to you as they crop up.

I am leaving for Gila tomorrow morning, March 30. I shall send you the Camouflage report on my return since things are still unsettled in the factory. The workers are accusing the contractor that he has not lived up to the terms of the contract and negotiations between the shop committee and the contractor are in progress.

Tamie

REVELATION

Tsuchiyama on the Recomposition of Community in Poston

Here I offer a brief description and analysis of three of Tsuchiyama's key topical reports. Above and beyond their substantive content, much of which documents forms of popular resistance on the part of Poston's residents, the reports provide important insights into Tsuchiyama's basic field methods. Even fifty years after the fact, Tsuchiyama's studies offer insights into what was really going on behind the scenes at Poston, especially in terms of political dynamics.

Although it is not dated, according to her correspondence with Director Thomas, the first report that Tsuchiyama wrote, "Chronological Account of the Poston Strike," was being composed immediately prior to Christmas 1942. Thirty-five double-spaced pages in length, the report is a running account of the developments that led up to the famed Poston strike of November 1942, which began on Sunday, November 15, and ended on November 23. Information concerning Wade Head's address to the City Planning Board on November 28 is included at the end of the report. Two sections, resembling appendixes, are also attached concerning Poston's administrators' responses to the strike and poststrike sentiments of Poston's Japanese American residents.

The strike was directly triggered by the November 15 arrest of two men who were accused of beating a suspected *inu*, or spy. The strike, however, reflected both general and specific complaints among Japanese Americans confined at Poston. Two key issues were central in this regard.

As previously indicated, Japanese Americans had deep concern about spies, since the FBI was empowered to enter the camp, interrogate whomever was suspected or accused in a given situation, and remove any individuals agents chose. All this could be carried out independently of the OIA and/or WRA, the officials of which ran Poston on a day-to-day basis from 1942 to 1943 and 1944 to 1945, respectively. Since individuals at Poston had already been picked up and interrogated by the FBI, tensions around spies and the act of spying were running high.

Above and beyond this immediate concern was the popular demand for self-government, largely in response to WRA rhetoric in this regard. In this instance, popular resistance was energized in terms of a push to test the WRA's actual commitment to principles of democracy. Many Poston residents supported the demand that the two men be subject to a fair trial conducted by a jury of their peers (i.e., other Japanese Americans confined at Poston). If, and only if, these men were found guilty by a jury of their peers would they then be turned over to the external authorities. At an equally significant level, Japanese Americans were demanding the right to take WRA policies for self-government seriously but in a fashion that was fully consistent with the actualities of hierarchy and power inside the community. In my view, this is one of the most significant points revealed in Tsuchiyama's JERS reports. Naturally, this assertion ran contrary to the ill-conceived WRA ruling in 1942 that Issei (first-generation Japanese immigrants) were ineligible to run for or hold elected office in terms of the formal institutions of self-governance at Poston.

Further study of Tsuchiyama's account indicates that a petition on behalf of the two imprisoned men—who resided in Unit I, Block 28—was generated by a predominantly Issei delegation, the members of which also lived in Block 28. Block 28 and contiguous blocks were predominantly composed of former residents of Orange County. The Orange County group in Poston was known to be led by a man (to whom I will give the pseudonym Murase) who had been arrested immediately after Pearl Harbor and sent to a special Justice Department internment camp, where he was held for some months before being released and allowed to join the rest of his family in Poston. Although Tsuchiyama noted that Murase stayed well behind the scenes, many of the Japanese Americans from Orange County were said to be obligated to this man, morally if not monetarily. What is significant is that, given the hierarchical setup of political organization in the Japanese American community before the war, Murase was one of the *yūshi*, or "public-spirited" men of influence, who could still sway popular opinion in camp, although he was very careful not to come out into the open for fear of further persecution. In short, in the context of this setup, the integrity of anyone from the Orange County blocks who did not sign the petition for the release of the two men became suspect; dissenters risked gaining a reputation as WRA "collaborators," at the very least, or receiving tangible retribution farther down the road.

The final point I'd like to make about Tsuchiyama's first JERS report concerns her already-evident dependence on Nishimoto for data as well as for interpretations. In the course of her thirty-five-page text, for example, Tsuchiyama makes at least five distinct references to Nishimoto, primarily recording what Nishimoto told Tsuchiyama he said or what he told her he saw. Remember that by January 3, 1943, just before Tsuchiyama mailed this report to Thomas, she had written that she had gained the confidence of Nishimoto, whom she believed to be and described as "one of the two most powerful figures in camp."

Tsuchiyama's Field Methodology

By the second of her six JERS field reports, a basic methodology—revolving around descriptions of Nishimoto as a prime political mover in Poston, along with transcriptions of his analyses and comments—was well established. Tsuchiyama wrote this report, entitled "The Visit of the Spanish Consul," in early 1943. (Because none of her field reports or research has ever been published before, it is reproduced in the Appendix.) Three points about this report are especially relevant here.

First, it should be emphasized that in 1942 Issei leaders agreed to ask the Spanish consul, Francisco de Amat, to inform the Japanese government that the conditions and treatment of people of Japanese descent in Poston were poor in some cases and unacceptable in others. This initiative developed into a broader movement to organize a request, directed toward the Japanese government, that Japan send $200 million to the Japanese American community at the end of the war in order to compensate for the latter's losses and to help with the postwar process of rehabilitation. Its proponents proposed that the request be transmitted to the Japanese government through the offices of the Spanish consul; since there was no official Japanese consulate in operation, Issei could only register protests or communications via the offices of Japan's allies who did have consulates open on the U.S. mainland. Nishimoto was dead set against this idea and proposal. The "Spanish Consul" report indicates that Nishimoto spearheaded the critique and ultimate rejection of this proposed request. The bulk of the report, then, is a close ethnographic description of Nishimoto's political methodology and political machinations.

Second, even before Nishimoto was hired on to the JERS project in order to be Tsuchiyama's Issei assistant, this report indicates that his role as a key informant was well established. Thus, Tsuchiyama's ethnographic reports, and this report in particular, are quite useful in terms of understanding Nishimoto's thoughts and activities relative to his role as a community leader.

Third, "The Visit of the Spanish Consul" manuscript establishes that there *was* an informal political structure in place in Poston that, unbeknownst to Euro-American authorities and researchers alike, was based on pre–World War II community organization and was dominated by Issei. This deserves further explication.

We know from his autobiographical accounts that Nishimoto had a wide exposure to both urban and rural Japanese American communities throughout California, since he had worked and lived in diverse areas such as San Francisco, Vacaville, Colusa, Palo Alto, Los Angeles, and Gardena, among other locales. Whether in rural or in urban settings, when their numbers permitted there was a stock set of groups often formed by the Issei. These included more particularistic regional associations (*kenjinkai*), rotating credit associations (*tanomoshi-kō*), and mutual aid groups (*kumiai*), all of which might be formed on a variety of bases from "common point of origin," common endeavor, propinquity in the United States, or a combination of the above, to more universalistic organizations like the Japanese Association of America (Nihon-jinkai). Undoubtedly, because of his different work experiences in diverse settings in California, Nishimoto was aware of the full range of such institutions that knit Japanese American individuals and families to the larger community.

One also learns from Tsuchiyama's report (plus information and commentary provided in Tsuchiyama's letters to Dorothy Thomas) that Nishimoto had formulated an analysis of the political organization of the prewar Japanese American communities. From Nishimoto's vantage point, in order to fully understand the politics inside a given Japanese American community, one had to identify the local *yūshi*. This is a Japanese term that literally means "public-spirited individuals," but it can be glossed here as "community leaders" as long as it is noted that such persons achieved their status on the basis of service, rather than on the basis of authority or command per se. In short, because of their public spirit and their good works on the behalf of their compatriots, *yūshi* were disproportionately influential within their local communities.

Beyond this, it must be remembered that in 1942, when people of Japanese descent were subject to mass removal, if nuclear or extended family members were living in the same point of origin, family units were basically moved together. Similarly, in many cases, members of prewar communities from a particular point of origin were often kept together and processed through the same assembly center and ultimately assigned to the same WRA camp. In the Poston case, people from the same prewar areas often wound up being assigned apartments in barracks in the same block. If they were a large group or otherwise didn't fit into a single block, they might also be situated in contiguous blocks.

Tsuchiyama's "Spanish Consul" report indicates that Nishimoto used his knowledge both of the organization of prewar communities as well as of the regionally based setup of housing in Poston's barracks, blocks, and quads to identify key *yūshi* inside the camp. Because of their prewar prominence, many *yūshi* apparently remained influential among community persons from their respective areas of origin on the West Coast. What is more, it is notable that *none* of the *yūshi* sought or played a role in Poston's formal political institutions, whether the Issei Advisory Board or the Central Executive Council. According to Tsuchiyama, *yūshi* preferred to remain well out of the limelight since, in some cases, prominence as a leader resulted in an initial period of incarceration, without one's family, in special internment camps run by the U.S. Justice Department.

Tsuchiyama's report details, at some length, Nishimoto's broader political methodology during the early days at Poston when he was still consolidating his power base. Basically, Nishimoto would target the key *yūshi* throughout Poston's Unit I and focus in on them in an attempt to sway them to his point of view. If successful, Nishimoto could usually count on the *yūshi* to bring their following into line, and entire blocks could be deployed to influence the formal decision-making structure of Poston's self-government. In this fashion, Tsuchiyama's report entails a unique account of Nishimoto's attempts to fashion himself into a major opinion leader in Poston—attempts that we now know were largely successful, at least in terms of the power politics of Unit I by 1944.

In short, as wholly dependent as I believe Tsuchiyama to have been on Nishimoto for the data and insights that make up this report (and this is another patent limitation that must be "read" back into the text), I propose that "The Visit of the Spanish Consul" provides the basis for some interesting hypotheses. The most important is that as early as 1942 the Issei had been able to reintroduce elements of their pre–World War II political organization into camp settings such as Poston, Unit I. Awareness of this informal and apparently hidden dimension of camp politics does not appear to be evident in the archival contributions of Euro-American bureaucrats or researchers on the scene, let alone in the secondary literature. This is a fact that must somehow be resolved, for example, with the extensive emphasis on "community disorganization" that frames large sections of Dr. Alexander H. Leighton's classic study of the first two years of Poston, *The Governing of Men*. In short, these two points offer a new perspective that can be utilized to reread as well as to creatively reinterpret the archival records and extant secondary literature, alike.

Another notable feature of the "Spanish Consul" report is a passage in which Tsuchiyama describes her own first-hand experience with this political methodology. This passage also prefigures Nishimoto's use of autoethnographic accounts, which he employed with much dramatic effect in his own field journals, reports, and JERS conference papers. In this particular instance, Nishimoto enlisted Tsuchiyama to help convince a certain *yūshi* to fall into line with his overall strategy—again, in this case, to undermine the Issei leaders who had petitioned the Spanish consul to bring their request for postwar compensation to the attention of the Japanese government. It is clear that Tsuchiyama felt that her gender, age, and generational status as a Nisei curtailed her ability to wield this political methodology effectively; she noted that Nishimoto had to come to her aid in order to successfully complete the mission.

I will only mention a few points about Tsuchiyama's third report, entitled "Aftermath of the Strike," which is undated but which was probably sent to Dorothy Thomas sometime around mid-January 1943. In this report, Tsuchiyama presents an ethnographic description of the new bodies that were created within Poston's evolving self-governmental order and also records who took what position in the debates that were an integral part of this process. It is critical to note that bureaucrats in both the OIA and the WRA believed that one of the redeeming aspects of mass incarceration was that the federal government could supervise and direct the exposure of Japanese Americans to the wonders of democracy and self-government. It was assumed that Japanese Americans had no real previous knowledge of or exposure to self-government before the war.

In terms of the WRA "community analysts" and the staff in Poston's BSR, I submit that researchers seriously underestimated the existence of a political infrastructure undergirding the social organization of the prewar Japanese American communities. Tsuchiyama's report indicates that the Issei generation effectively utilized this infrastructure in rejecting the imposition of the WRA's approach to self-governance, which initially empowered only young, second-generation Japanese Americans. In struggling to open new apertures for Issei political representation and participation, self-government was indeed being implemented, although not necessarily the kind of self-government that the authorities envisioned or intended.

On this basis, I conclude that, contrary to WRA policies, the Issei were able to reassert a significant amount of political influence within the larger community. This is certainly not to imply that the Issei were a monolithic group, however, in terms of either political position or action. In fact, Tsuchiyama's report clearly indicates the exact opposite.

In sum, what is striking about these three reports is that they demonstrate the extent to which, initially, Tsuchiyama was dependent upon Nishimoto's contacts, data, and interpretations. His aptitude, and his role at Poston as an insider and political broker, apparently fully compensated for his lack of advanced social science training. Even in light of Tsuchiyama's sometimes uncritical acceptance of Nishimoto's self-depictions of his actions and centrality, I submit that Tsuchiyama's JERS reports are still quite useful in reconstructing key dimensions of the social organization of Poston. Her reports definitely reveal that (1) the Issei did have informal mechanisms of political organization in place in their communities before the war, (2) these were reformulated in camp in order to respond to the new situation with its new challenges, and (3) one of the key dynamics in Poston before, during, and after the Poston strike in November 1942 was the assertion of Issei political power in the face of WRA policies. In effect, "self-government," as the WRA initially conceived it anyway, disenfranchised the Issei and put them under the control of their second-generation children, the majority of whom were in their teens or twenties and thirties at best. This is why, when the temporary community council was initially formed in Poston's Unit I with an all-Nisei membership, the Issei disparagingly referred to it as the "kids' council."

Finally, upon examining the overall time frame, it is striking that Tsuchiyama's six major field reports for the Poston phase of the JERS project were generated very quickly in what must have been a furious stint of analysis and writing. All six reports were essentially composed within a three-month period between the end of November 1942 and March 1, 1943. Because they were written on the spot and in terms of insider perspectives, they are quite rich in insights about the informal political organization and behind-the-scenes happenings of day-to-day political processes in Poston. One can only imagine that Dorothy Thomas was delighted with and impressed by Tsuchiyama's reports, although, as we shall see, Tsuchiyama's initial success also may have generated high expectations on Thomas's part for future research reports that Tsuchiyama, for whatever reason, was ultimately unable to fulfill.

Thus, Tsuchiyama's position as an ethnographer for JERS revolved around the fact that she was a second-generation woman trying to carry out research about political issues and community processes in a context that was largely dominated in Poston by men, including Nisei but also first-generation immigrant and Kibei men at that. Today, anthropologists are better equipped to appreciate the basic dynamics of gender vis-à-vis power and the production of knowledge. Unfortunately, Tsuchiyama did not have the benefit of a language or an analysis that might have helped her to understand or express the kinds of marginalization that she was to experience as a fledgling member of the academy, let alone in the field setting of Poston.

Nonetheless, it is clear that she was able to advance a substantive plan for fieldwork that went beyond the initial "notes and queries" outline produced by the Shibutanis in the assembly center at Tanforan, which was subsequently distributed by Dorothy Thomas as a preliminary data collection guide to JERS staff members who were assigned to one of the ten more permanent camps. In fact, by December 2, 1943, Tsuchiyama (along with Nishimoto?) had authored a comprehensive outline that clearly reflects her increasing command of the field, as well as the evolution of her interest in the specific topic of politics in Poston.

Nishimoto Is Hired as Tsuchiyama's Assistant

In early February 1943 Tsuchiyama mailed a copy of Nishimoto's "Firebreak Gang" report to Thomas. She noted that it might be of interest to her and invited her to make a copy if she liked and to send back the original. Replying only four days later, Thomas was very clearly impressed with Nishimoto's study of the Firebreak Gang, describing it as one of the "best participant-observation reports I have seen."

By March 26, 1943, as we have seen, correspondence in the JERS files indicates that Dorothy Thomas was worried that Tsuchiyama might be getting too close to Nishimoto, especially given the fact that Nishimoto was a married man. Thomas, in fact, explicitly warned Tsuchiyama about the potential dangers and sent Tsuchiyama's colleague, Robert Spencer, to Poston with a personal message to that effect for Tsuchiyama. Tsuchiyama, as always, denied that anything improper, beyond an ordinary and strictly professional relationship, had transpired.

In April 1943 Tsuchiyama wrote to Thomas, asking if JERS had the money to allow her to hire Nishimoto as her research assistant. From her letter, two things are apparent. One is that Tsuchiyama was staggering under her work load and felt that an assistant could help her with the basic task of keeping up with everything that was going on in camp. Second, Tsuchiyama clearly indicated that Nishimoto was valuable to her, both as a *oya-no-yobiyose* type who was bilingual and also as a block manager in Unit I, especially since in the latter capacity he received copies of all administrative orders and documents channeled through this medium. Because of this, Tsuchiyama proposed to Thomas that Nishimoto could gather data that were fully complementary to her own. In any case, since Tsuchiyama's letters firmly denied that she had anything but a professional relationship with Nishimoto, Thomas's concerns were apparently assuaged. Thomas agreed to hire Nishimoto as Tsuchiyama's research assistant, although since Nishimoto was an Issei, Thomas noted that technically speaking JERS could only pay him for his research products. This was fine with Nishimoto. His only request was that all JERS correspondence and reports conceal his actual name, identifying him only as "X." For the next year and a half, working as a team, Tsuchiyama and Nishimoto carried out field research in Poston on behalf of Dorothy Thomas and the JERS project. The accompanying letters suggest how dynamic and productive this collaborative relationship was. Dorothy Thomas was delighted, of course, especially in the beginning.

In September 1943 Thomas arranged for Tsuchiyama and Nishimoto to visit Rosalie Hankey, a Berkeley graduate student in anthropology who had been hired and sent to the WRA camp, Gila River, in south-central Arizona, in order to replace Robert Spencer, another Berkeley anthropology graduate student who had been at Gila but had resigned. The logistical arrangements behind the visit were apparently fairly easy to carry out. Permission to visit a neighboring camp such as Gila was obtainable, although Tsuchiyama's letters indicate that visits were limited in number; they were also sometimes restricted. Visits would have not caused any great suspicion since Nishimoto's brother and his wife were in the Gila River camp, and Tsuchiyama had friends there as well.

In her book on doing fieldwork (whose subtitle, *Warnings and Advice*, now seems prophetic), Rosalie Hankey Wax reports in great detail how miserable her initial fieldwork experience at Gila was. She also comments quite favorably on Nishimoto and his words of advice, offered during his and Tsuchiyama's stay: "Though it took me several weeks to appreciate and digest some of the things Nishimoto had told me, I was much heartened by his visit." Wax also observed that "much later . . . Nishimoto told me that on this occasion he had been sent to Gila by Dr. Thomas to report on whether or not I should be fired." The archival record supplements Wax's account. In September 1943 "Tamie and X" authored a report, titled "Administrative Notes [on Gila]" (the latter words are written by hand). The thirty-two typed pages present a "quick and dirty" ethnographic overview of that camp. No doubt Tsuchiyama and Nishimoto's ability to generate this document so quickly—and note here that Wax reported great frustration in terms of even approaching people in Gila, let alone collecting any viable data—had to do with at least three factors. First, they were Japanese Americans, more culturally attuned than Wax, who could only speak a few basic words of Japanese. Second, they had already been studying Poston, so their report on Gila revolves around the implicit and explicit similarities and differences between the two institutions. Third, Nishimoto's brother and other of his acquaintances could be quickly and conveniently interviewed in regard to the "inside story." In the context of these kinds of relationships, the initial steps that ethnographers take in order to gain rapport and trust—issues with which Wax was struggling mightily— were not germane.

Even so, in October 1943 Wax sent an eleven-page response to Dorothy Thomas regarding "Tamie and X," in terms of their report and their implicit criticisms of Wax's reports. As noted above, this was a key methodological device that Thomas utilized in order to cross-check field data. This visit and the materials it generated also provide a clear example of how Thomas's methodology exacerbated competition, division, and even a mild paranoia between members of the JERS field staff. Further, Thomas sent Wax's comments to both Nishimoto (who wrote back to Thomas in this regard on October 22) and to Tsuchiyama. In a letter dated October 22, 1943, Thomas noted to Tsuchiyama: "I am sending this, not so much because of her [i.e., Wax's] criticisms, which may or may not be valid, but in order to keep you informed about the situation that is developing so quickly in Gila. Hankey's last letter is quite incoherent, for she says that so much is happening that she is working day and night to get it done."

Even with Richard Nishimoto's assistance and the early successes of the Tsuchiyama and Nishimoto team in terms of both data collection and the production of topical field reports, Tsuchiyama's correspondence demonstrates that the strain on Tsuchiyama grew continually throughout her stay at Poston and soon became enormous. Thus in many of her letters from 1943 Tsuchiyama appears to have become more and more dissatisfied with her situation and increasingly willing to write to Thomas in order to express her feelings frankly.

On March 9 Dorothy Thomas wrote to Tsuchiyama and encouraged her to stay at Poston. Thomas made reference to "an important monograph" which she felt that Tsuchiyama was fully capable of writing. On April 8, 1943, Thomas also wrote to Robert Lowie, saying that "Tamie seems to be all right now" and indicating that "on the whole . . . Tamie is making a much better adjustment than formerly."

During the month of July 1943, however, things appeared to go downhill. On July 12 Tsuchiyama wrote a despairing letter to Thomas. Noting that the temperature was 118 degrees, Tsuchiyama stated: "I don't think I can 'take' the nervous strain of camp life much longer. If I had my way now I don't want to see another Jap face for a long, long time." On July 14 Thomas responded, and her letter contained both encouragement and warnings. Thomas asked that Tsuchiyama refrain from taking any "hasty action."

July 29 saw another desperate letter from Tsuchiyama. She began by emphasizing that she absolutely couldn't write up her notes from the past year in Poston. Her body covered with heat rash, Tsuchiyama said that she hadn't had a good night's sleep in four weeks. Indicating that her "mental and physical status . . . [make] it impossible to muster up sufficient detachment to write objectively," Tsuchiyama mentioned that Nishimoto felt she was on the "verge of a mental breakdown," and thus she needed to have a break from life in camp.

Given this overall situation, Tsuchiyama proposed an alternative plan. She asked Thomas for permission to leave Poston for three to four months to go to Chicago or Cleveland in order to write. By August 7 Tsuchiyama was suffering so much from the Arizona summer heat wave that she had checked into Poston's Unit I hospital. She wrote to Thomas: "Heat and malicious female gossip are two things which I [can't] stomach and those are the two very things in great abundance here."

Upon recovering enough to return to her barracks apartment, Tsuchiyama decided that she had to get out of Poston. On September 17, 1943, she wrote to Thomas concerning her plans to leave within the month in order to spend four months writing in Cleveland. Tsuchiyama promised that she would return to the camp to continue her research in February 1944. In the end, Tsuchiyama left Poston in mid-October 1943 with Thomas's permission (and apparently with the full knowledge and permission of WRA officials as well). It was agreed that Tsuchiyama would remain on staff and on the JERS payroll during this period. Her last letter to Thomas before departing from Poston is dated October 9, 1943, and ends with the following postscript: "I am leaving Poston with mixed feelings. One desire is to get out as quickly as possible and never again in my wildest dreams expect to return to a concentration camp again. The other is an intense curiosity (or more correctly, a deep sense of duty) to follow the whole thing through. It will be interesting to see which side will triumph in the next four months."

Interestingly enough, Thomas's correspondence with Richard Nishimoto—she had only written to him a few times before—really picked up when Tsuchiyama left camp. Had she already written Tsuchiyama off? Did she begin to cultivate Nishimoto as the most likely successor to Tsuchiyama as Poston's ethnographer? It is not easy to determine the answers to these questions from the Nishimoto-Thomas correspondence. In a letter of October 20 Nishimoto did comment on Tsuchiyama's vacillating emotions, which revolved around her self-image as a competent ethnographer. He also wrote: "I want to help her as much as I can, because she is the first person that I have met among all the people who are studying the Japanese who is best qualified to study the Japanese people. I say that because I found out that she is tolerant and she has no crack-pot prejudices and pre-conceived notions." A few days later, in his letter of October 22, 1943, Nishimoto again praised Tsuchiyama to Thomas: "Leighton knew and knows that Tamie has collected plenty of good stuff. He considers her as *the* rival. I wouldn't trade any of Tamie's for his" (emphasis in the original).

On November 1, 1943, Nishimoto wrote to Thomas: "I would like to make a few comments on your letter to the Chicago staff," referring to a rather stern memo that Thomas had sent to the JERS relocation study unit, set up in that city to collect data on Japanese Americans coming out of camp before the end of the war. Thomas had particularly upbraided two Nisei on the staff who were graduate students in sociology because they had raised questions about the theoretical bases of the JERS study; she had reemphasized that she wanted data. Nishimoto: "I am in a [sic] complete agreement with you. In fact I was surprised that you have insight into the Japanese problem, more than I have suspected. (This is not an empty compliment, although it's a [sic] kind of funny for me to pass a complement [sic] to my superior.)"

The triangulation of personal correspondence between JERS director and JERS staff provides rich insights into how Thomas managed her fieldworkers, European and Japanese American alike. The scenario at Poston appears to me to be as follows. Tamie Tsuchiyama was used as a "data collector" by Thomas, and, in turn, Tsuchiyama recruited Nishimoto in the same capacity after she had used him as a key informant for her own ethnographic work. They became associates and, for a period of time, close colleagues as they labored under the strain of documenting daily life and notable events in Poston. As we will see, however, within the space of less than a year Tsuchiyama, who would never actually return to Poston again, began to attack the quality and even the integrity of Nishimoto's fieldwork.

Letters from the Field, April–October 1943

Block 31, 11 B
Poston, Arizona
April 6, 1943

Dear Dorothy,

Your letter sent to Gila arrived in Poston yesterday. Denver is OK with me—in fact I prefer it to Salt Lake City. However, if I go to Denver, would you mind terribly if I knock off a week or two after the conference to visit Los Angeles friends at the Granada Relocation Center as a follow-up study of my Santa Anita report and also to determine how different Granada is from Gila and Poston? Granada interests me particularly because WRA "experts" like Embree have always contended that it is the "slowest of all the relocation centers"—a statement which I have always challenged from the type of people located there. Furthermore, the residents there seem to enjoy greater freedom of movement than in Manzanar, Gila or Poston so I want to find out whether there is any noticeable difference in the outlook of the people there. Granada, I'm told, is only a short distance from Denver.

Bob did not tell me about your "continued pleasure in the types of reports you are sending us" but he intimated that you were pretty sore at me for not transferring to Topaz last winter. I hope you have changed your mind somewhat and are reconciled to my remaining here indefinitely. I should confess that I have felt very guilty many times since I cannot send you reports more frequently but keeping up with current events consumes the greater part of my day. For instance from Friday to Monday I attended at least six camouflage meetings of several hours' duration apiece not to mention gathering data from other fields. I hope that when I return from Denver you will permit me to write up a comprehensive report of Poston taking into consideration all the odds and ends I have been throwing into my folders daily. That means of course that I won't be able to keep up with daily doings in camp.

In connection with the above Bob and I had a lengthy conversation in Gila and we wondered whether there were sufficient funds in the Study to permit me to take X as an Issei observer, just as Bob has Hikida and Okuno for his assistants. I sounded out X on my return in a round-about way and gathered that he would be perfectly willing to help me provided you would pay him ten or fifteen dollars monthly. As far as he is concerned he would be glad to do it gratis but he feels that if he could hand over this amount to his wife monthly he would have greater freedom of movement—that is family sanction to stay away from home practically every evening. . . . Since he works all day in the block manager's office he has only his evenings free. One advantage in "hiring" X is that I can have access to all the official memos sent out by the administration to the blocks. Furthermore he comes in daily contact with a great number of Issei and a certain type of Nisei that it will permit me to focus my attention on that type of Nisei he does not touch. So far I have found his material very reliable. If WRA will not permit you to add anyone to the staff here could he come under the classification of "clerical help"? If he will assist me in keeping up with current events I shall have more time to write up reports.

Miss Findley, Chief of Community Services, offered to let me go over all of her files on family welfare and other branches under her jurisdiction which she has not permitted the Bureau of Sociological

Research to touch. I have known Findley for over twenty years and since she feels I'm doing good work here she wants me to glance over them to extract any relevant data I might see. Since she is leaving for Hawaii soon I shall have to attack her files very shortly. Do you mind if I let some of my reports go for the time being and concentrate on things like this which have to be done immediately? I hope to have access to Dr. Cary's Education files soon also. Dr. Cary is the Director of Education here and my former high school principal. He and Findley are probably my staunchest supporters here. All of the administrative divisions are getting very secretive about their files so when there is an invitation you must grab it right away. Findley predicts that I'll be an accomplished thief before I leave the center. Incidentally, Bob tells me you are interested in *everything* so I'll throw in as many details as I can from now on into my reports.

With reference to Dr. Lowie seeing my reports you may show him everything I have sent so far. I do not care what you do with my reports provided they do not fall into the hands of the Tenney Committee, the F.B.I., the Senate Investigation Committee, the NSGW [the Native Sons of the Golden West], and other governmental and non-governmental agencies which may utilize them for propaganda purposes. I feel that anything given to me in confidence should be respected. Please give my regards to Dr. Lowie and Dr. Kroeber when you see them. I have been intending to write to them for some time but something always turns up to prevent me from doing it.

Re the "Who's Who in Poston" it's coming along. Since we must gather data on personalities rather cautiously it takes time to complete it. I have also written out the answers to your strike questionnaire but haven't had time to type them. I'm still looking around for a competent, trustworthy typist.

I received a letter from Mich and Anne yesterday. They maintain that the housing situation is pretty acute in Chicago and many of the Nisei, e.g. Charley's sisters are living in "holes in the wall." However, they say freedom is worth anything and encourage me to come out. Anne seems more or less [reconciled] to the situation but Mich appears to be chafing under the strain of coming in daily contact with Quakers who are fortunately not "ostentatiously pious" but "far removed from his war convictions." According to Anne "he superficially gets along well with them but underneath he must, I know, long for a chance to chat with fellows like Kennedy and Haas. Mich is looking forward to being in Cleveland as the Baptists, while quite conservative, number only a few pacifists. . . . "

Will send you a short comparison of Poston and Gila in a few days.

Tamie

Block 31, 11B
May 26, 1943

Dear Dorothy,

X had this paper on gambling ready for me when I returned two days ago. It is still in a rough draft but I thought you might want to see it before he rewrites it. Since this is the only copy we have will you please write comments along the margins wherever you encounter ambiguous statements and mail it back to us? If you feel that a revision is unnecessary please send us a carbon copy for our files.

Had a swell time at Granada. Got more dope than I expected.

Coming back to Poston I found the camp undergoing another F.B.I. scare. I'm informed that several F.B.I. agents are in camp and that two individuals have already been removed for possessing short-wave radio sets.

X is at present writing a report on private profiteering (private enterprises) which is the topic of the day in camp, as well as keeping up with current events.

[signed] Tamie

Block 31, 11 B
May 28, 1943

Dear Dorothy,

Immediately upon receipt of your letter I rushed over to the Leave Office and was informed that all leaves to Phoenix—indefinite as well as short-term—were frozen until further orders were received from Washington. It seems that so many Japanese were relocated in the Salt River Valley that the residents there who have never been kindly disposed toward the Japs became alarmed and requested Washington to do something about it. Consequently Dillon Myer wired Wade Head last week to stop the issuance of leaves to all parts of Arizona until he had thoroughly investigated the situation. . . .

I am very sorry to hear that Bob is leaving our study. As far as keeping an eye on Gila is concerned I shall be glad to do it but there are so many obstacles toward doing it efficiently. For one thing visits to Gila will be very infrequent since our project has an agreement with Gila that only eight from our camp will be permitted to enter Gila in a week. Even at that, there are frequent cancellations to suit the whims of the Arizona public. However, let me know your plans concerning the continuation of research there and I shall be glad to cooperate in whatever way I can. As you know I have many Santa Anita friends in the Butte camp so my stay there can always be disguised under a friendly visit. In the meantime X and I are scheming ways and means to continue our work there.

Poston at present is in a stage which X describes as one of "watchful waiting." The old fear of the F.B.I. has returned especially with the removal of two individuals for possessing short-wave radios last week. The much publicized segregation of the loyal from the disloyal is also giving jitters to many. The old talk of "Inus" is coming back now that the administration is rumored to have "issued a statement" that all those who answered "No" to question 28 as well as those whom the administration considers disloyal will be shipped to a camp in Winslow, Arizona, especially prepared for them. It is reported that those formerly confined at the Moab camp in Utah are already there. X informs me that a large number of people motivated by the fear of removal are requesting cancellation of their applications for repatriation. All in all the camp is in a very unsettled state, very receptive to rumors of all sorts. X believes that it is a very inopportune time for me to leave for if my departure should coincide with an F.B.I. raid or something equally dreaded it might have a disastrous effect on our study.

As far as my future plans are concerned I am seriously considering buying a cooler and remaining in Poston until things assume a more normal tone—that may mean anywhere from two to six months. I am intending, for the present anyway, to write my comprehensive report in camp since I consider bull-sessions with X invaluable along this line. . . .

[signed] Tamie

June 18, 1943

Dear Dorothy,

. . . The Dies Committee is reported to enter Poston sometime this week so I've had my hands full noting attitudes and reactions among the administrative staff and the evacuees. On Tuesday Wade Head sent a message *off the record* to the block managers to destroy all block records on the November strike and to announce in the mess halls that the Dies Committee was expected in Poston at any moment and to instruct block residents to destroy all semblance of "subversiveness." Our block manager's announcement was to the point: "If anyone has a Japanese flag or anything subversive in his possession please put it away in an obscure spot since the Dies Committee is supposed to come in at any minute." In the afternoon I saw my neighbor washing his tar paper walls and upon closer scrutiny noticed that they were scarred with swastika signs that his five-year-old son had scribbled. Yesterday it was reported by Nomura, chairman of the local council, that the vanguard of the Dies Committee had arrived in Parker to make preparations for the week's investigation of Poston by the committee. As far as the residents are concerned they are taking it as a grand joke—they claim that Poston is a "hell of a hole" already and even the Dies Committee cannot make the situation any worse. As far as the lowering of the subsistence appropriation to 31 cents is concerned they maintain that if conditions become more intolerable they will appeal to the Spanish consul. At present, the only ones genuinely worried about the impending visit are the administrative officials who are going around like chickens with their heads chopped off. . . .

The consternation in the administrative quarters is somewhat mirrored in the numerous official memos sent to block managers daily to destroy this or that and carrying the specific instruction that they must be delivered orally in the mess halls and must not be posted on the bulletin boards as customarily done. Yesterday the Adult Education Dept. which is under the supervision of John Powell requested all block managers to destroy all memos sent out by that department to date. Powell does not want his department investigated. All activities under Adult Education are suspended for the duration of the committee's sojourn. The police department also went around yesterday unofficially from block to block to request residents not to indulge in *kendō* (fencing) for a while.

I don't think I'll be subpoenaed but for precautionary measure (since the Dies Committee is threatening to make a barrack to barrack search) I've spirited away my notes for the duration of its stay. . . .

I was hoping that with the heat Poston would go into a state of "hibernation" but excitement never seems to subside here. In desperation I may have to chloroform the place if I ever expect to write that "comprehensive report."

Hastily,
[signed] Tamie

P.S.: W. I. might be interested to know that the "zoot-suit warfare" is in all its glory at Poston now. My sociological journal is crammed with incidents of rowdies crashing parties and breaking them up, "raping" girls, pushing sissies into the swimming pool, etc. The Judicial Commission, the block managers, the community council, and the C.E.C., are putting their heads together to solve the problem "once and for all."

The Dies Committee (3 Congressional representatives, Steadman, and 3 photographers) appeared at our mess hall at lunch today. We were having boiled cabbage, one wiener, tomato and cucumber salad, bread and jam. I was sorely tempted to invite them to partake of the food of the "best fed civilians in the world" but, thank God, held my peace.

Tamie

June 26, 1943

Dear Dorothy,

Things are happening so fast in Poston that I can't spare a minute to sit down and type a report on the Dies Committee—anyway, not for another week or so. Therefore I am sending you a copy of the 82-page sensational testimony of Harold H. Townsend, former Supply and Transportation Officer here, as a pacifier. The Dies Committee (including Costello, Eberharter, Mundt, Stedman and several photographers and reporters) blew in about 10:30 Friday morning, June 18 and blew out the same evening. They investigated no officials or evacuees but preoccupied themselves with peering under messhalls, noting the type of food served, and visiting the warehouses. Apparently they discovered no hidden caches with food for "Japanese paratroops" or any extravagant menus in the various mess halls. According to some reports the Committee's hasty exit from Poston was due to being called back to Washington by the main Dies Committee which feared that the stink its sub-committee was creating might result in hanging all of them.

As soon as I can I'll type out my sociological journal for the months of May and June so you can keep abreast of Poston activities. I can't send you the original because much of it needs annotation. There's positively no time to sit down and write up a formal report at present. When I reminded X yesterday after his lengthy dictation that I should be getting to my comprehensive report he retorted almost savagely: "What the hell does she think we're doing here anyway? Only two persons are working here and so many things are happening. The Bureau of Sociological Research has thirteen people on its staff but they are not getting half as much as we are. The events in camp won't wait for us. Hell, forget about the comprehensive report." So—please do not expect any formal reports from us in the next few weeks. We shall, however, send you a weekly journal to acquaint you with the trend of activities here.

Glad to hear that Miss Hankey is taking over Gila but certainly feel sorry for any *Keto* going to a relocation center at present. The tempo of the community is changing so rapidly that she'll be fortunate if she can get anything at all. More power to her. If she needs any moral support I'll be happy to make occasional visits to Gila to discuss common problems with her.

Dr. Miles E. Cary informed me a few nights ago that the relations between WRA and the Indian Service are at the breaking point and there is talk going on in the administrative quarters that the WRA will take sole charge of Poston within a few weeks. . . .

Hastily,
[signed] Tamie

July 12, 1943

Dear Dorothy,

Here is the sociological journal from June 1–14. The second half describing the visit of the Dies Committee, problems of juvenile delinquency, etc., will be ready for mailing, I hope, by the 15th.

Things have quieted down somewhat in camp. Except for the announcement of a drastic cut in project employment to conform with the quota set by the Washington WRA, and the removal of four juvenile gang leaders to Gila, there has been little excitement.

The heat is terrific. Last week my sweet potato vines began to curl up and die so I looked at the thermometer and found the room was 118 [degrees].

I don't think I can "take" the nervous strain of camp life much longer. If I had my way now I don't want to see another Jap face for a long, long time. As soon as my plans crystallize I'll inform you as to my future plans.

With the attached dollar could you get me two large packages of Lipton's orange [pekoe] tea in individual bags? X loves Lipton's tea and will work better when served some.

[signed] Tamie

P.S. I think we are definitely passing into the second phase of camp life so I am going to concentrate on getting that structural report done as quickly and as thoroughly as possible. This may be my last contribution to the "study."

[signed] Tamie

July 29, 1943

Dear Dorothy,

So Tule Lake has been selected as the segregation center. What is going to happen to the study there? Is Jimmy going to continue the study wherever he is sent or are you planning to have him transferred to Gila? I notice that Gila along with Poston and Manzanar is not on the list of centers to which Tuleans will be sent.

I have two specific plans for my future and I want you to make the final decision as soon as possible. The last two months have clearly demonstrated that it is impossible for me to write up my year's work in Poston. I feel, however, that it is vitally important that it be completed as soon as possible because in the physical condition I am in at present I don't know how long I can stick this out. Furthermore we are approaching the close of the first phase of relocation center life and it is important that the background be recorded before we launch into a study of the second. Therefore I am requesting you to give me a three to four month leave to go to Chicago or Cleveland beginning the first or second week of September to write up my comprehensive report. While I am gone X has promised to keep up with current events in camp to facilitate my return. In the mental and physical status I am in at present it is impossible to muster up sufficient detachment to write objectively. I feel that a change of environment would assist me tremendously in putting out a piece of work that would meet with your approval. X feels that I am on the verge of a nervous breakdown and strongly recommends my moving out before I become totally useless to the study. He believes that a three to four month sojourn among congenial friends would return me to normalcy and give me sufficient courage to return to jail again. He has also made arrangements so that I can have a private apartment in his block upon my return to release me from the [tortures] of residing in a rural block.

The second plan is to remain in Poston until the end of October to cover the segregation process. X and I are not expecting any fireworks but the atmosphere is definitely hostile at present. I feel X can handle the job adequately but if things break it might be too big an order to cover alone. According to Administrative Order 100 released last night segregation will begin in the northern centers first, then proceed to Arkansas, and Gila, Poston and Manzanar will be the last to be tackled. Since segregation is scheduled to begin on September 1 and terminate on October 20, I guess Poston will be hit sometime in October. The Instruction further states that repatriates will be the first to be moved out, then Kibei bachelors, and lastly those who require a hearing. If you want me to follow the second plan I should like to take a two-week vacation away from Poston in the near future to fortify myself for the coming ordeal. I must also caution you that the completion of the structural report will be delayed two months.

I heard from Walt Balderson, new head of the Community Activities division, this morning that John Embree has resigned from his present WRA job to teach in some sort of a colonial administrators' school to be opened shortly in Chicago. He also informed me that they are discussing the status of the Bureau of Sociological Research at the Denver conference this week. When the BSR staff left for Tuba City about three weeks ago to analyze the data they've collected since March of this year, Leighton moved out all of his belongings so they are not expecting him to return. Spicer will become the official Caucasian analyst for Poston on his return. Len Nelson at the last block managers' meeting announced that the BSR will be dissolved soon because it was an "unnecessary and unproductive" project. I don't know what the exact fate of the BSR will be but Walt claims that Leighton is trying to relocate all of his junior staff so it appears as though Spicer may have to work without evacuee help. . . .

Sincerely,
[signed] Tamie

P.S. Wish you could see me now. There isn't a square inch on my body not covered with heat rash. Haven't had a decent night's sleep for the last 4 weeks. Am beginning to agree with my family who have been admonishing me to relocate that "science should not come before life, liberty, and the pursuit of happiness."

Sept. 17, 1943

Dear Dorothy,

X and I returned last night from a profitable ten day visit in Gila. While there we had an interesting three-day session with Hankey, before she left for Berkeley Saturday morning. We were greatly pleased to see that she has made an admirable entree into the community. In our humble opinion she seemed to have a better grasp of the Gila situation than Bob [Spencer] ever did. (We reached this conclusion after talking to a number of our evacuee friends who are "in the know" there.) At present I am working up a brief comparative study of Gila which I hope to send to you sometime next week.

I presume Hankey explained to you in some detail our reluctance in getting statistics here. We consider it unwise to risk our reputation at this stage of the game collecting something which we feel is not sufficiently important to warrant it. Furthermore, if we were to collect such data we will have to do it ourselves. With so many important events occurring in the community simultaneously we feel that our time can be more profitably expended covering these than sitting in the census office copying somewhat unreliable data which probably will be more readily accessible later on.

In regards to Morton's trip to Washington X and I have thought up several questions which we hope to mail to him tomorrow.

I would be very much interested in receiving some samples of the material being collected in Chicago. As I told you in Phoenix I have a large collection of letters sent back to Poston by relocatees describing their first impressions of the outside and would be interested in comparing them with their material. Most of my letters come from Chicago, Cleveland, Salt Lake City and New York.

My future plans are these: I should like to leave Poston as soon as possible (preferably in the next three or four weeks) to spend at least four months writing up my year's research in Cleveland. Since we already have four capable workers in Chicago I believe it would be wiser to take up residence in Cleveland rather than Chicago so that incidentally while working on my report I might be able to collect some comparative material on relocation. Besides the letters from Mich and Anne describing the "disgusting" plight of the Nisei in adjusting themselves to the "American mode of living" in Cleveland have piqued my curiosity. Since both of them have a tendency to exaggerate I would like to see the existing situation for myself. X feels that in view of my inability to adapt myself to the summer heat of Poston, the chances of my wanting to return to jail would be greater if I leave here soon so that I will be ready to come back in early spring before the heat arrives. According to this plan I will return to camp sometime in February and spend the following four to four and a half months catching up on what I have lost and gathering new material to analyze on the outside during the latter half of June, July and August. If you still wish to continue our study after that period I will return again in September and spend the winter months here. Of course, a really comprehensive treatment of the material I have accumulated so far will require a year but I hope in the four months to analyze the basic structure of certain organizations for which I have detailed notes. I hope to work up the outline for my report before I leave but that depends on whether things break out in camp or not in the next few days. X believes that the segregation process will progress very smoothly and that there is no necessity for me to waste my time here. As long as I have the smallest desire to return to Poston to continue the study he has promised to keep up with current events to facilitate my reentry into the community. This, of course, all depends on whether you wish to continue his services or to close Poston with my departure. If the above plan seems highly unreasonable to you there is no other course for me to take but to hand in my resignation. I hope, however, that funds will be available for the next four months so that I can work up the data I have here to give you a more complete picture of the year's happenings in Poston. I hope you realize that I must get away from camp to obtain sufficient detachment to write that report. Even a ten day trip to Gila gave me a new perspective on Poston.

If the above plan, however, meets with your approval I would appreciate greatly if you would write a letter to Wade Head as soon as [possible] requesting permission for me to leave camp to go to Cleveland during the first week of October. The Leave Officer here has informed me that short-term leaves are granted only for sixty days at the very most—i.e., they are usually for a thirty-day period subject to renewal for another thirty days—and that I will have to go out on indefinite leave since the policy here is to refuse seasonal leave to anyone going further east than Nebraska or Kansas. Furthermore, within a few weeks no seasonal leaves will be granted anywhere. However, I do not believe that it will be very difficult for me to reenter camp in the spring. I talked to Vernon Kennedy, former Employment Chief and now relocation officer for the Kansas City area, on his way back from high-pressure advertising in Tule Lake and he informed me that the new policy of the WRA to be announced shortly will be to permit anyone to return to camp without any question if he cannot make a successful adjustment outside. According to this plan a relocatee simply presents himself to the relocation officer in his area and he will be given a permit without any investigation to return to his original camp. In this way the WRA hopes to induce fence-sitters to relocate. They feel that eight out of every 10 relocatees will want to remain on the outside once they get out of jail. At the worst I am perfectly willing to pay subsistence charges to the WRA from February if this plan does not go into effect. If you write that letter to Wade

Head will you please send me a carbon copy to attach to my application for indefinite leave as proof of outside employment?

As far as the Chicago conference is concerned I shall be glad to attend it if you feel that my presence is necessary. I definitely feel that Chicago is a much more logical site than Salt Lake City in view of the fact that five of us will be already in that area by November. Will you please let me know as soon as possible whether my future plans meet with your approval as I would like to file my application soon? If I go out on indefinite leave you will not have to pay my expenses since the WRA will attend to that. . . .

Sincerely,
[signed] Tamie

Oct. 9, 1943

Dear Dorothy,

I have just mailed you the sociological journal from Sept. 20 to Oct. 6, that X brought in yesterday. He was so busy with segregation that he could not get up to date sooner but promises to send in weekly reports to you and me from now on. He was quite taken aback by the amount you expected him to do while I was away and expressed the fear that he would never be able to satisfy you and suggested resigning from the study. I however, prevailed on him to stick it out until I returned to relieve him of part of his duties. X will eventually finish all of the reports you suggested in your letter but I hope you will not press on him to finish them soon because the recording of daily camp activities is a full-time job in itself and he is doing it more than adequately. As far as I can see he is a much more valuable person to the study than I am and contributing more monthly than his salary calls for.

X tells me I would be fortunate if I can complete the political structure of Poston before March but I'm hoping in my most optimistic mood to finish three other topics—social disorganization, education and relocation on the project level. I will send you a tentative outline of the work I intend to do within a few weeks.

Sincerely,
[signed] Tamie

P.S. I am leaving Poston with mixed feelings. One desire is to get out as quickly as possible and never in my wildest dreams expect to return to a concentration camp again. The other is an intense curiosity (or more correctly, a deep sense of duty) to follow the thing through. It will be interesting to see which side will triumph in the next four months.

6

REMOVAL

A Hiatus in Chicago

In the end, Tsuchiyama's original plans to go to Cleveland fell through because she was unable to find a suitable apartment there. After a two-week search, Tsuchiyama gave up, went to, and then settled in Chicago on November 1, 1943.

Around that same time Tsuchiyama also wrote to Thomas regarding an interesting prospect that opened up for her. Noting that her family had constantly implored her to get out of camp and come back to Hawaii, Tsuchiyama wrote that she now had a job prospect back home that tempted her. She stated that Charles Loomis, then head of the wartime Morale Section and active in policy circles on the islands, had written to her and offered her a position at the University of Hawaii. Loomis, in fact, was apparently so interested in hiring Tsuchiyama that he told her that she could write her own ticket. If she wouldn't come immediately, Tsuchiyama noted that Loomis had indicated that she need only let him know, and arrangements could and would be made. By January 1944, however, Tsuchiyama wondered if she should actually return to Poston in order to check as well as to gather more data. This possibility was clearly fraught with ambivalence for Tsuchiyama because she hated being at Poston.

When she learned that speculation and rumors apparently persisted in Poston concerning a personal relationship between her and Richard Nishimoto, this was the last straw. Tsuchiyama never returned to Arizona. What is more, instead of writing up her research as promised, correspondence indicates that she was unable to get much accomplished. (Tsuchiyama did note in a July 1944 letter that she planned to take a break and do some research and writing for her ongoing project on Athabascan folklore themes. This material would later be presented as her doctoral dissertation, which Tsuchiyama filed at the University of California at Berkeley in 1947.)

A document I obtained via the Freedom of Information Act indicates that, eight years later, neighbors living near Tsuchiyama at 5455 South Drexel Boulevard in Chicago still remembered her favorably, especially in terms of her disciplined work habits. The report summarizes the impressions of several individuals who lived in the same apartment complex and who remembered that "Tsuchiyama was writing a book dealing with the effect of the relocation upon the Japanese during the war. They stated that she did this work in her room as if she was working in an office. She had regular hours for research in the morning and then did typing in the afternoon and night."

One wonders what might have happened to this material, as correspondence indicates that little was ever sent throughout the year to Dorothy Thomas back at Berkeley. Ultimately, Tsuchiyama's failure to produce additional data and reports precipitated a marked decline in her relationship with Dorothy Thomas and, ultimately, Tsuchiyama's association with the JERS project.

Letters from the Field, November 1943–July 1944

441 Wrightwood Avenue
Chicago, Illinois
November 1, 1943

Dear Dorothy,

My address until further notice will be 441 Wrightwood Avenue, Chicago, Illinois. I am at present sharing a two-room apartment with a nineteen year old girl from Poston who is taking a two-week vacation between jobs. I had hoped to secure an apartment all to myself so I could work as my spirits moved me but this was the best arrangement I could find in a hurry. As soon as she commences, work conditions will undoubtedly improve since I shall probably be able to work undisturbed for at least nine hours during the day. Under this arrangement I can look for another apartment at leisure and still accomplish some work on the report. I spent all Friday morning surveying vacant apartments near the university with Frank but they were all so dark and dingy that I decided to try other areas. In the afternoon I encountered a young girl who had come to the hostel in quest of a room-mate since she could ill-afford a $40 apartment which she had located the day before. The apartment is light and cheery and has more modern conveniences than I had expected at that price. There is a possibility she may get married within the next few weeks and move out in which case I may not have to look for another apartment.

Enclosed is Dr. Redfield's letter which you wanted returned for your files. It is interesting that Leighton who considered X and me his greatest enemies and who toward the end of his stay would scarcely recognize us when we met in the street should suddenly become very magnanimous and want to surrender his files to us for the "furtherance of science." In all probability I have more detailed notes than he on many subjects but would be extremely interested to see Spicer's study of block 34 (A.P. block), minutes of administrative staff meetings, and Leighton's personality studies—provided there are no strings attached. The Bureau members spent practically two months during the summer at Tuba City going over their notes and writing up a "Handbook for Administrators" and according to Spicer, Scotty Matsumoto, the best of the evacuee staff, was going to spend several months in Chicago going over the notes and writing up a sociological study of Poston. I should think in that case most of their material when published will be available to the public without our assistance. I should appreciate greatly if you will send me a copy of that handbook as soon as it is released by the Dept. of Interior. I can almost imagine what it will be like after listening to Spicer's swan song last August.

I was much interested in Hankey's comments on our Gila report. X's answer more or less coincides with my general sentiment so I will refrain from writing another. Is Hankey coming to our Chicago conference?

I am at present busily absorbed in going over my notes and making an outline of the report I intend to write out here. I doubt if I will have much accomplished by the time you and W. I. arrive. Please let me know any definite plans you may have concerning the conference since I rarely go out to the office. I feel like a stranger and an intruder there— besides it takes me from 45 minutes to an hour by subway to get there.

I miss Poston and my fights with X very much. Wish I were there now. Things seem to happen whenever I'm absent.

My best regards to W. I. I'm looking forward to seeing both of you soon.

Sincerely,
[signed] Tamie

5455 So. Drexel Ave.
Chicago, Illinois
Nov. 15, 1943

Dear Dorothy,

. . . My new address is 5455 So. Drexel Ave. I moved here Saturday afternoon because life with Alice [a pseudonym] was unbearable and unproductive. I was practically running a boarding house at the Wrightwood address for her Nisei boy friends. I decided it was more expedient for me to move than to wait for her to move out.

Will write you a detailed letter concerning my future plans tomorrow. My Poston friends inform me that there has been a decided change in sentiments among the Issei concerning the outcome of the war which I have been waiting for (and on which my study is focused) which, coupled with the scheduled transfer of Poston from Indian Service to WRA hands, may necessitate my return to camp soon.

Hastily,
[signed] Tamie

5455 So. Drexel Ave.
Chicago 37, Ill.
Nov. 19, 1943

Dear Dorothy,

For the past week I have been enjoying some degree of peace for the first time since Dec. 7, 1941. I did not realize the extent of my mental fatigue until I located this apartment and had an opportunity to relax. I am gradually pulling myself together to make a stab at the work I have set out to do in the next few months.

Aside from going through my files and attempting to bring my notes up to date, I have accomplished very little since coming out. At present I am working on an outline for an "ideal" study of Poston to give me an idea what gaps will have to be filled when I return to Poston.

Ever since coming out I have been receiving urgent appeals from my Poston friends to return to camp as quickly as possible. Apparently I chose a very inopportune time to dash out. I will discuss my future plans with you in detail when you arrive in Chicago.

Will you please request the accounting office to mail my checks to

45-2-C, Poston, instead of my old address? I am as yet uncertain when I shall return to Poston so it is probably more advisable to have them sent to X's address than to my Chicago address.

Hastily,
[signed] Tamie

Jan. 3, [1944]

Dear Dorothy,

Thanks for your Xmas card. I must admit that the sight of the Golden Gate Bridge made me a little homesick for that damned state called California.

This letter is primarily a request to start negotiations immediately with Shirrel for my return to Poston. I should like to be back in camp by the middle of February at the latest and government red-tape may take longer than you suspect. For the past two weeks I have been slicing up X's journal and throwing it into different folders. I hope to spend all of this week rearranging my files and then making a detailed outline of the political structure I intend to write next week. The week after that I hope to do some shopping and then I should be ready to return to camp. I believe it will be wiser for me not to make an attempt at writing out here but to go back as quickly as possible, settle down, and then write without interruption for several months. I am determined to finish that detailed structural report of Poston before I come out again, heat or no heat. For this purpose, I have asked X to scout around for a cooler for me. I fully realized only a few weeks ago that my soul will not be my own again until I have this report ready for you. Only after it is completed can I make up my mind whether to continue with the Study or to pull out. Besides moving in and out of camp is too time-consuming. I waste so much valuable time trying to get adjusted to different situations.

I had fully intended not to let you know about the following since I still remember the fuss you made in Phoenix at the time Bob Spencer pulled out of the Study but when I casually mentioned it to Frank after you left he insisted that I tell you so that we would all be prepared for your reaction in a case a similar situation cropped up again. You noticed during the conference that I was terribly dejected and you even made an attempt to comfort me before you left. You may probably be interested to know that during the conference I had to make the biggest decision in my life since February, 1942, when I learned I could not return to Hawaii. Ever since I came out in October I have been receiving letters from Hawaii urging me to return to conduct a research among the Japanese there under the auspices of the Morale Section under the military governor. During the conference, Mr. Charles Loomis, the head of the Morale Section, offered me an instructorship in anthropology at the University of Hawaii giving me the choice of delivering classroom lectures or conducting research among the different racial groups. He wanted me to wire my decision by Dec. 15th since they were holding up the next six months waiting list in San Francisco. If I decided to accept their offer, the military intelligence had promised to give me priority over that list so that I could return sometime in December or January. Of course I wanted to go home terribly. My family has been entreating me in every letter since Dec. 7, 1941, to return home and I also have become tired of marking time among strangers—some of them hostile, I admit. I've often wondered in the last two years how it would feel to go back among trusted friends on friendly soil again. But I knew it wouldn't be fair to you to pull out at this time—that I really couldn't leave the Study until I had written up a detailed study of Poston. So I decided not to confide in you—although I was tempted to several times during the conference—but to make the decision myself since there could be but one decision. However, after I had wired Loomis he had replied that the job would be held open for me indefinitely, and after I had my talk with Frank, I began to question my value to your study. Since both Hankey and Sakoda seem to be doing admirably in their respective fields I wondered whether there would be any loss in the closing of Poston. You realize, of course, that my leaving would also mean the termination of X's services since he has always maintained that he will "fold up" the same day I resign. If I could only be satisfied with the work I am producing in Poston I would have just cause to continue but as you know I have been terribly disappointed with the results. There is something lacking in my reports which constantly frustrates me. Whenever I proofread my reports before sending them to you I feel like an outsider peering at the evacuees from a telescope. I had hoped in the beginning that being a member of the "in-group" by necessity, I would be able to make an "ideal" study of it but the results have been far from satisfactory. Perhaps the detailed report will help to portray the evacuees as a complete picture rather than bits of humanity thrown indiscriminately in space as I have been picturing them. Perhaps my anthropological approach is at fault—it may not be dynamic enough to give a truer picture of camp. Anyway, all this rambling leads up to the following: Please contact Shirrel immediately and arrange my return to Poston as soon as possible. I want to get that report out of the way as quickly as I can so I can regain my freedom. Once it is completed I can make my decision whether to continue with the Study or to pull out. In all probability I will stick it out to the bitter end "between tears and laughter" but it would be a grand feeling to know that I am free to do as I please. At times I chuckle to think that a misanthrope like me should be studying humanity when I really belong in the front lines shooting down every two-legged creature that comes my way and enjoying it. But maybe one must become a misanthrope to get sufficient objectivity to view the hypocritical actions of man with equanimity.

X wrote yesterday asking for instructions on the disposal of the single copy of the journal from now on so I advised him to mail it to me so I can read it immediately on receipt and forward it to you on the same day. If you were to receive it first it would probably take several weeks before your secretary will have time to make carbon copies and dispatch one to me. I find it imperative to keep up with Poston. Besides this arrangement will last only for a few weeks. As soon as I reach Poston we will mail it to you directly. My regards to W. I. I hope you had a pleasant trip back.

[signed] Tamie

Jan. 24, [1944]

Dear Dorothy,

Just received your wire. I was debating whether to write you or not without waiting for X's letter when your wire arrived.

I'm in a hell of a fix. I don't know why I attract more trouble than others on the study. I wrote a letter to X Friday saying that I was returning on Feb. 3 or 5 depending on whether Hankey could meet me in Phoenix and the next day I received a letter from him saying his wife had opened my Jan. 15th letter informing him that I was planning to return by the middle of February. Apparently she had thought she had gotten rid of me when I left Poston in October and was quite disturbed about my intention to return. She demanded explanations from X and accused him of being in love with me else he would not be working so hard on the Study. . . . This reaction was an entirely new one to me since I had assumed she liked me since she appeared amicable to me whenever I encountered her in Poston. I thought it was quite evident to everyone that I had no more intentions on capturing X than marrying a hippopotamus but strange things happen in this world. Knowing X and his techniques I'm certain everything is under control but I dread the idea of facing an insanely jealous woman. I don't know if I had the choice of facing a lynching mob or a jealous wife which I would select.

The purpose of this letter is to ask you what I should do. Should I go back to Poston and take the chance of endangering the study, or shall I remain in Chicago and write up the report without any disturbance? My return to Poston is further complicated by the shortage of apartments. Seasonal workers are not too anxious to go out again this spring and the blocks are still very crowded. Block 31 has only one large apartment vacant which X is certain I cannot get. Block 45 is closed to me because of X's wife who is reputed to be the block's greatest gossiper. That leaves me only blocks where I know no one and it will take weeks before I can settle down and get work done. If I had my way I would like to have X continue his journal as usual and I remain in Chicago to finish that report without much loss of precious time. After that is completed I should like to throw in the sponge. I'm thoroughly disgusted with everything. I'm going to buy a small farm in Hawaii and raise vegetables for the duration. After that I'll head for my coral atoll. I don't want to deal with human beings again in my life. I have reached the conclusion the Japs in Poston do not care to be helped, do not want to be helped, and do not deserve to be helped. If you insist on my returning to camp I will do so, but you will have to take the chance of my walking out on you without finishing the overall report if I get mad enough. (At present I feel like Tom Shibutani and Charlie Kikuchi who felt they could no longer be of help to you in the centers. [This sentence was crossed out in the original; however, it is still readable.]) (Censored by myself.)

I'll probably cool off in a few days and become a little more "sane" again. Meanwhile will you let me know by return mail whether I should go back to camp or remain in Chicago? I am requesting the WRA tomorrow to withhold the wire to the project announcing my arrival.

Hastily,
[signed] Tamie

P.S. You might save a few gray hairs by firing me outright for causing you so much trouble.

T.T.

January 28, 1944

DR. D. S. THOMAS
PREFER TO REMAIN IN CHICAGO. YESTERDAY'S WIRE WAS LAST ATTEMPT TO CONTINUE POSTON STUDY FOR YOU. PLEASE DON'T WRITE TO DICK UNTIL YOU HEAR FROM ME. HAVE STARTED REPORT. LETTER FOLLOWING. TAMIE
    Received 9:40 A.M.

Jan. 31, 1944

Dear Dorothy,
I had full intentions of writing you a letter immediately after sending you the wire Thursday evening but on second thought decided to wait a day or two for X's letter which might clarify matters. This morning I received one which makes no mention of the unfortunate incident and appears to be his usual gossipy type of informing me of camp affairs and inquiring when I am returning.

I am extremely sorry to have caused you that scare last week. But I was scared too. Apparently I made a mountain out of a mole hole. As far as X and his spouse are concerned it seems to be a closed incident. On Wednesday—the first time after informing me of the incident—he sent me a very brief letter saying: "Everything is alright out here. The weather is very warm." On the strength of this I wired you that evening that Poston was under control and that I could meet Hankey in Phoenix on Feb. 9. You had just cause to assume that this was another tantrum of mine and that you should emphasize the seriousness of the situation. But the change in plans was motivated by something deeper than mere capriciousness. I've repeated to you on several occasions, if I recall correctly, that X had told me many times that he would "fold up" the day I resigned from the study. When I left Poston in October he asked me to inform him of my decision as soon as I decided not to return to Poston because he would quit then. His policy up to now has been: "I'm willing to help a Jap to the best of my ability to gather material to write up a history of the Japanese in California as the Japanese see it, but by God I won't lift a finger to help a *Keto* to do the same thing." Hence I was afraid X would resign as soon as he learned I was not returning to Poston in the spring. He could interpret such a decision as a desire on my part to pull out of the study as soon as the over-all report is completed—which would be a correct interpretation for if I remain in Chicago until that time I would certainly have no desire to return to "the Black Hole of Calcutta" again. After I sent you that memorable Jan. 24th letter my conscience began to hurt because I knew deep down in my heart that I couldn't give up this easily, that I should make another attempt to keep that study going for you in Poston. I, by myself, could contribute very little to the understanding of the Japanese in California, but with X's help I knew we could produce something worthwhile. If this were so, then the only course for me to take would be to keep my promise of returning to Poston in February or March. When his letter arrived on Wednesday saying "everything is alright out here" I took for granted that I had exaggerated the seriousness of the situation and wired you that I could meet Hankey in Phoenix as originally planned. I hope this will explain to your satisfaction the incongruity between my letter of Jan. 24th and my wire Wednesday evening.

On Saturday I sent a registered letter to X asking him to answer frankly the following questions so that on the basis of his reply I could make up my mind whether to return to Poston to continue the study or to abandon it at this point. I requested that he answer by return mail since I had already bought a train ticket which will expire on Feb. 19, and since the Chicago WRA had already wired the project to expect me on Feb. 5th.

"1. If I remain in Chicago indefinitely to finish writing up the over-all report would you be willing to continue with your journal as usual, or would you resign as you have been previously stating? The chances of my returning to Poston at a later date to continue the study in this case will be practically nil.

2. If I were intending to return to Poston in the near future when is the most advisable time? Since I had planned to leave Chicago on Jan. 31st my things are practically packed and I can leave at a minute's notice.

3. If I returned to Poston in the near future will there be some sort of temporary housing for me until I locate an apartment somewhere? Some assurance of housing the first night is important since I arrive late at night.

4. How serious was your quarrel with your wife regarding my Jan. 15th letter? Do you think she will make it extremely unpleasant for me if I returned—enough to endanger the future of the study in Poston?"

His reply to these questions will give us an insight into the Poston situation to enable us to formulate our plans. If his replies are favorable I am perfectly willing, leaving all personal considerations aside, to go back and keep the study going for you, if you wish. We have some darn good material in our files and it would be tragic to abandon the study at this point (i.e. if X sticks to his word and walks out on us). My return may mean some delay in finishing the over-all report but in the long run we may be compensated. It may be taking a chance, but—between taking a chance to keep the study going and having to close it because of X's resignation—it might be worth it.

I'll send you X's answer as soon as I receive it. Meanwhile I shall be interested in hearing your comments.

Sincerely,
[signed] Tamie

P.S. Please don't worry about my walking out on you in the near future. No matter what happens I'll finish that over-all report for you before I undertake anything "softer" in Hawaii or elsewhere. I have that much decency still left.

Feb. 2, 1944
(RSN to TT)

Dear Tamie:
I have received your letter, air mail and registered. It's a long story to explain the questions asked by you. But as it stands now, it might [be]

deemed same as the time you left Poston. Her suspicion began with rumors about us in Block 31. And on top of it your letter of January 15 arrived.

Everything has been settled now, and I don't think it is necessary to go into them. I shall explain the detail to you when you come here.

About your residence in Block 31, there is some rumor as stated above. I don't think it is wise for me to contact Joe Hayashi [a pseudonym] on your behalf. If, however, you don't mind [residing] in some other block, I will be glad to contact the manager. Let me tell you frankly, although it might hurt you, that you were not a bit popular in Block 31. You seem to have antagonized inadvertently quite many people, including the Ito [a pseudonym] family.

As to your temporary apartment, there should not be any worry. There are many apartment vacant in many blocks here. I had suggested Block 42, because it is a mind-your-own-business block and Tom Sakai lived there.

Therefore, the Poston situation should not alter your plan in coming back here.

Hurriedly,

(X)

The above letter appears in the JERS correspondence file, perhaps because it was passed on to Dorothy Thomas by Tsuchiyama; see the handwritten note dated February 5, 1944, from Tsuchiyama to Thomas: "Here it [the letter] is; it's [the decision is] in your hands."

> 5455 So. Drexel Ave.
> Chicago, 37, Illinois
> Feb. 8, 1944

Dear Dorothy,

I infer from your wire today that you would rather have me remain in Chicago and finish the report at once than return to Poston in the near future (the only feasible way as I see it) and attempt to keep the study going for you there. If that is what you really want, that is perfectly satisfactory to me.

Living up to my promise made to X last October that I would notify him as soon as I decided to withdraw from the study, I am writing him today that I have decided to remain in Chicago indefinitely to write up the overall report and do not intend to return to Poston at a later date to continue my work. It is your job now as director of the study, if you desire to retain his services, to impress upon him the importance of the study and persuade him to continue his journal. I fear I am in no position to induce him to stay when I, myself, am planning to resign upon completion of my report.

Will you be kind enough to request the accounting department to mail all future checks to my Chicago address?

Very sincerely yours,
[signed] Tamie

7

REJECTION

A Parting of the Ways

As evidence of the decline in Thomas and Tsuchiyama's professional relationship, one need only peruse a letter of late July 1944. Thomas wrote to Tsuchiyama expressing her concern and disappointment that the quality of
Tsuchiyama's penultimate report was "distinctly below standard." While noting
that her baseline for this evaluation was, in fact, Tsuchiyama's previous work,
Thomas emphasized that

> the interests of the [JERS] study quite clearly call for "production." I
> would define "production" as a finished performance, utilizing all the
> wealth of detail that you must have at hand. I would naturally expect a
> report superior in both quality and quantity to the 40-odd pages that
> represent your total output over the last nine months.
>
> If you are willing to face the implications of this situation with
> complete frankness and to do the professional job of which your earlier
> performance indicates you are capable, I hope you will continue [working
> for JERS]. May I hear from you about this by return mail?

Tsuchiyama's reply must have been fired off on the same day that she
received Thomas's letter. Beginning with "Dear Dorothy" (as she had addressed
Thomas in her correspondence ever since late 1942), Tsuchiyama sarcastically
acknowledged that her work was not up to Thomas's standards but noted that
the two had never agreed about the best way to proceed with the research
project at hand in the first place. Tsuchiyama then asked for permission to
resign from JERS as of July 15, 1944, noting that, in light of Thomas's lack
of confidence in her work, Tsuchiyama preferred to pursue other endeavors
more to her liking. Probably unbeknownst to Tsuchiyama, Thomas had already
been writing to Nishimoto on the side, asking for his advice about how to

handle Tsuchiyama and trying to obtain his explicit commitment to continue as a JERS fieldworker for the Poston dimension of the project should Tsuchiyama decide to leave.

As the letters reveal, however, Thomas was interested in keeping Tsuchiyama on as a fieldworker, even when things were clearly "not going very well." On the one hand, this is because Thomas was afraid that Tsuchiyama might actually leave before she had written up what she had researched in Poston, which would be a great loss for the project, in Thomas's opinion. On the other hand, Thomas thought well of Tsuchiyama's previous field reports and felt confident that subsequent reports could and would measure up to their predecessors, if only Tsuchiyama would buckle down and get to work.

Thomas's actual method of getting Tsuchiyama to produce fieldnotes and topical reports, however, was characterized by a carrot-and-stick approach throughout their relationship. As is clear from her correspondence, Thomas would alternately praise and encourage and then pressure and threaten Tsuchiyama in order to make the latter produce the goods. My best guess is that, once in Chicago, Tsuchiyama's removal from Poston, Nishimoto, and the larger set of field relationships gave her the time and distance to reflect upon her situation. By that point, Tsuchiyama may have already been feeling a measure of distrust, if not outright betrayal, in regard to Nishimoto, Thomas, or both. It is not possible to say exactly what such feelings engendered. It is possible that she thought "to hell with it" and simply decided not to write anything up. (This is the conclusion that Nishimoto came to after reviewing the notes that Tsuchiyama had sent to Thomas at Berkeley and that Thomas in turn sent on to Nishimoto in Poston for his assessment and evaluation.)

Having actually obtained Nishimoto's commitment, as early as January 11, 1944, in regard to continuing in Poston as a fieldworker should Tsuchiyama fail to return to the camp, Thomas finally agreed to go along with Tsuchiyama's request to resign from the project. August 1, 1945, marked the end of Tsuchiyama's affiliation with JERS.

Incidentally, Hisako, Tamie's elder sister, does not remember Tsuchiyama writing about JERS matters or personnel during the war: "Our letters [during the war were] subject to censorship. Tamie, by nature, was not one to write of anything that might throw a bad light on anyone." Hisako also noted that by the time she came to Texas in the mid-1950s, "she [Tamie] was silent on 'relocation,'" did not care to speak about this period in her life, and when asked about it point blank simply refused to answer. Hisako suggested that, in this regard, "[w]e have a tendency not to talk of anything we want to forget." Thus, Tsuchiyama apparently did not make contact again with any of her Poston JERS, BSR, or WRA colleagues after the war.

On their part, as might be expected, both Nishimoto and Thomas were quite uncharitable in regard to Tsuchiyama's output after she left Poston for her stay in Chicago. In essence, Thomas commented that what had actually been written up looked flimsy and weak. Nishimoto wrote back that, upon inspection, the data Tsuchiyama had submitted upon her resignation were "lousy" and that her work overall "stank." At the same time, in a somewhat mysterious letter from the same general period, Nishimoto blamed himself for the negative turn that Tsuchiyama's attitude and work had taken, acknowledging to Thomas that some of what had happened was "my fault."

Nonetheless, when all was said and done, Thomas and Nishimoto did draw from Tsuchiyama's fieldwork in their well-known text *The Spoilage*. An overview of the Poston strike, attributed to Tsuchiyama's field report, appears in that book, as well as a shorter excerpt from a study Tsuchiyama wrote on selective service registration and draft resistance.

Did Dorothy Thomas's methodology for cross-checking data, ostensibly for the purpose of increasing the validity and reliability of fieldworkers' ethnographic observations, create an aperture for Nishimoto to win Thomas's confidence? I suspect so. Did Thomas and Nishimoto "cannibalize" the research of the JERS fieldworkers—European and Japanese American alike—for their own ends? On the basis of cases like Tsuchiyama's and Wax's, my response would be, yes. Was this inappropriate? I think it was, especially because Tsuchiyama's professional career did not take off after the war, in part, I assume, because she had no original, independently authored publications. But let's pursue this story further. Ultimately, when we return to the issue of the politics and ethics of ethnographic fieldwork, I invite readers to judge for themselves.

Letters from the Field, July–August 1944

July 17, 1944

Dear Dorothy:

In reply to your letter of July 15 I am sending you by railway express, insured, all of my notes, including my field notes, as soon as Frank returns the notes he has borrowed from me from time to time. I've been trying to contact him all day but no one appears to have shown up at the office today.

Your letter of July 15 clearly indicates that you do not trust me and feel that a constant surveillance is necessary. Since it is impossible for me to work under the conditions you set forth, and since it has been my policy as long as I can remember never to work for an employer that distrusts me, I am resigning from the Study as of July 15, 1944.

Regarding future plans I had intended to remain in Chicago as long as necessary to complete the report to your satisfaction, and then resign. When the military authorities warned me in May that unless I returned to Hawaii then they could not guarantee passage for me for the duration, I forfeited my right to return for the duration so I could finish the report for you. After reading your letter of July 15, however, I feel that I am under no ethical compulsion to continue any longer. Furthermore, I consider a trip to Berkeley wholly unnecessary. From an ethical stand-point, I feel I am under no obligation to do so, and from the practical point of view, I believe that my field notes are sufficiently full—perhaps too full—for an armchair social scientist to evolve fanciful theories.

I am sorry that I have so little completed on paper (since most of my work has been confined to mulling over facts in my mind) but I am certain you or X can do a much better job in a much shorter time. With best wishes for the success of the Study,

[signed] Tamie Tsuchiyama

July 21, 1944

Dear Dorothy,

Since the railway express office informs me that due to shortage of workers it will not be able to call for the box containing my field notes before the beginning of next week, I have decided to send the completed portion of my report separately. If there are any questions you would like to have answered after reading the report, I shall be glad to do so.

[signed] Tamie Tsuchiyama

July 26, 1944

Dear Dorothy,

If, after reading the completed report sent last week, you are still desirous of having me finish the Poston report I shall be willing to resume work on August 1, 1944, provided I do not have to send reports more frequently than once every two weeks. Having been accustomed for the last eight years to the working methods of the Department of Anthropology where accuracy of detail is highly stressed, I find it extremely difficult to conform overnight to the mass production techniques of some other departments.

I shall withhold sending my field notes to Berkeley until I hear from you again.

Very sincerely yours,
[signed] Tamie Tsuchiyama

July 31, 1944

Dear Dorothy,

Since I am reluctant to make any promises which I may not be able to fulfill *to your satisfaction*, I am requesting for the last time to be released from the study as of July 15, 1944, to pursue other activities which are more acceptable to me. From the very beginning we have not seen eye to eye on how the Japanese should be studied so I see no advantage to you in my continuing further.

The railway express office has promised to call for my field notes within the next three days so they should arrive in Berkeley within the next two or three weeks. If there are any questions you would like to ask me concerning them I suggest that you contact me soon since I expect to leave Chicago before the end of August.

Very sincerely yours,
[signed] Tamie Tsuchiyama

RESTORATION

Serving Her Country: Tsuchiyama in the WAC

After leaving the JERS project, Tsuchiyama's hope was to be assigned to G2, or Army Intelligence. According to her sister, Tsuchiyama was on her way to Officer Training School with the ultimate hope of being assigned to work in Polynesia when orders came down that all personnel of Japanese descent were, in fact, going to be assigned to Fort Snelling, Minnesota.

Military records indicate that in Chicago on November 9, 1944, Tamie Tsuchiyama officially enlisted in the United States Army. (Incidentally, as of 1943, the army was the only branch of the armed forces that accepted persons of Japanese descent who were willing to enlist.) Thirteen days later she entered into active service as a private in the Women's Army Corps (WAC; a member of this corps was referred to as a "Wac"). Tsuchiyama reported for duty and began six weeks of basic training. Upon completion, she was promoted to Tech 5 on September 24, 1945.

In mid-January 1945, along with her WAC compatriots of Japanese descent, Tsuchiyama was assigned to the Military Intelligence Service at Fort Snelling, Minnesota. The assignment was designed to generate a group of women proficient enough in Japanese to be able to translate documents accurately from Japanese to English. Like her colleagues, Tsuchiyama took classes and studied intensively during this period in order to raise her Japanese-language proficiency to the required level.

Interestingly enough, although she was somewhat older and had advanced farther in terms of her studies, in many respects Tsuchiyama's background resembled those of her Japanese American colleagues at Fort Snelling. As we know, Tsuchiyama was educated, a Christian, and quite Americanized in terms of her orientations and life-style; so were most of the other Japanese American Wacs. Like the other Wacs, although Tsuchiyama had some exposure to the

Tamie Tsuchiyama at Fort Snelling, April 1945. (Courtesy of Hisako T. Roberts)

Japanese language, she was not fully bilingual or biliterate. Tsuchiyama also came from a family where her mother was head of the household and could be characterized as a dynamic if not strong person, a characteristic that appears in the background of a number of the Japanese American Wacs.

Her colleagues remember the course of studies at Fort Snelling as quite intensive. Ms. Miwako Yanamoto remembered that the Japanese American Wacs studied from morning through dinner. Then they returned to their rooms in order to study some more until it was time for bed. At Fort Snelling, Tsuchiyama ran into Nisei women from Hawaii, as well as her old friend Edith Kodama from Los Angeles with whom she had stayed at Santa Anita in 1942. Under this kind of pressure, however, Yanamoto remembered that there wasn't a great deal of time for Wacs to socialize even if they knew one another or to get to know one another if they didn't.

Subsequently, in mid-December 1945 Tsuchiyama was reassigned to the Pacific Military Intelligence Research Section (PACMIRS), located at Camp Ritchie, Maryland. PACMIRS had been created in August 1944 to centralize the analysis of all available Japanese-language documents in order to better conceptualize "strategic planning and action." In April 1946 Tsuchiyama was assigned to a PACMIRS unit at Fort Myer, Maryland. In a similar capacity, Tsuchiyama was also posted in Washington, D.C., at the War Documents Center. According to various army documents, including her U.S. Army Separation Qualification Record, Tsuchiyama served a total of twenty-one months as a Tech 5–level translator. The latter document lists her military occupations as "Translator: Assigned to Army Military Intelligence units in various parts of the country. Translated official Japanese documents." Tsuchiyama's service records indicate that during this period she also served as a "voice translator." For reasons I will detail below, it is likely that she continued to think about, if not actually work on, her anthropological research on Athabascan folklore during this period.

Within five months, Tsuchiyama was honorably discharged on August 25, 1946, at Fort Sheridan, Illinois. She was presented with various awards for her service, including the Good Conduct Medal, the World War Two Victory Medal, and an American Theatre Service Ribbon. A civilian again, and now thirty-one years old, Tsuchiyama decided she would go back to Berkeley, reenroll, and finish up her doctorate in anthropology. As of July 1946 her military records list her permanent address as the International House, University of California at Berkeley.

Tamie Tsuchiyama at Fort Snelling, 1945. (Courtesy of Frances F. Kawano)

Between 1946 and 1947, in less than one academic year, Tsuchiyama was able to complete her Ph.D. work in the field of sociocultural anthropology at the University of California at Berkeley. Tsuchiyama became the first Japanese American *and* the first Asian American of either gender to have ever done so. That she had almost finished her doctorate by the end of 1941 helps to explain why her two-hundred-page Ph.D. dissertation, which was filed in June 1947, was entitled "A Comparison of the Folklore of the Northern, Southern and

Pacific Athabaskans: A Study in the Stability of Folklore within a Linguistic Stock," and obviously had nothing at all to do with her research on Japanese Americans in the WRA camps during the 1940s. Tsuchiyama's Berkeley transcripts indicate that she was awarded her Ph.D. degree on June 19, 1947. As she finished her doctorate, Tsuchiyama applied to go overseas as a researcher attached to the U.S. occupation forces in Japan. This led to the next major step in her career.

Back to the Field

In December 1947 Tsuchiyama was employed under the broad auspices of the General Headquarters, the Supreme Commander for the Allied Powers (SCAP), and spent some three years in occupied Japan on this basis. Hired as a social science research analyst (at the grade of G5-11, 5-2), she was assigned to the Public Opinion and Sociological Research Division of the Civil Information and Education Section. She met up with acquaintances from Poston such as anthropologist Iwao Ishino, the only other Nisei in the unit as of 1949. She was also able to reestablish contact with her old friend Edith Kodama, and, although Edith worked elsewhere, the two became very close friends while stationed in Japan.

In 1948 Tsuchiyama joined a research project initiated by the Natural Resources Section of the SCAP. This section was engaged in implementing agrarian legislation and land reform in occupied Japan. As part of its efforts, the Natural Resources Section had invited Dr. Arthur F. Raper of the Bureau of Agricultural Economics, the U.S. Department of Agriculture, "to make observations on the effects of land reform and other agrarian programs upon rural institutions and organizations." Raper arrived in Japan in 1947 and in May and June conducted a survey of some thirteen villages throughout Japan in order to gather data pertaining to the Natural Resource Section's interest. Land reform itself wasn't implemented until 1948, and so the idea was to gather data both before and after the implementation of reforms. In October 1948 Raper returned to Japan in order to resurvey most of the same villages, and at this point Dr. Tsuchiyama joined the project as a member of Raper's survey party. Tsuchiyama's own description of the project is that it involved "approximately 50" Japanese researchers and translators. Their task involved "making intensive sociological studies of rural communities throughout Japan, to determine the effect of Occupation politics on the political economy and social structure of these communities. Duties consisted primarily of planning research programs, directing research of Japanese scholars in the field, and writing reports for publication." When Raper returned to the States the following January, the field team continued to collect additional data and began to write up their research.

In May 1949 Raper returned and along with Tsuchiyama, Herbert Passin, and David L. Sills began to write up the final report. According to the preface of the resulting book, "Drs. Raper and Tsuchiyama undertook the major responsibility for the preparation of the preliminary version of the manuscript. Dr. Raper prepared those chapters dealing with agricultural problems and over-all changes, and Dr. Tsuchiyama wrote those chapters concerning the social and community aspects of village life. Messrs Passin and Sills rewrote portions of these chapters and added materials." Published in 1950, the resultant survey, *The Japanese Village in Transition*, is a comprehensive yet very readable survey, containing text and photographs illustrating the continuities and changes that Japanese families and communities in rural settings were experiencing after World War II.

Apparently, in tandem with *The Japanese Village in Transition* survey, Tsuchiyama was conducting her own fieldwork project and trying to assess the impact of legal reforms in regard to a set of Japanese fishing villages along the inland sea. Unfortunately, I have been unable to find any evidence that this study was ever completed or published.

In retrospect, memories even of one's colleagues grow dim after almost fifty years. One of her peers in this team project remembered her as being "competent," "quiet," "shy," "withdrawn," as well as "small." Two members of the team remembered her as having her own set of Japanese friends; rather than socializing with the team and attending their dinner parties, Tsuchiyama preferred to go off on her own. Nonetheless, one is struck by three points. Even after her disastrous experiences with Dorothy Thomas's JERS project, Tsuchiyama joined up with yet another interdisciplinary team research project in which her duties involved fieldwork and ethnography. Second, once again, basic data and text produced by one team member would be taken, edited, and reworked by other team members. Third, Tsuchiyama's individual contributions ended up being buried in anonymity, although this may have had to do with the military sponsorship and hierarchy that characterized the setup of the Natural Resources Section.

The Oriental Library

Following her return to the United States in late 1951, Dr. Tsuchiyama tried to obtain new employment. As far as I can determine, she sought an academic position in the field of anthropology as well as a possible position overseas with the Voice of America program. Biding her time as she investigated different possibilities, Tsuchiyama took on a temporary position in the library at the University of California at Berkeley. Her superior was so pleased with her performance that Tsuchiyama was offered a high-level position on a permanent basis even though she had no formal training as a librarian. According to her sister, Hisako, Tsuchiyama's friends and colleagues advised her to wait a bit longer to see if an anthropology position would come up and thus encouraged her to turn the library opportunity down. A month later, when no offers were forthcoming and other job applications did not come through, Tsuchiyama decided to accept the library's proposal. When she returned, though, Tsuchiyama was told that she was "ungrateful" for not having accepted to begin with and that the position was no longer available.

Since no anthropology positions opened up for her, Tsuchiyama decided to apply for work again as a librarian; because there were positions in this field and because this was where she had received her first tangible job offer, it seemed like a more viable occupational field than anthropology. Tsuchiyama then reentered the University of California at Berkeley in September 1953. During the 1953–54 academic year she took four courses a semester in librarianship. According to her transcripts, on June 17, 1954, she earned yet another degree, this time a bachelor of library science. Unfortunately, the job offers she received after she completed her degree were all at lower pay and status than her initial offer from the University of California.

Over the next five years, Tsuchiyama worked as a librarian on three different campuses. She first obtained employment as a librarian at Fresno State College in Fresno, California, but apparently didn't care for it very much there. From Fresno Tsuchiyama went to Washington State College at Pullman, Washington. Her sister, Hisako, reports that Tsuchiyama felt favorable about the campus, the faculty, and the people there and that this was a very pleasant experience for her. Tsuchiyama felt, however, that this position lacked the status that her education merited, so she decided to move again, this time to Stanford University in Palo Alto, California. Ultimately, although this was a better position, Tsuchiyama wasn't very happy at Stanford and reported to her sister that the general climate was less than friendly.

According to Hisako, Dr. Tsuchiyama then joined her in Texas around 1956. There, Dr. Tsuchiyama started the Oriental Library at the University of Texas at Austin. Tsuchiyama was initially hired to catalog some ten thousand volumes that the university had purchased from the University of Minnesota, sight unseen. After sorting, cataloging, and shelving these books, Tsuchiyama's expertise resulted in her eventually being hired as the first director of the collection.

Hisako reported that this was another period in her life when Tsuchiyama was basically very happy. She felt great satisfaction in helping to organize and then work as a librarian for the collection, as her education and training were put to use for the benefit of others. At some point, however, and certainly by the 1950s, Tsuchiyama discovered that her early childhood illness had damaged her body quite seriously. A medical examination had revealed that her kidneys were operating at less than half their normal capacity. As in her early years, Tsuchiyama again seemed to be living on borrowed time.

The Final Years

In the mid-1970s, Tsuchiyama retired and lived in a small town outside of Austin, Texas. As she aged, she became increasingly blind. She refused to use a white cane and for the last years of her life continued to walk down to the local grocery store, about two blocks from her house. Her sister, Hisako, remembered:

> The store [personnel] liked and admired her. The manager or an assigned helper would lead her among the shelves and select the items that she desired. They also suggested what vegetables or fruit were in prime condition. She was touched that on her birthday, May 8, the store had presented her with some luscious strawberries. Small touches of genuine appreciation meant so much to her. Poor Tamie who all her life, except possibly in Japan, had not received any recognition or appreciation for the work she had done.

Still in Texas, at the age of sixty-nine Dr. Tamie Tsuchiyama passed away in her sleep on May 12, 1984.

If she were still alive, one wonders what her response would be to the tremendous interest (and controversy) that the JERS materials—the journals, reports, and letters alike—are generating among professors, researchers, and students today. Perhaps the JERS project's long-deserved recognition and the recognition accorded to JERS staff researchers like Tamie Tsuchiyama and Richard S. Nishimoto—along with the intervening years and Dr. Tsuchiyama's other accomplishments—would have served as a measure of compensation for the sacrifice and suffering that her stay as well as her ethnographic fieldwork at Poston clearly entailed.

9

REDUX

Interpretations

The interpretation I have in mind of JERS director Dorothy Thomas, of Tsuchi-yama's work for her during the 1940s, and of the implications of this dimension of the JERS project for the ethics and politics of ethnographic fieldwork is necessarily partial; that is, it revolves around Tsuchiyama's story. I acknowledge that full accounts of Dorothy Thomas's relationships with other JERS field-workers have yet to be written and that these may reveal other dimensions of Thomas's character, motives, and role as project director.

To begin with, I have shown that Tamie Tsuchiyama's experiences with JERS generally support Roger Sanjek's finding that a division of labor separates the general tasks of fieldwork from those of writing formal ethnography—at least historically in situations in which Europeans or Euro-Americans have utilized field assistants who were people of color. Moreover, Sanjek is right in stipulating that such a division of labor becomes colonial in nature when and if those who gathered field data are not credited fully if they are credited at all. The colonial dimension is exacerbated when those who are in a position to develop and publish ethnographies are the European or Euro-American scholars, not the field assistants of color.

To develop these points further, I draw from the work of Pierre Bourdieu. Bourdieu's discussion of "colonial science" incorporates a method that can be used to explore the often hidden histories of social science and ethnography in colonial situations. This, in turn, helps us to understand more fully the biases and limitations of research produced under such circumstances.

Colonial Science

In an address given in Paris in 1975, French anthropologist-turned-sociologist Pierre Bourdieu indicated that in order to understand a discipline, it is of critical importance to command that discipline's past: "Knowing what one is doing when one does science—that's a simple definition of epistemology—presupposes knowing how the problems, tools, methods, and concepts that one uses have been historically formed."

Interestingly enough, although his comments are fully relevant to "normal science," Bourdieu was addressing the role of sociology as a "colonial science" in terms of the maintenance of empire during the period of French rule in Algeria. Bourdieu proposed, then, that a critical sociocultural analysis of colonial science is imperative if we aspire to utilize in any form or fashion the data generated by such science.

As an integral step, one must examine the research process in terms of a semiautonomous scientific field that has its own rules and dynamics regulating the relationships within that field. (Bourdieu's concept is not to be confused with the idea of "field," the physical site of research, as in the term "fieldwork.") In Bourdieu's terms, a field is "a structured space of social forces and struggles" or "a set of objective, historical relations anchored in certain forms of power/capital." Note here that "capital" is not money alone but, rather, a matter of resources that provide power to a specific group or segment of society to facilitate its interests, including "reproduction," broadly speaking. In Bourdieu's corpus, "capital" comes in a range of "species," including economic, social, cultural, and symbolic (or political) capital.

According to Bourdieu, the scientific field is integral to how research is structured and implemented. He suggests that "whatever object the sociologist or the historian chooses, this object, his way of constructing the object, raises the question not of the historian or the sociologist as an individual subject, but of the objective relationship between the pertinent social characteristics of the sociologist and the social characteristics of the object." Beyond this, while noting that "the colonizers, in a sense—dominated by their domination—[are] the first victims of their own intellectual instruments," Bourdieu warns that "those instruments can still 'trap' those who merely 'react' against them without understanding [them]." Specifically, Bourdieu emphasizes that any research project is necessarily based on systems of classification, as well as on *doxa*, or tacit belief; together these preconstructed representations determine what is relevant, what is irrelevant, and even what is not worth mentioning. Analysis of conceptual schema, however, is "not a question of setting oneself up as a judge ["one wants to do something more than distribute praise or blame"], but of understanding [these systems of classification . . . as well as why researchers] could not understand certain things, could not raise certain problems, of determining what are the social conditions of error—necessary error, inasmuch as it is the product of historical conditions [and] determinations." In addition, Bourdieu notes that "at every moment, there is a hierarchy of the objects of research and a hierarchy of . . . the subjects [in this case, researchers] which makes a decisive contribution to the distribution of the objects among the subjects. . . . [In this sense] nothing is less socially neutral than the relationship between the subject and the object."

My interpretation of this framework is that, for any given project such as JERS, we need to elucidate the hierarchy of researchers based on the kinds of resources or capital they can deploy within the scientific field and correlate this hierarchy with the conceptualization of a given research project and its foci, including the way that relationships of status and power determine who studies what, when, where, how, and why.

Finally, Bourdieu encourages us to seek the "social conditions," as well as the "social relations," undergirding the production of social science data because these are precisely what become erased in colonial science. In an especially insightful passage, Bourdieu offers this trenchant commentary: "*[T]he unconscious of a discipline is its history; [further,] its unconscious is made up of its social conditions of production, masked and forgotten.* The product [i.e., data], separated from its social conditions of production, changes its meaning and exerts an ideological effect" (my emphasis). This characterization of colonial science has *very* rich implications for the reanalysis of the three research projects orchestrated by JERS, the BSR, and the WRA on Japanese Americans that I mentioned previously. Using Bourdieu's discussion of colonial science as a conceptual framework, I will apply the elements of this approach to JERS—specifically to the research that Tsuchiyama carried out in Poston for Dorothy S. Thomas.

The Politics of Fieldwork in an American Concentration Camp

TAMIE TSUCHIYAMA

Thomas appears to have selected Tamie Tsuchiyama because of her status as an advanced graduate student who Thomas felt would fit into the camp milieu and (on the basis of a trial period in the Santa Anita assembly center) be able to do fieldwork and collect the necessary data under such circumstances. Because Tsuchiyama was also a Japanese American, albeit from Hawaii, Thomas must have also seen Tsuchiyama as a terrific potential resource, since Thomas believed that Tsuchiyama would have the ability to interpret data from the standpoint of a denizen of Poston. However, this did not turn out to be the case.

Tamie Tsuchiyama, then, was one of the most extensively educated, in terms of professional criteria, members of the Japanese American staff who was willing to carry out participant observation in the field. However, Tsuchiyama had little or no prior fieldwork experience. With only a limited knowledge of the mainland Japanese American community, Tsuchiyama—who was a relatively young graduate student and a Nisei woman to boot—decided to focus on the political dynamics of Poston, a domain overtly characterized by power struggles between men. Handicapped because she had to work on a semiclandestine basis, Tsuchiyama simply did not have the personality or the kinds of interpersonal skills needed to get the inside story, at least in terms of her interest in politics.

Passionately committed to the discipline of anthropology and having ignored her sister's advice not to pursue a doctoral degree, Tsuchiyama was willing (at least in the beginning) to endure all kinds of deprivations in order to do firsthand fieldwork and prove she was a competent professional. In the bulk of this book, I have drawn on a biographical reconstruction and her correspondence to illustrate specific aspects of Tsuchiyama's experience as an ethnographic fieldworker, including (1) the day-to-day physical challenges Tsuchiyama endured in order to live and to carry out fieldwork in Poston; (2) the emotional challenges of doing semiclandestine fieldwork in a climate that was oppressive and even, on occasion, dangerous; (3) Tsuchiyama's ambivalent reactions to Japanese Americans in Poston—for example, her feelings of both sympathy and contempt; (4) the tension between Tsuchiyama's desire to carry out her own ethnographic research independently as opposed to the team-oriented setup of fieldwork in Poston; (5) the constant and unremitting pressure from Dorothy Thomas to produce both raw data and thematic field reports congruent with the study's missions; and (6) Tsuchiyama's recruitment of Richard S. Nishimoto in response to Dorothy Thomas's demands.

Initially, Tsuchiyama recruited Richard Nishimoto to help her gather more data. In fact, Nishimoto had many skills and attributes that made him an ideal assistant. Tsuchiyama, in turn, introduced Nishimoto to Thomas. Thomas came, in time, to rely heavily on Nishimoto's counsel while he was still in Poston, as well as after his release. Given Nishimoto's growing importance to Thomas, Tsuchiyama, who was under a great deal of physical and psychological pressure, must have felt that she was gradually being superseded. She even began to criticize the validity of Nishimoto's work in her letters to Thomas, at the same time that she began to openly indicate her increasing dissatisfaction with JERS. By 1944, Tsuchiyama's letters show that she had become totally alienated. Whether as a partial result of these growing tensions or not, when Tsuchiyama left Poston and went to Chicago to write, she was unable to produce the fieldnotes and reports that she had promised to Dorothy Thomas.

That Tsuchiyama often felt she was a failure as a fieldworker makes her letters especially poignant. I never found any indication that Tsuchiyama was told that this is a very common feeling among neophyte and even experienced fieldworkers. Concomitantly, by the end of Tsuchiyama's tenure with the JERS project, Thomas's correspondence indicates that Thomas also thought of Tsuchiyama as a failure—someone whose utility, in an instrumental sense, had evaporated. Exhibiting little of the friendship or personal concern she may once have actually felt, by 1944 Thomas's only goal seems to have been to get access to whatever empirical data Tsuchiyama had already gathered and written up but had not yet turned in.

DOROTHY S. THOMAS

As JERS director, we have seen that Thomas held much of the capital at play within the scientific field that encompassed JERS. As the chief academician of JERS, she conceptualized and designed the research project. She also not only controlled all the economic resources, but she handpicked recruits and had the power (as she once baldly put it to Tsuchiyama) to shape the educational and career trajectories of the students who worked for her, depending on the caliber of their performance.

As a scholar, Thomas was interested in accounting for the mixed responses of Japanese Americans to WRA policies and procedures. As her initial memo to fieldworkers indicates, Thomas was keenly interested in "raw" data in order to assess this topic. Thomas did no fieldwork herself, but via her husband, the eminent sociologist W. I. Thomas, she was aware that accounts of action must be contextualized in terms of the actor's "definition of the situation." Thus Thomas, as we have seen, continually pressured her fieldworkers for more and more field data, as well as for topical field reports. (This interpretation would certainly help to account for the ambivalence that is visible in Thomas's letters to Tsuchiyama. Her tone shifts: Thomas was friendly and solicitous when she wanted to solidify Tsuchiyama's role as a collaborator; her letters become more authoritarian and, finally, threatening when she felt that Tsuchiyama was not producing the quantity and quality of data that Thomas believed her to be "clearly capable of.")

Thomas's experiences as a researcher stand in marked contrast to Tsuchiyama's. They entailed (1) complete freedom, the ordinary amenities, and the relative safety and security of home, neighborhood, and campus; (2) the security of being a "white," tenured full professor who, although having experienced disadvantages as a woman, was highly successful in her own right by the 1940s; (3) the emotional luxury of not being of Japanese ancestry, not having to live in a WRA camp, and not having to get her hands dirty by handling difficult legal, policy, or applied dilemmas; (4) not having to do firsthand fieldwork; and (5) having many varied burdens while trying to coordinate a complex, multisite, team research enterprise (including keeping sometimes recalcitrant employees, like Tsuchiyama, in line).

Despite a potentially symbiotic relationship between director and staff, the actual division of labor in JERS was exploitative and then hidden from public view. One of the main published accounts of how the JERS project was carried out—the preface to *The Spoilage*, pp. v–xx—delineates the multidisciplinary basis of the study and the method of deploying multiple fieldworkers but avoids commentary regarding the primary role of Dorothy Thomas in analyzing, synthesizing, writing, and publishing the data. This, in turn, can be seen as a rhetorical device utilized to heighten the readers' confidence in the data's validity and reliability, even as it disguised the very real risks and costs that were borne by those who actually collected the material upon which JERS publications like *The Spoilage* were based. To account for this, we need only remember that Thomas saw herself as a scientist, deserving of the recognition and status that went along with being a senior university professor. This desire—for recognition as a scientist and in terms of doing everything to consolidate and advance that status—seems to have energized her self-image and her strategies, at least in terms of the period and the project under consideration here.

In terms of these same criteria, field data, based on notes derived from participant observation, were used to generate the lowest level in the JERS hierarchy of scientific objects. For example, in terms of Tsuchiyama's "Visit of the Spanish Consul" report, the objects constructed for study included, among other things, the field of Unit I politics, the factions as well as the individual leaders who struggled to shape political strategies, and perhaps even former engineer Richard S. Nishimoto's methods of "influence brokering" in order to sway public opinion. In any case, the menial task of collecting such materials was relegated to the lowest level of the hierarchy of researchers—a few Euro-American graduate students, but also, even lower still in terms of overall prestige, the Japanese American staff, including graduate students, college undergraduates, and their assistants.

Much of the JERS data, then, were generated by "natives," on site, for the ultimate use of a Euro-American scholar who was not, herself, physically present. This person, Dorothy Thomas, paid minimal wages, expropriated the data, and took control of the final analysis as well as the production of formal studies (as products) and their publication. In the end, Thomas simply forced the raw data that JERS fieldworkers had gathered back into a conceptual framework with which she was familiar. I have argued that Thomas's "scientific objects" had to do with the reification of demographic characteristics that were then projected as significant attributes upon the Japanese American population in the WRA camps. Thomas thus utilized variables such as generation, religion, community of origin (urban versus rural), and so on in order to explain which sectors of the camp population did what, politically speaking, in response to WRA and federal policies. As far as I can determine, no actual use was ever made of Tsuchiyama's field report on the Spanish consul, whether at a conceptual, substantive, or theoretical level. It is interesting to conjecture whether senior scholars' practices along these lines engender a dramatic narrowing of perspectives, potentially very deleterious to social sciences that revolve around a deep commitment to a comparative understanding of societies, cultures, and worldviews.

Once stated as such, it appears that all this was tied to both Thomas's training as well as to her perceptions of what the production of knowledge was all about vis-à-vis the scientific field. This, after all, was the kind of detached, objective research that would be rewarded by her colleagues in the academy.

Implications

In sum, the social conditions of production pertaining to the Poston phase of JERS fieldwork had many features that parallel a colonial arrangement. And for whatever conscious or unconscious reasons, the pertinent details that might have suggested this conclusion were conveniently omitted from the official JERS publications. This point seems especially critical given the totally self-serving way that Thomas characterized JERS methodology in research articles, four years and then eight years, respectively, after she had used and discarded both Tsuchiyama and Nishimoto.

That Thomas was able to get away with this and win the 1952 presidency of the American Sociological Association has much to do with the fact that many key members of the disciplines of sociology and anthropology were interested in applied issues that harnessed their academic skills in the service of their country. In other words, especially in light of the setup and activities of the BSR and the WRA's "community analysis" section, there was hardly an institutional space in the domestic (or even international) scientific communities that would allow, let alone promote, critique of Thomas's research practices. But at the same time that we scrutinize Thomas and her contemporaries, we can't and shouldn't let the Japanese Americans who did fieldwork for JERS off the hook.

Perhaps the general point here is that, in a colonial research setup (where a native comprador group works in complicity with an imperial power and facilitates the extraction of resources on behalf of that power), the overall relationship must necessarily have two sides. Dorothy Thomas did not, after all, *force* Tsuchiyama to play the role of principal fieldworker for JERS in Poston. Tsuchiyama chose that role voluntarily, although we have now seen that this choice was a complex one that took on different forms, the penultimate of which was Tsuchiyama's resignation under protest.

In this sense, Tsuchiyama's role, and that of many of the Japanese Americans who carried out ethnographic fieldwork for JERS, can be reexamined in terms of another set of desires that were generated by the colonial setup of the JERS project. For example, one kind of escape hatch to which young Nisei academic types had recourse was, like Thomas, to envision themselves as scientists who were in a position to exercise their training and their status as students to study the impact of mass incarceration. It is not very hard to see other desires at play here, whether in terms of the short-term psychological relief that "scientific objectification" of fellow prisoners might have afforded or in terms of the hope for future academic opportunities. (It may be taken as a partial index of her level of awareness that, in her published accounts, Thomas offered no commentary or reflections on her Nisei fieldworkers' motivations to work for JERS.)

In any case, we know now in retrospect that Tsuchiyama and Nishimoto collected an enormous amount of primary data that spanned almost the whole institutional life of Poston, from 1942 to 1945. What strikes me in the final analysis is that because of its colonial matrix, one of the most exciting JERS projects, and one that would certainly have complemented the three books that did come out of JERS, was never completed. This would have been Tsuchiyama's and Nishimoto's full-scale ethnography of the political dynamics of Poston, which could—if Dorothy Thomas had supported their original plan, as well as her two Poston fieldworkers, more assiduously—have been put together by a talented pair of bilingual ethnographers with extensive ties to two generations of Japanese Americans, Issei and Nisei, in the United States.

Tsuchiyama's outline for a book about life and politics in Poston and her and Nishimoto's data are still available (as are the data from the two other research projects operating in Poston, which was the most thoroughly studied of the ten WRA camps by 1945). Such a book remains to be written. So although some have objected to the clandestine fashion in which JERS personnel did their research (and I agree, by the way, that this is not a desirable or acceptable methodology in terms of today's ethical standards), I propose that if we contextualize and historicize JERS and other related materials, there are still invaluable data and interpretations we can wring from the archives. First, however, as I hope to have demonstrated here, we need to determine who collected the data and how, as well as how we can best mine these data today in a critical and reflexive fashion.

Redux

Let me re-emphasize my belief that Tsuchiyama's story has lessons that are relevant for social scientists and others today. One is that the manifestations of colonial science have differential outcomes with regard to gender: of the serious JERS fieldworkers without Ph.D. degrees (they can be identified by their lengthy correspondence files in the JERS collection), the Euro-American men and the Nisei men who were interested in pursuing graduate training and academic careers in the social sciences seem to have been able to realize their aspirations.

Another lesson is that, given the prevalence of sexism in the academy, women of color who are put in the situation of having to gather data on "their own people" for a senior scholar are structurally the least able to speak up, let alone to confront and accuse their superiors if and when something goes wrong. I sense that Tsuchiyama may have decided it was easier to move on to other things rather than try to battle Dorothy Thomas publicly, given the resources that Thomas had at her command: professional status, in combination with a superior class position and racial privilege.

In point of fact, even with the critical and legal advances brought on by the women's movement, cases involving the appropriation of women's scholarship have occurred often enough in the academy up through the 1990s. Even today, if discussed at all, the resulting hurt, despair, and anger are typically confined to informal conversations between friends and peers. Junior scholars are justifiably worried that even a hint of complaint might cause a senior scholar to thwart or to even destroy their careers before they really begin (which may help to explain why I have been unable to find any documented cases of exploitation exactly along these lines even though I have heard about a number of such cases informally over the years).

My recommendations are largely a matter of common sense. First, I submit that senior scholars should eschew asking a junior scholar under their supervision to carry out field research on the latter's own community for the former's benefit. If they find that they must, senior scholars should ask no more of junior scholars than they are prepared to do themselves. In any case, junior scholars should not be required to carry out research in settings that are controversial or dangerous. Too much is at stake, and too much can go wrong. If junior scholars are asked to gather such data, senior scholars should protect them fully and reward them well for services rendered, including giving them the opportunity to publish either jointly or individually authored works.

Similarly, for their own part, junior scholars, whether graduate students or assistant professors, should avoid agreeing to collect data on their own communities for a senior scholar unless their own research interests and professional needs are directly served in the process. Even if the overall context is positive, junior scholars should realize that they may get caught between the proverbial rock and a hard place if aspects of data collection, analysis, and publication are not to community members' liking. Junior scholars should also protect themselves by asking for appropriate remuneration for their labor, including the right to publish accounts based on the data they have helped to gather.

In short, if we are able to examine the Tsuchiyama-Thomas case in retrospect and can develop a clearer understanding of the kinds of political and ethical principals that should govern the professional relationships between junior and senior scholars, then perhaps the ultimately tragic story of their JERS collaboration can serve a beneficial purpose after all.

APPENDIX

The Visit of the Spanish Consul

Dec. 12, 1942

The Spanish Consul, Señor Francisco de Amat, accompanied by a representative of the State Department, arrived in Poston about 10:00 A.M. Evans, the assistant project director, notified the Central Executive Committee which was in session at the time of his arrival and requested that it contact at least four or five Issei to interview him. The Committee thereupon invited the Issei members of the Labor Relations Board (Kadowaki, Mitani, Matsumoto and Nakachi) and the chairman (Kato) and vice-chairman (Mizushima) of the Issei Advisory Board to sit in with that body (Nagai; Okamoto; Nakamura; and Niiseki) to draw up a few proposals for the Spanish consul to transmit to the two governments. The first proposal introduced by Nagai, former chairman of the Issei Advisory Board and at present the most prominent member of the Central Executive Committee, requested the Japanese government to send two hundred million dollars to the Issei immediately after the war to be utilized for rehabilitation. He argued that all of them had lost practically everything with evacuation and since the WRA ruled that all relocation centers must be vacated within fourteen days after the cessation of hostilities that sum was vitally necessary in reestablishing themselves. His proposal is said to have been received with great enthusiasm at that time but it is interesting to note that a few days later when those who had sat in the conference were approached individually concerning it they invariably expressed the sentiment that they were opposed to it but were drowned out by the others.

The following proposals to the United States government were also framed at that time:

1. Storage of a three-month food supply in Poston. (The reason given for this was that rainstorms at certain seasons might prevent the needed food supply from reaching the camp.)
2. Improvement of living quarters: a) the restriction of one family to each apartment, b) The installation of toilet facilities in each barrack, and c) The installation of heating facilities in each apartment.
3. Payment of wages on time. Payment should be made within two weeks after the end of the month.

4. The immediate erection of school buildings. (The WRA had promised at one time that school buildings would be constructed as soon as the school term began but this promise like all "Poston promises" had not been fulfilled. If they depended on adobe bricks the rate of production was such that they would not be completed for another two or three years. Furthermore adobe bricks were unsafe for immediate occupancy— a certain length of time must be set aside for the setting of the bricks.)

5. Improvement of the hospital: a) The installation of more optical and dental equipment, b) An increase in the medical staff—the present number was inadequate for so large a population.

6. The installation of [a] telephone in the block managers' offices. It is reported by those "in the know" that Nagai was most instrumental in the formation of the above proposals, strongly supported by his stooge, Rev. Mitani.

As far as the majority of camp residents were concerned, the arrival of the Spanish consul on Saturday made little impression. Reports here and there claimed that the Spanish consul was in camp and was interviewing relatives of internees. The news of the proposals "drawn up by ten prominent men" did not become public property until the agitation against the first proposal initiated in block G spread to adjoining blocks on Tuesday and Wednesday. Even then some blocks remained unaware of the agitation and were informed of it only when their Issei representative heard about it for the first time in the Issei Advisory Board meeting Thursday afternoon and reported that fact to the residents that evening.

On Saturday evening Mizushima, the vice-chairman of the Issei Advisory Board and a participant in the conference, gave a report on the proposals to his block (G) at dinnertime. There was much hand-clapping after his speech. X sitting at one of the tables was greatly perturbed about the first proposal but decided the time was unripe for public comment so merely remarked to the person sitting next to him: "That's the silliest proposal I've heard of." That night he analyzed it from all angles and wondered how much influence he wielded in camp. At the same time he feared adverse publicity for the Nisei if the newspapers obtained the information.

Sunday, Dec. 13, 1942

At breakfast X sought out Mizushima and warned him that the opposition to the first proposal would in all probability come soon from the *kyoko-ha* (radicals or "the militant faction") in camp. He replied: "Well, I expected that. I opposed the plan strenuously during the conference but was overwhelmed by the others."

While they were still conversing No. 14, a *yūshi* of the block, strolled along and attacked the proposal from the economic standpoint. A little later Mizushima instructed Nomura, the Nisei councilman, to get hold of a member of the Central Executive Committee to address the block residents since a strong opposition to the first proposal was in evidence.

No. 18 of block N [see the key at the end of this report] was finally persuaded to talk to block G at lunchtime. As he got up on a bench to speak he received a big hand from the audience. He passed over the controversial proposal rather lightly and emphasized in great detail the other six proposals transmitted to the United States government. He mentioned at that time that the Spanish consul had informed them that he had been negotiating with the army for a permit to visit relocation centers since June and this was the first time he had been able to procure one. He had also voiced the hope that there would be cooperation between the evacuees and the administration since another rupture would prevent him from reentering camp to work for their behalf. As soon as he ceased speaking No. 14 stood up and began attacking the first proposal basing his arguments on the pre-war gold reserve situation in Japan. He claimed that sometime before the war he had met the zaimukan (a sort of Fiscal Officer) attached to the New York consulate and had been told that it would be an ideal situation if the Japanese government could store a five million dollar gold reserve in the United States. If that meagre amount could not be shipped here at that time was it not preposterous to expect the Japanese government to send two hundred million dollars after the war? Should Japan lose the war would it not be asking indemnity from their own government? Etc. etc. No. 18's retort at this point was that they were not asking the Japanese government to send this amount—in actuality it was asking the United States government to pay them that sum as an indemnity for everything they had lost in the process of evacuation. He then proceeded to explain that there were approximately 45,000 Issei in the United States and figuring about $4500 for each person they had arrived at two million dollars. They had wanted to include the Nisei also but had desisted[,] fearing international complications. The sum, however, was intended to be divided with the Nisei when they actually gained possession of it. No. 14, however, remained adamant and demanded the retraction of such a preposterous proposal. At this time he also opposed the storage of a three-month food supply in Poston claiming that since people on the outside were suffering food-shortages such a request would create ill-feeling toward them. No. 18 then promised No. 14 that he would pass the criticism to the Central Executive Committee but he gave the impression to his listeners that he would do it in such a fashion that it would appear as though one individual had voiced such an opinion and not the block as a whole.

Another block resident then wished to know how many American prisoners were interned in Japan since he was convinced there was a direct correlation between the number of Americans held there and the treatment of evacuees in relocation centers. No. 18 replied that the only information available to the Spanish consul at this time was that war prisoners in Shanghai, contrary to public opinion, had been treated humanely by the Japanese. Another person then suggested that a vote be taken on the proposal. Since no one made any move X stood up and began: "I do not know the real motive of the Central Executive Committee in desiring to have such a proposal transmitted to Japan but as I see it there are two apparent motives: If they wished to report to the Japanese government the conditions of evacuation and the sufferings resulting from it that is an unnecessary step. The details were known to Ambassador Nomura who relayed them to the Japanese government. According to reports some of these facts were broadcast in Japan and created a tremendous furor among the Japanese people. They know how we have suffered. Another point I would like to emphasize is this: If they actually wanted money from Japan I will say that no true Japanese will ask for such at a time like this. Needless to say, our brothers are falling in the battlefields. Fathers and mothers in Japan are sending forth their sons for the sake of [the] survival of Japan. They are sacrificing every comfort toward such an end. Their motto is: To forget oneself and serve the country. How could the Central Executive Committee ask for money at a time like this? How can we call ourselves true Japanese? Are we forgetting the real convictions and determination we had at the outbreak of the war? When this proposal is transmitted to the Japanese government and made known to the people what will they think of us? Will they consider us worthy of their brotherhood? Our true Japanese spirit has not decayed although we have remained in this country for twenty or thirty years. I am beseeching the wise members of the Central Executive Committee to reflect again and reconsider the Proposal." X's speech was received with great enthusiasm. No. 18 had no ready reply to such a challenge. At this point Nomura moved that the meeting be adjourned. Everyone filed out of the mess hall in great indignation. No. 18 walked out like a meek lamb although he had arrived at the meeting confident that he could push this over the residents of block G. Although no vote was taken on the proposal it is interesting to note that the people of the block invariably remarked with pride later that "we in the block decided on retraction 100 percent."

Residents of block G expected No. 18 to transmit the message to the Central Executive Committee so considered their duty done and dropped the matter from their minds.

Monday, Dec. 14, 1942

About noon, a friend of No. 18 residing in block G informed X that No. 18 had contacted Nagai that morning but could get nowhere with him. Nagai had insisted that his stand was justifiable and that he was willing to fight it out. Moreover he was confident that if he made a round of quads and explained the proposal to the people they would appreciate his convictions. In fact he had spoken in block C on Sunday night and had received a tremendous applause from the residents. Even if block G were opposed to it there were thirty-five other blocks in Camp I which supported his stand. Therefore he contended the opposition from block G could not be considered.

X decided to verify the statements made by No. 18's friend so after supper visited No. 1 in block I and explained the situation to him. No. 1 informed him that he himself had listened to Nagai's speech the evening before and had been impressed by it. He had not realized how serious the situation was. He was willing to cooperate with X but the job of swinging camp opinion was much too big for him. Since X knew No. 2 in the same block why not contact him? He therefore visited No. 2 but he was not at home so dropped in to see No. 3, the Issei advisor of that block and a personal friend of his. He promised to see Nagai next morning to persuade him into retracting the proposal before the opposition grew beyond control. With No. 3 at that time was No. 4, a *yūshi* from block Z who was greatly moved by X's argument (the others being loyalty and economic reasons): The Central Executive Committee was acting on behalf of 45,000 Issei whom it did not represent. If the Committee wished to do so it was its duty to consult other Issei in other relocation centers. What about Camps II and III here in Poston? They had not even been consulted.

X then proceeded to block L and talked to No. 5 and No. 6 who introduced him to No. 7, the Issei advisor of that block. No. 7 had recently returned from internment camp and was in complete accord with X's plan. In fact he informed X that he had wanted to oppose the proposal himself but had feared it was a sentiment of the minority. He promised to work on the adjoining blocks K and M and at the same time requested him to stir up as much opposition as possible in the remainder of camp. No. 5 and No. 6 were instructed to line up block L. No. 5 further promised to swing everyone at his place of work and instruct him to work in his respective block. (According to X this was very effective.)

Before coming home X intercepted No. 8 from block O in the northwestern corner of camp. Since he was a very influential person that section was left completely in his hands. Block P nearby was assigned to No. 6.

When he returned to block G he reported his progress to No. 14 who offered to take charge of the adjoining blocks A, B, and F.

Tuesday, Dec. 15, 1942

In the morning X encountered Mizushima in the latrine and requested his coopera-tion since a little more work seemed necessary. He replied that that was impossible because more exertion on his part would cause him to lose his "balance as a councilman." X reminded him that it was his duty as the Issei advisor to carry out the wishes of the block residents. He further warned him that if he refused to do so he would proceed to do it himself. Mizushima replied: "Go ahead." On that day X heard a number of accusations against him such as: "He doesn't deserve to be a councilman," "We should kick him out," etc.

About noon reports began to drift in (all reports were brought to X by stooges of the *yūshi*). No. 3 claimed that he had talked to Nagai but could not induce him to retract his proposal. No. 6 maintained that block P was well under control. No. 5 reported that he had intended to call a block meeting but the residents of this block informed him that it was unnecessary since they would stand 100% back of him. He also related that at his place of work one person had been in favor of the proposal but the rest ganged up on him so he was now innocuous. Furthermore, all of them had consented to stir up opposition in their respective blocks. No. 7 claimed that many in his section were strongly in favor of the proposal so requested X to agitate in other parts of camp to compensate for it.

Therefore in the evening X began working on the Salinas strongholds which he had ignored up to this time. He visited No. 9 in block Q who introduced him to No. 10, the Issei advisor. Between themselves they decided to take full responsibility of Q, S, T, and U. X personally contacted No. 11, the Issei advisor of block R who was easily convinced. He purposely skipped adjoining block 2 since its Issei representative, Nagai, was a good friend and former employee of No. 14.

He next strolled over to block I since the report from No. 3 indicated an uncertainty as to the position of the block. There he sought out No. 2 who had not been home the night before and No. 12 who both promised to take charge of the block. No. 12 then introduced X to the Issei advisor of block C and further offered to take full responsibility of block D. No. 13, the Issei advisor of block E informed X that his block was well under control. He then returned to block L and assembled 5, 6, and 7. No. 7 reported at that time that blocks K and M were so strongly in favor of the first proposal that he was unable to swing them completely to his side but had rendered them innocuous by neutralizing them. (In other words the Issei advisors had promised to cast the deciding votes when the proposal came up for a vote in the Issei Advisory Board meeting next day.) He proceeded to explain that Nagai had come to block M on December 14 and had received much ovation from the crowd. He suggested that X also talk to that block to persuade it to change its mind. X, however, felt that in view of such limited time it was unnecessary to bother with individuals especially when the block had already been neutralized. No. 7 was then selected to deliver the keynote speech at the council meeting next day to be followed by minor orations by other stooges. He was specifically commanded by X at this time not to go after Nagai's scalp. On discovering then that No. 6 was a relative of Nagai, the Issei advisor of block 2, X instructed him to "neutralize" him since he appeared to be on the other side of the fence. When he returned home to block G late that night No. 14 informed him that there had been a great deal of excitement in blocks A, B, and F, but they were safely in tow.

Wednesday, Dec. 16, 1942

No. 6 reported to X at noon that he could do nothing with Nagai of block 2 since he was so much in favor of the proposal. X therefore sent No. 14 to intercept him before the council meeting (which happened to be a joint session of the Issei Advisory Board and the City Council) but it had already commenced and he was unable to see Nagai. About 4:30 P.M. X encountered No. 7 in front of the hospital and was informed that since Kennedy, the Employment Chief, had delivered such a lengthy address at the opening session of the council the matter of the two hundred million dollars could not come up for discussion. However, they were holding an exclusive Issei Advisory Board meeting (to which Caucasians and Nisei would be barred) in Sumo Headquarters in block 27 next day to deal specifically with this problem. X highly pleased with the turn of events strolled toward Ward 7 of the hospital and requested his young friend, Tsuchiyama, to aid him in swinging her Issei advisor into line. The arguments she was to use were to be based on the adverse criticism the Nisei would receive should such a proposal become publicized. She only consented to do so since her Issei advisor was her next-door neighbor and a good friend.

Immediately after supper Mizushima accosted X and chided him: "Don't agitate so much. Block 28 was having a big fuss today claiming they were going to chase Nagai out of camp." X's answer at this point: "Alright. Shall I agitate in Camps II and III also?"

X sought out No. 12 in block I soon after and was told that blocks X, W, and Y had been wooed to their side. He had also sent someone to block C and D and had been reassured that they were well in line. He also related that at that time blocks H, I, and C were holding block meetings to discuss the proposal. X then visited No. 7, his keynote speaker, and informed him that he calculated at least twenty-four blocks had been completely swung over or neutralized by this time (of that number only three or four had to be neutralized). No. 7 cautioned that block X seemed to be only lukewarm in its opposition so he hastened to send No. 13 from block E to clinch it, in which he succeeded.

On the way home he feared that his young friend, Tsuchiyama, unversed in political intrigues, might have got into hot water and failed in her task, so primarily to reestablish her prestige in the eyes of her Issei advisor (it did not matter by this time whether block 31 opposed or favored the proposal since twenty-four blocks had already been won over) dropped in at block 31 and accosted the Issei advisor just as he was about to leave her apartment. Meanwhile for the past two hours she had been trying to convince him of the advisability of opposing the proposal but he believed that she was making a mountain out of a mole hole [sic] and that the issue was not so serious as she imagined. Furthermore, he had not even heard of such a proposal. If it were really true it was a swell idea—they would need it after the war. When she retorted that she believed it was not the appropriate time to make such a request when people of Japan were sacrificing so much for the "survival of Japan" he replied: "Oh, the matter will not go beyond the government officials. They will probably get a big laugh out of it interpreting that the Japanese in America were entertaining themselves in concentration camps by thinking up such fantastic proposals." This was the situation when X arrived at the scene. He first requested Tsuchiyama to leave the apartment (explaining after her departure to the Issei representative that he wished to tell him a few things not meant for Nisei ears) and then quietly presented the arguments he had utilized elsewhere (only in stronger terms) to change his attitude. When she returned to her room some thirty minutes later she was struck with the change in the Issei advisor. (I do not know exactly what X told him but his comments after the Issei's departure was interesting: "Well, you don't have to worry about your position in your block or in camp for that matter. I settled it for you tonight. Your Issei representative will have greater respect for you from now on." He intimated at this time that he would even have risked an open debate with Nagai in his block to convince the residents that he was wrong. He felt this step was unnecessary by Wednesday night, however, when twenty-four blocks appeared to be on his side. This confession as well as his appearance in the Issei Advisory Board meeting Thursday afternoon indicates how serious he regarded the issue since his greatest desire is to work behind the scenes.) From there X proceeded to block Q but No. 9 was already asleep. He was confident, however, that it was under control realizing his friend's influence. When he returned to block G No. 14 related that the residents were becoming pretty sore at Mizushima. X then instructed him to work a little more on his friend, Nagai of block 2.

Thursday, Dec. 17, 1942

About noon No. 14 reported to X that he had finally succeeded in neutralizing Nagai. Since many of the Issei advisors did not seem to realize the full significance of transmitting such a message to Japan he suggested that it might be a wise step for X to appear at the meeting and explain to them. In such a case Nagai had offered to propose an "emergency motion" to assure the floor for him (this was necessary since X is not an Issei advisor). X's reaction to this was that there was already sufficient opposition in camp to kill the proposal so it was an unnecessary step. Furthermore, he preferred to remain inconspicuous. But realizing that over-confidence could be as equally harmful as lack of confidence both of them finally decided to attend the council meeting that afternoon. The question then arose as to whether they should go as block representatives or as individuals. They eventually decided to take it up with the Issei in the block at a special meeting directly after lunch.

Before lunch X hopped over to block I and reported that both No. 14 and he would be present at the meeting. Block I as a result decided to send a special observer also. Then he proceeded to block L and acquainted No. 7 with the change in plans.

In the block meeting held after lunch No. 14 explained what he and X proposed to do in case of danger of defeat. A vote was taken and the Issei decided to send both men as special block representatives. At that point Mizushima interrupted: "Where are you two going anyway?" When informed he simply uttered, "Oh," and walked out of the mess hall (a political faux pas on his part). To defend him an Issei got up and explained that the reason Mizushima had not appeared at the special meeting Sunday was that he had induced him to go to the ironwood forest with him that morning. He hoped that the Issei advisor would not be blamed for his absence. He further requested that when X and No. 14 appeared at the council meeting that afternoon they remember that he was the official representative of the block and cooperate with him. Two or three dissenting voices broke out from the group at this point so X proceeded to explain that he had encountered Mizushima two days before and had asked him to work a little more since Nagai was insistent [on] having the first proposal accepted. He had replied that he could do nothing more so X had gained his permission to go ahead and contact a few influential persons. If the block objected to their going as official block observers they would just as soon go as individuals. The Issei answered that he was only working for the harmony of the block and was satisfied to have them go in an official capacity. Rev. Niisato, the blind Evangelist, offered a piece of advice at this point: When a flood had destroyed certain sections of Imperial Valley several years ago they had requested the Japanese government to send them fifty thousand dollars which was refused. Hence he figured it was useless to ask for so large a sum at this time.

At the Issei Advisory Board meeting held in Sumo Headquarters in block 27 that afternoon, Nagai of the Central Executive Committee appeared extremely uneasy from the very beginning. No. 18 of block N was conspicuously absent. About 3:30 after certain routine matters had been disposed of a young Issei advisor (X cannot recall his name) casually inquired whether there was any report concerning the Spanish consul who it was rumored had visited Poston on Saturday. Mizushima as acting chairman proceeded to enlighten him but was soon interrupted by Nagai who asked permission to do it himself. He then simply stated that the proposal requesting the Japanese government to send them two hundred million dollars was being withheld. He could not tell them his real reason for making such a request but he felt that since the people here would be destitute after the war it was the wise thing to do. Since there seemed to be much opposition to the proposal he considered it wise to withhold it. As soon as he ceased speaking the Issei advisor from block A, No. 14's spokesman, jumped up and began attacking the proposal from the standpoint of international finance: that the outflow of gold to the amount of two hundred million dollars, i.e., 860 million yen, from Japan would create an acute internal problem; that it was outrageous even to assume that such an outflow of gold was possible. (He proceeded to elaborate this point.)

No. 7 (X's chosen speaker) then presented his arguments: that when people of their own blood were falling on the battlefields it was improper to be thinking of something so mercenary as money to be sent them for rehabilitation. The national policy of Japan at present was: "Ichi-oku isshin messhi hoko (One hundred million [i.e., the entire population of Japan] with one spirit; forget oneself; serve [the country])." The transmission of such a proposal was against this principle. He then demanded retraction.

The Issei advisor from block B followed in a similar vein: "The idea of my going out to gather ironwood is not to make a collection of ironwood stumps but for the training of an iron will. An iron will means to forbear and to withstand sufferings that come our way. It is the Japanese spirit to receive all sorts of persecution with a smile. The Central Executive Committee acted without proper authority. They did not even consult the Issei Advisory Board. The proposal should be retracted immediately." (He spoke in a highly emotional tone.)

Nagai replied simply: "Well, the proposal has been retracted already." Someone inquired suspiciously: "How did you retract it?" Nagai referred the question to his stooge, Rev. Mitani: "How did you phrase the message, Mr. Mitani?" (Meanwhile those who had participated in the conference were squirming uncomfortably in their seats.) Mitani pretended to feel his pockets saying, "Maybe I have a copy here." Then not finding it he related that he had simply wired the Spanish consul to retract the first proposal. He added that he had a copy in his office and would read it to the group [on] another occasion if they so desired. The representative from block A jumped up excitedly at this point and shouted: "Retraction is not enough. Apologize to the group." Nagai sprang up from his chair speechless with surprise.

At this stage the advisor from block 3 (Nagai's block) stood up in defense of Nagai: "I wish you would interpret the whole affair in a good-natured way. Mr. Nagai was greatly concerned with the situation that might arise after the war. He was worried about the people who would be destitute after the war. He acted in the sincere belief that this would help the people. Please do not accuse the Central Executive Committee." No. 7 interrupted: "Well, if you had said in the first place that you had retracted the proposal I would not have said anything. Since you simply said that it was being withheld, the word necessitated my speech." (He laughed to break the tension—even Nagai was compelled to smile.) The representative from block F echoed: "It's okay, if it has been retracted." No. 7 continued: "I am willing to support the Central Executive Committee's policy 100% but that does not mean we have to follow it blindly. It is the duty of the Issei advisors to point out their mistakes and ask for corrections. There is a tendency on the part of the Central Executive Committee to neglect or forget our existence. From now on we won't hesitate to criticize their policies. We let it be known that we have that right."

Nagai replied in a very humble tone: "We are liable to make mistakes although our intentions are good. After all our experiences and our capabilities are limited. We intend to carry on our heavy burden with your able advice and assistance. We are always willing to cooperate with your representative body. Please do not hesitate to guide us. I beg you to lead us with your great ability."

When the meeting resumed its discussion of routine matters X sneaked out of the building and went around thanking the *yūshi* who had helped him. A little later he met the Issei advisor of block F who confessed to him: "Nagai seemed so weak I didn't want to mistreat him. When a person is down I don't want to hit him." He added that since he knew that the agitation against the proposal started in block G and had spread to A, B, F, he was intending to bring Nagai to a quad meeting that night. He would act as chairman and let the quad people attack Nagai as much as they wished and embarrass him into resigning from the Central Executive Committee. X reminded him that he was only interested in the retraction of the proposal and not the scalping of Nagai. Therefore the bringing of Nagai to the quad meeting was unnecessary.

After the meeting X knew that Mizushima wished to resign as Issei representative of block G so sought him out. He told him: "If you do such a thing we shall be in a quandary. What we have done to help you has been in vain. What I did day and night was intended to further your political career. I have no political ambitions and I promise to support you. From now on you must do your best for us." Mizushima greatly touched responded: "Alright. Instead of accusing you I should thank you. Let me thank you from deep in my heart." (Mizushima informed X the following night that he had a run-in with the C.E.C. members that day and they had inquired: "Do you want to quarrel with us?" He had answered, "Sure, if you want to. I have lots of backing." The C.E.C. knows that block G initiated the agitation against the proposal and is rumored to be afraid of it. X informed me with great amusement the other day that Mizushima told him that the C.E.C. comes up to him whenever it has something up its sleeve to sound out his reaction and to request his cooperation.)

Friday, Dec. 18, 1942

X contacted the man in charge of telegrams in the administration building and learned that the retraction wire had been sent only this morning. Hence Nagai and Mitani, as he had suspected, were lying when they claimed that the proposal had been retracted. X, however, did not divulge the secret to anyone lest the people become infuriated and molest the members of the Central Executive Committee.

That day the residents of block A were still agitated and insisted on scalping Nagai. They maintained that the milk had been spilt and that wiping of [sic] the puddle would not restore the liquid into the bottle. They therefore sent K. Matsumoto of the Labor Relations Board and Karakane, the Issei advisor of block A, to invite Nagai to speak at a quad meeting that night. Blocks G, B, and F were rather lukewarm in their support of the plan. Nagai informed Matsumoto that there was a funeral in his block that day and [he] was unable to accept the invitation. At the same time he sent the Issei representative from his block to explain the situation to the people. Meanwhile, it is rumored that Nagai contacted the Issei advisors of the quad and entreated them to quiet the agitation.

Analysis

As far as the administration was concerned the visit of the Spanish consul made only a slight impression. Here and there according to Spicer a few officials cursed the Japs for their audacity in framing the first proposal but no one knew or was sufficiently interested in discovering what happened to it after it left the conference room. As far as the Press Bulletin was concerned the news of the Spanish consul's visit was restricted to the following meagre lines in December 15th's edition:

> Spanish Consul to Report Poston Center Problems, Activities. Señor F. de
> Amat, consul of Spain representing the government, which is the "protective"

power for Japanese interests in the U.S., arrived last Saturday here to "talk with the enemy alien evacuees" on problems regarding center activities.

The consul who makes the report from all relocation centers to Spain made his rounds in Poston, observing various projects. From the standpoint of research the report is of great significance since:

1. it affords an insight into the mechanics of camp policies;

2. it gives the reasons [for] the ascendancy in power of the Issei Advisory Board over the Central Executive Committee enabling us to appreciate more fully the present struggle for existence of the Central Executive Committee (which will be discussed in detail in the report on the aftermath of the strike to be sent in a few days);

3. it explains the "rise" of Mizushima (a political figure to watch in the next two months) from his lowly position after the strike;

4. it presents an invaluable collection of prevailing Issei sentiments in camp; and

5. it illustrates to a certain extent the helplessness of the Nisei in changing Issei attitudes.

1. INSIGHT INTO CAMP POLITICS:

The report discusses for the most part the technique employed by X, one of the most influential political leaders in attaining his ends. The small number of *yūshi* (literally "public-spirited men") contacted by X to aid him in swinging public opinion from one extreme to the other indicates that there are only a very few really influential men in camp. In fact X confessed to me a few days ago in a strictly confidential conversation that only four persons (with X as coordinator) representing four different pre-evacuation geographical areas are necessary to mold public opinion in camp. Thus in any crisis No. 12 can be depended on to control the Orange county sections; No. 14, the Los Angeles groups; No. 9, the Salinas blocks, and No. 7, the Imperial Valley areas. These four *yūshi*, with the exception of No. 7 whose position as Issei advisor sometimes necessitates his intervention in petty politics, rarely if ever participate in politics aside from those bearing international complications, e.g., the November strike and the two hundred million dollar incident. The report also bears out my earlier contention that the real leaders are not represented in the Issei Advisory Board—that many of the block representatives are merely spokesmen or stooges for the *yūshi*.

An analysis of the distribution of *yūshi* mentioned above shows rather clear-cut geographical groupings (a small circle after a numeral denotes that that individual is an Issei advisor):

[nearby]	Block I—1, 2, 3°, 12
	Block E—13°
	Block L—5, 6, 7°
	Block G—14, X
[contiguous]	Block R—11°
	Block Q—9, 10°
[contiguous]	Block O—8
	Block Z—4

According to X a scattered distribution of *yūshi* is highly advantageous in preventing a coalition of leaders turning against him. Thus 7, 12, 9, and 14 are politically unknown to each other and the probability to their uniting against him is rather remote. So far X's ideas have been in perfect conformity with those of the four just mentioned so there has been no cause for friction to appear. It is interesting to note that not all of the fifteen *yūshi* cited in the report are Issei— two of them, according to X, are Kibei.

2. ASCENDANCY IN POWER OF THE ISSEI ADVISORY BOARD:

On Friday, Dec. 4, 1942, at a meeting of the City Planning Board, an unsuccessful coup d'etat was staged by a small number of Issei (the same group that is attempting at present to dethrone the Central Executive Committee) who accused the existence of the Labor Relations Board as being undemocratic since its members had been appointed by the C.E.C., and not elected by the delegates. At that time Rev. Mitani, the executive secretary of the L.R.B., maintained that its existence was based on democratic principles since the C.E.C. which had appointed them had been elected by the 78 delegates of the City Planning Board who in turn had been elected by the people in their respective blocks. As a result of the fiery accusation which lasted several hours the L.R.B. and the C.E.C. resigned but were returned to power by a vote of confidence from the Nisei and the majority of Issei delegates who feared adverse publicity from the administrative side if they gave up in three days after formation. At that time the delegates promised full cooperation and support in whatever the C.E.C. and L.R.B. decided to do.

Page 20 [p. 185, above] of my report therefore is of great significance since it indicates a complete round-about face in the attitude of the Issei delegates toward the C.E.C. No. 7's assertion that the I.A.B. would not hesitate from then on to criticize the policies of the C.E.C. and Nagai's humble acceptance of the fact demonstrate the rise in power of the I.A.B. over the C.E.C. (At present a few members of the I.A.B. led by Mizushima are attempting to dethrone the C.E.C.

in the hope of attaining the position themselves. This will become more comprehensive to you after you read my report on the aftermath of the strike.)

3. THE "RISE" OF MIZUSHIMA:

At the beginning of the November strike Mizushima's political career was at its peak but due to a faux pas he committed on the first day of the strike he was branded an "Inu" or a dog and his prestige was considerably lowered. Thus during the strike he was only chairman of the Ground Patrol, a minor committee of the Emergency Council. After the strike he was reelected Issei representative of his block merely because X, the only other likely candidate, wished to remain inconspicuous and unhampered in his political movements (attachments to the I.A.B. will considerably restrict his actions). Mizushima again incurred the resentment of his block during the two hundred million dollar incident because of his passive opposition to the first proposal and his resignation from the I.A.B. was prevented solely because X did not wish to replace him as block representative. Mizushima's present "rise" in power is based on the C.E.C.'s and the I.A.B.'s knowledge that the agitation against the first proposal began in his block and spread to adjoining areas. According to X these two bodies feel that he has strong backing in camp, especially in his block. (X is wondering at present whether it might not have been wiser for him to have "killed" Mizushima politically at that time to have avoided the current unpleasantness between the I.A.B. and the C.E.C. It appears from conversations with him that he is anxious to see Mizushima rise to the very top of the C.E.C. since in all probability Nakamura of the present C.E.C. with the aid of two or three kenjinkai (prefectural organizations) will dethrone him within two months with such a bang that he will be politically dead for the duration and the block will not have to be bothered with him.)

4. SENTIMENT OF THE PEOPLE:

I believe that the sentiments and attitudes expressed in this report are representative of a large number of Issei in camp. The extremely "subversive" utterances of X, however, are not quite indicative of his character. The time limitation compelled him to utilize the most potent and unchallengeable arguments to which as an individual he may not subscribe.

5. NISEI INFLUENCE ON ISSEI:

Pages 13 and 14 of the report [p. 182] indicate to some extent the helplessness of the Nisei in changing Issei attitudes. In this case the situation was of a more exaggerated nature than usual since as a hakase (literally a Ph.D. but frequently employed to denote a person who has had several years of post-graduate work) she is considered one of the foremost Nisei in camp whose opinions are generally respected. If such an individual could not sufficiently impress an Issei advisor, who has the highest regard for her, to change his attitude one can appreciate the apparent timidity of the Nisei council in the face of Issei opposition. [January 10, 1943]

Key

Hereafter in reports of a confidential nature the same alphabetical letters will be assigned to the blocks and the same numerals to the individuals mentioned in this report. Thus block G will always be block 45, and no. 14 will always be the same individual in block 45.

BLOCKS

A—35	N—60
B—36	O—5
C—37	P—13
D—38	Q—16
E—39	R—15
F—46	S—17
G—45	T—18
H—44	U—32
I—43	V—2
J—42	W—27
K—53	X—28
L—59	Y—26
M—54	Z—12

BIBLIOGRAPHIC ESSAY

Chapter 1. Introduction

Since I could find no published account of either her life or work, primary materials have been central to the biographical reconstruction of Tamie Tsuchiyama presented here.

Most of the familial and biographical details about Tsuchiyama's life before and after World War II were provided by her sister, Mrs. Hisako Tsuchiyama Roberts. Between 1993 and 1998, I carried out an extensive discourse with Mrs. Roberts via repeated phone interviews, correspondence, and her commentary on primary documents and on my drafts. Whenever possible, I confirmed Mrs. Roberts's accounts through checking with archival sources as well as conducting additional personal interviews with Tsuchiyama's colleagues and acquaintances from the 1940s.

Beyond this, I have drawn heavily from Tamie Tsuchiyama's correspondence with JERS director Dorothy S. Thomas, which can be found in the Japanese American Evacuation and Resettlement Records, BANC MSS 64/14c, Bancroft Library, University of California, Berkeley: JERS file J 6.32. It is my impression that a good deal of the correspondence is personal; I do not think that Tsuchiyama necessarily realized that her letters were going to be placed on the record in the JERS collection after the war. I also found, however, that some of the letters referred to appear to be missing.

Although it focuses primarily on her research and observations at Poston, Tamie Tsuchiyama's personal correspondence also contains autobiographical information and many details about professional and interpersonal relationships between the JERS staff members. Beyond juxtaposing claims made in her correspondence with the record established in the published literature, I have correlated these letters with similar correspondence exchanged between Dorothy S. Thomas and other staff members, particularly letters between Thomas and Richard S. Nishimoto (JERS files W 1.25A, and W 1.25B). The correspondence of other pertinent affiliates such as Robert Lowie (in JERS file W 1.29), who, as Tsuchiyama's main advisor in the Department of Anthropology, was in touch with both her and Thomas, provides other interesting insights about the "management" of younger scholars in a team-research situation.

The only known collection of Tsuchiyama's research data from this period is held at the Bancroft Library at the University of California at Berkeley and includes her letters, field reports, and massive "sociological journal." Other Tsuchiyama materials are contained in files pertaining to JERS staff reports (for example, JERS file W 1.10).

The only other contemporaneous source of information on Tsuchiyama is found in the unpublished fieldnotes and diaries of professional colleagues who were also engaged in research at Poston, particularly Alexander H. Leighton and Edward H. Spicer. Leighton's comments appear in his field diaries for the months of November and December 1942, Series 20, box 13, held in the Department of Manuscripts and University Archives, Cornell University Libraries, Ithaca, New York, MS 830. Spicer's comments regarding Tamie Tsuchiyama's reactions to the Poston strike of November 1942 also appear in his fieldnotes, held in "U.S. War Relocation Authority, papers of Edward H. Spicer, Head of the Community Analysis Section, WRA, 1942–1946," MS 42, box 12, December 6, 1942, pp. 1–4, Special Collections, University of Arizona Library.

Although cursory, Tsuchiyama's official military records and a copy of her 1952 job application to "Voice of America" obtained through the Freedom of Information Act provided key data about the dates and the sites of her military training and activities between 1944 and 1947.

Finally, I have followed the same basic approach to transcription as delineated in "A Note on Transcription and Terminology," which appears in Richard S. Nishimoto, *Inside an American Concentration Camp*, ed. Lane Ryo Hirabayashi (Tucson: University of Arizona Press, 1995), xix–xxiv. Tsuchiyama's letters are reproduced in their original form except that minor typing errors have been silently corrected. For the most part, I have selected from Tsuchiyama's JERS correspondence file letters that pertain directly to her fieldwork experience or that contain especially insightful observations about Poston. Because the content of her letters is varied, I have also chosen to delete portions of some letters; these deletions are indicated by ellipses. The complete correspondence file is available at the Bancroft Library; see the complete citation listed above.

THE SIGNIFICANCE OF TAMIE TSUCHIYAMA

Professor Rosemund B. Spicer related her memories of Tamie Tsuchiyama to me in a letter of May 6, 1995.

Although I could find no corroborating evidence, Mrs. Hisako Roberts said that a friend told her that her sister once gave spirited testimony in defense of Dr. J. Robert Oppenheimer (probably in 1954, at Oppenheimer's security clearance revocation hearing)—so spirited that it amazed peers who had never seen that side of Tsuchiyama's personality.

Professor Nelson H. H. Graburn, one of my mentors and former chair of the

Department of Anthropology at the University of California at Berkeley, searched the graduate files at my request. In a letter to me (undated, but circa January 1995), Graburn reported that Tamie Tsuchiyama was the first person of Asian descent to get a Ph.D. from that department, and that no other Asian American followed in her footsteps until the 1970s.

AN ETHNOGRAPHER'S EPIPHANY

This correspondence can be found in the Japanese American Evacuation and Resettlement Study Collection, Bancroft Library, University of California, Berkeley: JERS file J 6.32.

The citation for Roger Sanjek's seminal article is "Anthropology's Hidden Colonialism: Assistants and Their Ethnographers," *Anthropology Today* 9 (April 1993): 13–18. Two of Pierre Bourdieu's extended discussions of colonialism appear in his books *The Algerians* (Boston: Beacon Press; original edition in French, 1958) and *Algeria, 1960* (Cambridge: Cambridge University Press, 1979). His Algerian research clearly provided the basis for Bourdieu's subsequent formulations concerning "colonial science."

TSUCHIYAMA'S CORRESPONDENCE

I discuss a social science approach to the concept of bias in the preface to *Inside an American Concentration Camp: Japanese American Resistance in Poston, Arizona* (University of Arizona Press, 1995), xi–xv.

For other pertinent discussions of JERS analysts, see *Views from Within: The Japanese American Evacuation and Resettlement Study*, ed. Yuji Ichioka (Los Angeles: UCLA Asian American Studies Center, 1989); *Japanese American World War II Evacuation Oral History Project*, Part 3: *Analysts*, ed. Arthur A. Hansen (Munich: K. G. Saur, 1994); and Peter T. Suzuki, "The University of California Japanese Evacuation and Resettlement Study: A Prolegomenon," *Dialectical Anthropology* 10 (1986): 189–213.

I offer more discussion of the ethics and politics of social research later in the text, as well as in the notes for chapter 4.

Chapter 2. Roots

Tsuchiyama's childhood and family background were largely reconstructed on the basis of my interviews with her sister, Mrs. Hisako Tsuchiyama Roberts.

Tsuchiyama's transcripts from the University of California provide information about her high school classes, her University of Hawaii, UCLA, and Berkeley undergraduate career and honors, as well as her graduate work, her Ph.D., and her postwar studies toward a degree in library science.

Some supporting data were also drawn from Tsuchiyama's camp records. It is worth noting that WRA "intake" records (such as those contained in "Individual Records, WRA Form 26") are sometimes inexact, in part because they were based on information compiled during the tumultuous period when individuals were first incarcerated. For example, for some reason WRA records indicate that Tsuchiyama had a dual major in social sciences and mathematics. Perusal of Tsuchiyama's University of California transcripts, however, belies this point. An additional reference that is quite useful for understanding the overall impact of the educational system on young Japanese Americans in Hawaii is Eileen H. Tamura's book *Americanization, Acculturation, and Ethnic Identity: The Nisei Generation in Hawaii* (Chicago: University of Illinois Press, 1994).

STUDYING ANTHROPOLOGY

Dr. Leonard Mason, professor emeritus of the University of Hawaii, Manoa, gave me leads that allowed me to determine that the late professor Felix Maxwell Keesing was the first chairperson of the Department of Anthropology at Hawaii, Manoa, and the person who first inspired Tsuchiyama's enthusiasm for the field of anthropology. Keesing's obituary appeared in the *American Anthropologist* 64 (1962): 351–54.

Information about Professor Ralph L. Beals, who founded the Department of Anthropology at UCLA, appears in *International Dictionary of Anthropologists*, ed. Christopher Winters (New York: Garland, 1991).

Overviews of the careers of Kroeber, Radin, and Lowie, all of whom worked with Tsuchiyama at the University of California, Berkeley, can also be found in Winters's *International Dictionary of Anthropologists*.

Chapter 3. Recruitment

The temporary camp (a.k.a. "assembly center") at the then Santa Anita Racetrack has been described in a short monograph by Anthony L. Lehman, *Birthright behind Barbed Wire: The Santa Anita Assembly Center for the Japanese* (Los Angeles: Westernlore Press, 1970).

According to official records, the Kodamas were assigned the WRA family number 18254 in Santa Anita; Tamie Tsuchiyama's personal identification number was 18254-C.

For details about Tsuchiyama's hiring, see Thomas to Leighton, August 3, 1942, JERS W1.26, and two letters by Leighton to Thomas of August 7 and 26, 1942, JERS W1.21.

Tsuchiyama's two-part report on Santa Anita is held in the Bancroft Library, Japanese American Evacuation and Resettlement Study, B 8.05.

TSUCHIYAMA'S INITIAL FIELDWORK

According to the anthropologist Roger Sanjek, ethnography is a *process* of gathering data that revolves around long-term fieldwork and participant-observation in order to record a sociocultural group's "design for living." It is also a *product*, that is, a "comprehensive account" of that group's way of life. See his anthology *Fieldnotes: The Makings of Anthropology* (Ithaca: Cornell University Press, 1990), as well as his trenchant encyclopedia entry "Ethnography" in the *Encyclopedic Dictionary of Social and Cultural Anthropology*, Alan Barnard and Jonathan Spencer, general eds. (New York: Routledge, 1996). In this sense, research in anthropology is said to be structured by the traditions of the discipline. Basic concepts, methods, and even topics of interest are framed by ethnology, or cultural theory, as a whole. In addition, anthropologists rely upon long-term fieldwork in order to develop ethnography, that is, a holistic description of a group's life and design for living. Fieldwork involves studying a culture firsthand and *in situ* by means of the method of participant-observation, ideally over a period of at least a year. Fieldwork thus involves studying a particular culture in depth through a combined process of observing and participating in the daily rounds of life, interviewing, and collecting a wide range of quantitative and qualitative data. Fieldwork as a process is empirical, naturalistic if not "realistic" in orientation, and holistic in scope. Interested readers can pursue a comprehensive presentation of contemporary research design and quantitative and qualitative data-gathering techniques in H. Russell Bernard, *Research Methods in Cultural Anthropology* (Newbury Park, Calif: Sage, 1988).

Maps of the location and physical layout of the Poston camp can be found in *Inside an American Concentration Camp*, pp. xxxiv, xxxvi, 54.

Accounts of the camouflage net workers' strike can be found in Lehman's *Birthright behind Barbed Wire*; Audrie Girdner and Anne Loftis, *The Great Betrayal: The Evacuation of Japanese-Americans during World War Two* (London: Macmillan, 1969), 179–83, 191–94; and *Japanese American History: An A-to-Z Reference from 1868 to the Present*, ed. Brian Niiya (New York: Facts on File, 1993), 305.

A Parker, Arizona, resident, J. G. Fuqua, once stated for the record that he personally knew two or three Japanese Americans who were spying in the Poston camp on behalf of the FBI; see *Japanese American World War II Evacuation Oral History Project, Part 5: Guards and Townspeople*, ed. Arthur A. Hansen and Nora M. Jesch (New Providence, N.J.: K. G. Saur, 1993), 635. Edward Spicer also noted that Office of Naval Intelligence (ONI) investigations in the camps included the use of "informers"; see Spicer Papers, MS 42, box 2, folder 3, Special Collections, University of Arizona Library. I find it unfortunate that no Japanese American has been willing to come forward, even anonymously, to put a statement on the record in regard to intelligence work for the FBI or the ONI.

In terms of the *inu* phenomenon at Poston specifically and the WRA camps generally, it is important to remember that incarceration itself appears to generate certain characteristic dynamics. An instructive illustration is Gresham M. Sykes's classic study *The Society of Captives: A Study of a Maximum Security Prison* (New York: Atheneum, 1966). Sykes's discussion of the roles of "rats," "squealers," and "center men," as well as "ball-busters" and "real men" in the New Jersey State Maximum Security Prison near Trenton could easily be extended to an analysis of similar types in Poston. Moreover, certain of Sykes's findings (e.g., that even prisoners in "high security conditions" can have a considerable influence in and on "the joint" or that riots are most likely to occur if and when officials destabilize the equilibrium of the social order) have rich implications for understanding the dynamics of daily life at Poston.

LETTERS TO LOWIE, 1942

Robert H. Lowie, who was born in Vienna on June 12, 1883, was a senior scholar in the Department of Anthropology at the University of California at Berkeley and Tamie Tsuchiyama's principal graduate advisor.

In her letter of July 8, 1942, Tsuchiyama refers to an individual of Korean descent who apparently decided to enter Santa Anita in order to seek and identify Japanese Americans who were voicing "pro-Japanese" sentiments. Korea, of course, was a colony of Japan, and between 1910 and the end of World War II, Koreans in the United States used a variety of tactics to protest and resist this state of affairs; see Sucheng Chan, *Asian Americans: An Interpretive History* (Boston: Twayne Publishers, 1991), 98–99.

Robert Spencer, mentioned in the same letter, was a graduate student in the Department of Anthropology at the University of California at Berkeley who was also recruited to serve as a fieldworker for the JERS project. He was assigned to the WRA Gila River camp in south-central Arizona. See "Robert Spencer," in *Japanese American World War II Evacuation Oral History Project*, Part 3: *Analysts*, 175–327.

AN ETHNOGRAPHER OF MASS INCARCERATION

Tsuchiyama's thoughts and activities here are largely reconstructed via her letters to Professor Robert Lowie, JERS file W 1.29.

Although no full-length assessment of the BSR has been published to date, a brief account that is relatively accessible can be found in an appendix in Alexander H. Leighton, *The Governing of Men: General Principles and Recommendations Based on Experience at a Japanese Relocation Camp* (Princeton: Princeton University Press, 1945), 371–97, authored by Leighton and his colleague, Edward H. Spicer. Although I have been able only to sample their contents, the BSR files at Cornell University—

held in the Japanese American Relocation Papers, Department of Manuscripts and Archives, Cornell University Library—include transcripts from BSR staff meetings that include full-length reports as well as comments offered by Tsuchiyama. Five cartons of BSR materials, apparently duplicate papers, are also held in the Bancroft Library under the call number 72/233. Other BSR materials are in JERS files J 1.15 and J 1.16.

As noted in an appendix to Alexander H. Leighton's book *The Governing of Men,* the Office of Indian Affairs director, John Collier, Sr., had set up the bureau in order to study and monitor Poston's "residents." On this basis, the BSR was supposed to advise Poston's administrators as to short- and long-term policy options. While this description is probably true enough, it may elide other dimensions of the bureau. See, for example, the section "The Research Project," in Lt. Alexander H. Leighton et al., "Assessing Public Opinion in a Dislocated Community," *Public Opinion Quarterly* 7 (1943): 656–57. The third goal of the BSR was to "train a research staff that would be capable of working in occupied areas and providing the government body there with the same kind of service it gave the [Poston] Center Administration."

Tsuchiyama's ties to the BSR are outlined in her correspondence; see, for example, Tsuchiyama to Lowie, August 26, 1942. Also see Leighton to Thomas, August 7 and 26, 1942, JERS W 1.21. For examples of the tensions that Tsuchiyama's dual employment status generated, see Thomas to Leighton, August 3, 1942, JERS W 1.21; and Morton Grodzins to Tamie Tsuchiyama, August 12, 1942, held in JERS file J 6.32. For data concerning her employment arrangements, see Tsuchiyama's letters to Dorothy S. Thomas, March 3 and May 21, 1943, in the same file. In the end, to the best of my knowledge, Tsuchiyama never gave any of her JERS field reports to Leighton, perhaps because Tsuchiyama resigned from the BSR before she completed any such work.

Because most of them pursued professional careers after World War II and many became distinguished scholars, basic biographies on many of the Euro-American scholars involved in the BSR are available in the *International Dictionary of Anthropologists.* Much work remains to be done on the Japanese American field-workers; what materials exist can be found largely in the article by Peter T. Suzuki, the anthology by Yuji Ichioka, and the oral histories of Arthur A. Hansen, cited above.

For Tsuchiyama's comments on Alexander H. Leighton, see her letters to Dorothy S. Thomas, November 2 and December 1, 1942. Leighton comments on Tsuchiyama in his field diary, cited above, deposited in the Department of Manuscripts and Archives, Cornell University Library, Ithaca, New York, and in his various letters of late 1942 and early 1943 to Thomas, which are held in JERS W 1.21.

LETTERS TO THOMAS AND LOWIE, 1942

The Shibutani-Najima-Shibutani outline was developed by a Japanese American graduate student of sociology, Tamotsu Shibutani, his wife Tomika Shibutani, and Haruo Najima, a colleague at the Tanforan, California, center, where they were incarcerated. Formally titled "Proposed Outline for the Study of Japanese Evacuees in the Assembly Centers" (JERS file W 1.20), the four-page outline presents a short rationale for field research, as well as a systematically conceptualized list of topics to cover. Apparently this was done in an effort to ensure that field research was comprehensive, holistic, and consistent across the different research sites.

Toward the end of her letter of December 1, 1942, Tsuchiyama is undoubtedly referring to Richard S. Nishimoto.

In her letter of December 15, 1942, Tsuchiyama refers to Morton Grodzins, who was a graduate student in political science at the University of California at Berkeley. Grodzins served as Dorothy Thomas's administrative assistant for the JERS project. He also carried out research for Thomas and the JERS fieldworkers in terms of the WRA and federal bureaucracies in Washington, D.C., among other places.

Chapter 4. Research Setting

Information on the JERS project is based on a number of informative accounts, especially Yuji Ichioka's anthology *Views from Within*. Ichioka's introduction and the chapter by S. Frank Miyamoto offer invaluable analyses of the study and its director.

As with the BSR, the director's own account of JERS remains useful at a basic chronological level, although it is also uncritical and unreflexive; see Thomas and Nishimoto, *The Spoilage*.

In addition to her two JERS studies, *The Spoilage* (Berkeley: University of California Press, 1946) and *The Salvage* (Berkeley: University of California Press, 1952), Dorothy S. Thomas's statements about her wartime research include her "Experiences in Interdisciplinary Research," *American Sociological Review* 17 (1952): 663–69. Thomas's perspectives and practices between 1942 and 1945 are best revealed through an analysis of her correspondence with JERS fieldworkers, much of which is included in the JERS collection, her memos about the study to fieldworkers (e.g., "Memorandum to Field Collaborators," August 27, 1942, JERS file W 1.20), and transcriptions of the JERS staff meetings (e.g., "Chicago Staff Meetings," December 2, 1943, JERS file W 1.10).

Information on pre–World War II team research projects and methodologies can be found in Margaret Barron Luszki, *Interdisciplinary Team Research: Methods and Problems* (Washington, D.C.: National Training Laboratories, 1958). Judith Fiedler,

Field Research: A Manual for Logistics and Management of Scientific Studies in Natural Settings (San Francisco: Jossey-Bass, 1978) indicates that other scholars have continued to work with research methods pioneered by Dorothy Thomas.

Not a great deal of biographical information is available on Dorothy Thomas. Two useful publications in this regard are by Steven O. Murray: "W. I. Thomas, Behavioral Ethnologist," *Journal of the History of the Behavioral Sciences* 24 (1988): 381–91; and "Resistance to Sociology at Berkeley," *Journal of the History of Sociology* 2 (1980): 61–84. Stephen O. Murray published an interesting account of Thomas's attempts to block the publications and professional career of Morton Grodzins, her former JERS administrative assistant; see his article "The Rights of Research Assistants and the Rhetoric of Political Suppression: Morton Grodzins and the University of California Japanese-American Evacuation and Resettlement Study," *Journal of the History of the Behavioral Sciences* 27 (1991): 130–56.

Also controversy emerged with the publication of R. S. Smith's study "Giving Credit Where Credit Is Due: Dorothy Swaine Thomas and the 'Thomas Theorem,'" *American Sociologist* 26 (1995): 9–28. Smith argues that only sexism can account for citations that credited only one of the famous academic couple. Robert Merton's trenchant rejoinder, however, in a subsequent issue of the journal casts doubt on the validity of Smith's thesis.

The most comprehensive statement, designed to address evolving dimensions of ethics in the field of anthropology, is "Code of Ethics of the American Anthropological Association," *Anthropology Newsletter* 39 (Sept. 1988): 19–20. See also the accompanying bibliography under "VIII. Other Relevant Codes of Ethics," p. 20.

In regard to Tsuchiyama's plans for fieldwork early on, see Tsuchiyama to Thomas, September 17 and November 2, 1942. Tsuchiyama notes that she intended to follow "Shibutani's outline" in carrying out her field research, probably referring to the previously cited document "Proposed Outline for the Study of Japanese Evacuees in Assembly Centers" (JERS file W 1.20).

It is very possible, as Tsuchiyama claims, that she met both Dr. Miles Cary and Nell Findley in Hawaii, although I could find no corroborating evidence. The former ran the educational program at Poston, and the latter, the only woman on the staff, was Poston's chief of community services; see Paul Bailey, *City in the Sun: The Japanese Concentration Camp at Poston, Arizona* (Los Angeles: Westernlore Press, 1971), 81, 95.

POSTON

I've cited a number of secondary sources pertinent to Poston in my edited volume, *Inside an American Concentration Camp*, liii nn. 30, 35. For publications generated under the auspices of the BSR and the WRA, interested readers can consult Edward H. Spicer et al., *Impounded People: Japanese Americans in the Relocation Centers* (Tucson:

University of Arizona Press, 1969), appendixes I, II, 301–31. Another useful resource is Jean Nudd, "Japanese Internment Camps in Arizona: Sources for Original Documents," in *Casa Grande Valley Histories* (Casa Grande, Ariz.: Casa Grande Valley Historical Society, 1992).

The wonderful pictures that appear herein are the work of an amateur Issei artist. According to Eddy Masato Kurushima, his nephew, the late Jitsuo Kurushima was born in Hiroshima prefecture in 1905 and came to the United States in 1920. Mr. Kurushima studied in the United States, completing elementary and high school and a year of college at the University of Southern California. As a first-generation Japanese immigrant, however, ineligible by law for naturalization, Kurushima was unable to pursue his chosen career of architecture. Before the war, he worked in Los Angeles as a printer for the Japanese American newspaper *Nichi Bei*.

Incarcerated at Poston along with his wife and three children, Kurushima was able to indulge his passion for art. His wife told me that he drew constantly, even on napkins in the mess hall, and Eddy Kurushima reports that his uncle made use of his considerable artistic talents while working for Poston's Educational Department.

Kurushima's artwork reproduced here was originally published in a special issue of the Issei poetry magazine, the *Poston Bungei*. Edited by Issei poet Aikira Togawa, the *Bungei*, which ran from February 1943 to September 1945, was reproduced via an offset printing process; thus Kurushima's brush strokes appear with some fidelity. I would like to thank Professor Yuji Ichioka, who contacted Kibei-Nisei printer Roy Matsumura, who offered his expert comments in this regard.

The Poston strike has received a good deal of attention. Interested readers can find the entry "Poston Strike" and an accompanying bibliography in *Japanese American History*, 286. After the Poston strike had been resolved, camp director Wade Head publicly emphasized that it was in everyone's broader interests to keep things calm, because the FBI agents could interrogate and remove suspicious persons at any time they pleased.

TSUCHIYAMA AS A FIELDWORKER FOR JERS

In addition to Sanjek's publications on fieldwork and ethnography cited above, qualitative sociologists have also offered interesting analyses of this method; see, for example, John Lofland, "Analytic Ethnography: Features, Failings, and Futures," *Journal of Contemporary Ethnography* 24 (1995): 30–67; and Jack Katz, "Ethnography's Warrants," *Sociological Methods and Research* 25 (1997): 391–423. The recent anthology *Fieldwork in Developing Countries*, ed. Stephen Devereux and John Hoddinott (Boulder, Colo.: Lynne Rienner Publishers, 1993), is also useful in terms of a step-by-step account of how anthropologists conceptualize and carry out research; see especially Part 1, "Overview: Fieldwork from Start to Finish."

My observations concerning Tsuchiyama's fieldwork in this section are based largely on an analysis of her letters and reports compared to available literature on the same or similar topics. Biographical information on Nishimoto is available in *Inside an American Concentration Camp.*

Good examples of Tsuchiyama's displaced hostility include statements about "Japs" made in two letters: Tsuchiyama to Thomas, July 12, 1943, and January 24, 1945. To be fair, I note that in another letter reprinted here Tsuchiyama states that members of Poston's Euro-American staff, who failed to understand the total frustration and alienation that many among the Issei generation harbored, were fools. For background on Nisei educational training in Hawaii, which also helps to account for Tsuchiyama's "Americanized" response to Poston, interested readers should consult Eileen H. Tamura, *Americanization, Acculturation, and Ethnic Identity: The Nisei Generation in Hawaii* (Chicago: University of Illinois Press, 1994), esp. chapters 3 and 4.

My interpretation—that the sedimentation of "Old World" value orientations as well as the Issei's nostalgia toward Meiji- and Taishō-era Japan must be understood in the larger context of anti-Asian/anti-Japanese racism on the U.S. mainland—is based on UCLA professor Yuji Ichioka's research, e.g., *The Issei: The World of the First Generation Japanese Immigrants, 1885–1924* (New York: Free Press, 1988), esp. 244–54.

Stress, as generated by fieldwork settings and experience, has been the subject of much inquiry in anthropology. For example, see the very pertinent discussion offered by Rosalie H. Wax in her book *Doing Fieldwork: Warnings and Advice* (Chicago: University of Chicago Press, 1971), 59–174. Wax's article-length meditations on stress in fieldwork, from which she drew for her 1971 book, go back to the 1950s and are based on her stressful fieldwork done in the WRA camp at Tule Lake. It is imperative, however, also to consult Violet Kazue de Cristoforo's article "J'Accuse," *Rikka* 13 (1992): 16–30, for a fascinating and disturbing account of a former Tulean's experiences as an anthropological "informant/subject." In retrospect, it is clear that Tsuchiyama, like Wax, tried to carry out fieldwork in an anomalous and occasionally dangerous research setting; see Raymond M. Lee, *Dangerous Fieldwork* (Thousand Oaks, Calif.: Sage, 1995).

Texts that discuss the more typical and mundane strains faced by anthropologists can be found in the anthology *Stress and Response in Fieldwork*, ed. Frances Henry and Satish Saberwal (New York: Holt, Rinehart and Winston, 1969). More recently, Nancy Howell has written a comprehensive monograph on the subject: *Surviving Fieldwork: A Report of the Advisory Panel on Health and Safety in Fieldwork,*

American Anthropological Association, American Anthropological Association, special publication series, no. 26 (Washington, D.C., 1990).

It has really been only since the 1970s that accounts have been published that explicitly treat the dynamics of gender in field research. Three examples of this literature are *Women in the Field: Anthropological Experiences*, ed. Peggy Golde (Chicago: Aldine, 1970); Carol A. B. Warren, *Gender Issues in Field Research* (Newbury Park, Calif.: Sage, 1988); and the recent anthology *Gendered Fields: Women, Men and Ethnography*, ed. Diane Bell, Pat Caplan, and Wazir Jahan Karim (New York: Routledge, 1993).

Finally, gender dynamics in Tsuchiyama's field situation may need special consideration in terms of the "involuntary" setting that Poston represented and also because researchers in WRA camps were sometimes regarded as *inu*, or spies. Apropos of this, see Raymond M. Lee, *Dangerous Fieldwork* (Thousand Oaks, Calif.: Sage, 1995), 1–14, 53–63.

RENEWING AN ACQUAINTANCE: TIES TO NISHIMOTO

Information on Nishimoto is drawn, in part, from *Inside an American Concentration Camp*, as well as from Tsuchiyama's correspondence.

LETTERS FROM THE FIELD, JANUARY–MARCH 1943

Throughout Tsuchiyama's correspondence, "X" was the code name that she utilized to disguise the identity of her Issei assistant, Richard S. Nishimoto. See my discussion of this point in *Inside an American Concentration Camp*, xlv.

Beginning with her letter of January 11, 1943, Tsuchiyama uses acronyms in this set of letters, including I.A.B. (Issei Advisory Board), C.E.C. (Central Executive Committee), L.R.B. (Labor Relations Board), T.C.C. (Temporary Community Council), and O.W.I. (Office of War Information). I offer a brief discussion and a diagram of the bodies of "self-government" in *Inside an American Concentration Camp*, xxxvii–xl. I have since come to realize, however, that Poston's "city council" was actually the body representing all three units of the camp.

A biographical entry on Saburo Kido is available in *Japanese American History*, 201–2. His beating is generally regarded as a sign that the larger Japanese American community did not accept the leadership of the Japanese American Citizens League (JACL).

The Japanese term *keto* (literally, "hairy barbarian") is an insulting term, sometimes used to refer to Caucasians.

Chapter 5. Revelation

Tsuchiyama's field reports are as follows: (1) "Chronological Account of the Poston Strike" (JERS file J 6.24); (2) "The Visit of the Spanish Consul" (JERS file J 6.28); (3) "Aftermath of the Strike" (JERS file J 6.18); (4) "The Beating of Saburo Kido" (JERS file J 6.19); (5) "History of the Central Executive Committee" (JERS file J 6.20); and (6) "Notes on Selective Service Registration" (JERS file J 6.23). A seventh "article," listed under Tsuchiyama's name and pertaining to the impact of Japanese-language radio broadcasts on Poston's residents, turns out to be an excerpt from her correspondence with Dorothy Thomas. Her massive "Sociological Journal," which is divided into twelve folders, can be found in JERS files J 6.25A–J 6.25L.

References to Richard S. Nishimoto can be found in Tsuchiyama's "Chronological Account of the Poston Strike," 4–5, 9–10, 14–15, 19–20, and 27.

TSUCHIYAMA'S FIELD METHODOLOGY

For evidence supporting the third claim about an informal political structure in Poston, see the Appendix, Tsuchiyama's "Visit of the Spanish Consul." In contrast, it is informative to reexamine the conclusions advanced by Tsuchiyama's former colleague and contemporary, BSR director Dr. Alexander H. Leighton, M.D. His book *The Governing of Men* focuses largely on the early days of Poston up through the November strike. Leighton identifies a number of the administration's key policies and aims:

> 4. It was thought to be important to show that the United States could carry out a program of evacuation and relocation in a democratic manner that would provide a useful basis for future responsibilities of a similar nature and the greatest possible contrast to population shifts in Axis countries.
>
> 5. To accomplish these policies, it seemed that adequate incentives would have to be created, that the Japanese must be brought to feel some security, some opportunity, and some acceptance as fellow Americans and friendly aliens. A program of self-government was envisaged that would develop gradually and enable the Project Administration to withdraw for the most part. (*The Governing of Men*, 242)

While acknowledging that some of the envisioned aims had failed, Leighton assigned full credit for the transition from a state of (what he called) "social disorganization" to a state of enlightened "self-management" to Euro-American bureaucrats. Leighton concluded, "In the sphere of developing self-government . . . among the evacuees, *the Administration may be said to have achieved its aims*" (*The Governing of Men*, 243, my emphasis). A number of his JERS contemporaries reported that, during the 1940s, Leighton was basically an outsider in terms of the Japanese

American community at Poston; see, for example, Tsuchiyama to Thomas, November 2, 1942. Nor was Leighton able to get access to JERS field reports or other JERS materials before he wrote his classic study. This case, then, suggests that Euro-American ethnographers were denied access to data concerning sensitive topics such as Issei influence over informal political dynamics in the WRA camps.

This is not to suggest that all anthropological analysis carried out in Poston was necessarily faulty. Compare, for example, Leighton's interpretations of the Poston strike to those advanced in Edward H. Spicer et al., *Impounded People: Japanese Americans in the Relocation Centers* (Tucson: University of Arizona Press, 1969), 129–35. Given that they had almost twenty-five years to think their data over, perhaps it is not surprising that the latter were very much more on target, although, in terms of Issei involvement in Poston's politics, it is possible that they overemphasized the role and significance of the Issei Advisory Board. By contrast, Tsuchiyama's assertion was that the "real" Issei leaders in Poston were not members of the board.

NISHIMOTO IS HIRED AS TSUCHIYAMA'S ASSISTANT

Before the war, Robert Spencer, like Tsuchiyama, was a graduate student in the Department of Anthropology at the University of California at Berkeley. Dorothy Thomas had hired Spencer to be a JERS fieldworker at the Gila River Relocation Center, a WRA camp also in Arizona. An interesting, if occasionally contemptible, oral history interview with Spencer, concerning his background, philosophy, and ethnographic fieldwork at Gila, has recently been published by the historian Arthur Hansen; see "Robert Spencer," in *Japanese American World War II Evacuation Oral History Project*, 175–327.

Information on Nishimoto is drawn in part from *Inside an American Concentration Camp*.

In a letter from Tsuchiyama to Thomas dated March 26, 1943, Tsuchiyama noted, "I've known X for about eight years in San Francisco and Los Angeles, and his wife has known my sister for a much longer time. They think of me as 'Hisako's kid sister.'" Also see Thomas to Tsuchiyama, February 4, 1943. In the same correspondence, Thomas wrote, "I am developing a great respect for X." Although he was quite open about his JERS affiliation after the war, while he was in Poston Nishimoto insisted on anonymity. In part, he wanted to keep the confidence he had won through his political stands and action; but at the same time, Nishimoto was well aware that popular opinions concerning his JERS research contributions might be negative.

LETTERS FROM THE FIELD, APRIL—OCTOBER 1943

The *Pacific Citizen* was, and still is, the official organ of the JACL.

As explained in the text, Gila was the Gila River Relocation Center, which was the other major WRA camp located in southern Arizona.

Tsuchiyama's letter of September 19, 1943, to Morton Grozdins is of interest because it illustrates the kind of research that he carried out for Dorothy Thomas and the JERS fieldworkers in Washington, D.C.

"A.P." is the acronym for "appointed personnel," the term often used by Japanese Americans to designate Euro-American staff members of the WRA (and, in Poston, the staff of the Office of Indian Affairs).

John Embree was a distinguished anthropologist who had carried out one of the first "community studies" in Japan before the war. As a staff member of the WRA, Embree was based in Washington, D.C., and served as the first head of the Community Analysis Section, although Edward H. Spicer was subsequently appointed to that position.

Chapter 6. Removal

The information in this section is drawn largely from Tsuchiyama's correspondence; see, for example, Tsuchiyama to Thomas, October 28, 1943. Her family, it might be noted, knew little about what was happening at the time.

Chicago was the site of a team of JERS researchers with whom Tsuchiyama, in fact, did have contact. S. (Shotaro) Frank Miyamoto, Tamotsu (Tom) Shibutani, and Charles (Charlie) Kikuchi, among others, were there on assignment, gathering data for the JERS project on "The Salvage," or those Japanese Americans who had left camp as early as 1943 to resettle in the Midwest and back east. According to a letter (Thomas to Nishimoto, January 8, 1944), Tsuchiyama did not get along very well with the JERS staff members in Chicago, although inquiries of surviving JERS staff members revealed that more than fifty years later no one could remember any specifics.

Chapter 7. Rejection

Points raised in this section are based primarily on Thomas's correspondence with Tsuchiyama. Despite many efforts to find family, friends, or colleagues who might be able to verify or expand on what happened, only one Euro-American researcher, who preferred to remain anonymous, would or could comment. Although he could not remember the specifics, he wrote, "I had the feeling that she resigned because she was unhappy about what she was doing." Tsuchiyama, who was a private person anyway, never talked about JERS after she quit. None of her SCAP colleagues whom I interviewed remembered her discussing Thomas or JERS; nor does her sister, Hisako.

LETTERS FROM THE FIELD, JULY—AUGUST 1944

Most of Dorothy Thomas's replies to these letters were included in Tsuchiyama's correspondence file and can be found in JERS file J 6.32. I am uncertain as to whether Tsuchiyama and Nishimoto were ever more than friends. Tsuchiyama certainly denied this. What is more, Edward H. Spicer's fieldnotes document the fact that Tsuchiyama was fully aware of all the potential problems that could result from having more than a professional relationship with Nishimoto. See Spicer Papers, MS 42, box 12, January 2, 1942, Special Collections, University of Arizona Library.

Chapter 8. Restoration

I would like to acknowledge helpful interviews with Mrs. Roberts and former WAC Miwako Yanomoto in regard to this period of Tsuchiyama's career. I have also cited and cross-referenced data listed in Tsuchiyama's military record and official discharge papers, as well as the "Employment" and "Military Training" sections of her 1952 "Voice of America" job application.

For background about Nisei women's participation in the WAC, see the entry by Stacey Hirose, "WACs," in *Japanese American History*, 345. Additional sources from which I have drawn to cross-check my data include *The Pacific War and Peace: Americans of Japanese Ancestry in Military Intelligence Service, 1941 to 1952*, ed. Clifford Uyeda and Barry Saiki (San Francisco: National Japanese American Historical Society, 1991); and *MIS in the War against Japan*, ed. Stanley L. Falk and Warren M. Tsuneishi (Washington, D.C.: Japanese American Veterans Association, 1995).

BACK TO THE FIELD

The full citation of the publication discussed in this section is Arthur Raper et al., *The Japanese Village in Transition*, General Headquarters, Supreme Commander for the Allied Powers, Natural Resources Section, Report No. 136 (Tokyo, 1950). The book's preface is the basic source for the data about this project. I was also able to interview three staff members—Professors Herbert Passin, David Sills, and John Bennett—by phone in order to discuss the data presented here. Incidentally, a fascinating study remains to be done in regard to WRA and BSR researchers, Euro-American and Japanese American alike, who went to Japan during the postwar period of occupation in order to carry out research for the U.S. government. For one example, see Appendix D, "The Development of the Research Methods of the Foreign Morale Analysis Division," in Alexander H. Leighton, *Human Relations in a Changing World* (New York: E. P. Dutton and Co., 1949), 299.

According to Hisako Tsuchiyama Roberts, a second study was in preparation by the SCAP team of field researchers, including Tsuchiyama, but this was ordered to be destroyed when the U.S. Armed Forces left occupied Japan. Professor Herbert Passin, who was initially Tsuchiyama's immediate supervisor, disagrees but does remember that Tsuchiyama was very active in a similar but smaller survey that focused on the impact of reforms on Japanese fishing communities. Tsuchiyama apparently devoted a great deal of her spare time to that project, but as far as I can determine, no publication ever resulted from this research.

THE ORIENTAL LIBRARY

Information on Tsuchiyama's career as a professional librarian is based on interviews with Hisako Tsuchiyama Roberts. Without going into detail, I find it very significant that Tsuchiyama ended her academic career as a librarian for the Oriental collection at the University of Texas. This was apparently a fairly common career trajectory for women with "higher education" and even graduate degrees, vis-à-vis sexism in the academy, before the war and for decades after.

THE FINAL YEARS

This information is also based primarily on interviews with Hisako Tsuchiyama Roberts.

Chapter 9. Redux

An oft-cited definition of "colonialism," from which I have drawn here, is presented in Michael Burawoy, "Race, Class, and Colonialism," *Social and Economic Studies* 24 (1974): 546: "the conquest and administration by a metropolitan country of a geographically separated territory in order to utilize available resources . . . for the creation of surplus which is repatriated to the metropolis." The application of this definition to social science research is a bit of a stretch, but as I argue herein, it is of heuristic value—that is, it elucidates many elements of Dorothy Thomas's relationship with the Japanese American staff members of JERS, including Tsuchiyama.

In discussing Pierre Bourdieu's concept of "colonial science," as well as his epistemological views of knowledge and science, I have drawn from the two books mentioned above, along with the following sources: "The Specificity of the Scientific Field and the Social Conditions of the Progress of Reason," *Social Science Information* 14 (December 1975): 19–47; "The Scholastic Point of View," *Cultural Anthropology* 5 (1990): 380–91; "Rethinking the State: Genesis and Structure of the Bureaucracy" *Sociological Theory* 12 (1994): 1–18; and his seminal essay, "Les Conditions sociales de la production sociologique: Sociologie coloniale et décolonisation de la sociologie," in *Le Mal de voir*, Cahiers Jussieu 2 (Paris: Union Générale d'Editions, 1976), 416–27. An English-language version of this piece appears in Bourdieu, *Sociology in Question* (Thousand Oaks, Calif.: Sage, 1993), 49–53.

Useful guides to Bourdieu's overall corpus are his own books, including *An Invitation to Reflexive Sociology* (Chicago: University of Chicago Press, 1992) and *Sociology in Question* (Thousand Oaks, Calif.: Sage, 1993); *An Introduction to the Work of Pierre Bourdieu: The Practice of Theory*, ed. Richard Harker, Cheleen Mahar, and Chris Wilkes (New York: Saint Martin's Press, 1990); and Ruben Urbizagastegui, *Pierre Bourdieu: Bibliographic Database* (Pittsburgh: University of Pittsburgh, 1991). Although in my view some of his interpretations exhibit a kind of "bad faith," a useful critique of Bourdieu's work is offered by UCLA sociologist Jeffrey C. Alexander in his recent book, *Fin de Siècle Social Theory: Relativism, Reduction, and the Problem of Reason* (London: Verso, 1995), 128–94. In an appendix, "A Note on Intellectual Chronology," in the same book, Alexander is able to generate a fascinating account of the French anthropologist-turned-sociologist by applying a Bourdieuian-style analysis to Bourdieu.

It is interesting that another famous sociologist, Robert E. Park, along with his colleagues at the University of Chicago, utilized students of Asian ancestry as informants and researchers to study the "Oriental problem" in the United States; see Henry Yu, "The 'Oriental Problem' in America, 1920–1960: Linking the Identities of Chinese American and Japanese American Intellectuals," in *Claiming America: Constructing Chinese American Identities during the Exclusion Era*, ed. K. Scott Wong and Sucheng Chan (Philadelphia: Temple University Press, 1998). According to Yu, these students were very grateful to Park et al. insofar as concepts like "the race relations cycle" and "the marginal man" enabled them to understand their situation in America in more depth.

JERS folder W 1.1.0 contains three key documents that together specify Tsuchiyama's research focus: her three-page statement "Problems for Future Research at Poston"; a transcription of her report to the JERS "Chicago Staff Meeting," December 2, 1943; and especially a six-page document, "Outline for a Preliminary Report on the Colorado River War Relocation Project."

Dorothy Thomas's proprietary interest in JERS research and her attempts to block the publications of junior colleagues are given thoughtful treatment in Stephen O. Murray's case study of Morton Grodzins, "The Rights of Research Assistants and the Rhetoric of Political Suppression."

For a contemporary case of a then-junior African (Ugandan) anthropologist who was pressured to surrender her fieldnotes by Western anthropological colleagues—who were also working in Uganda and who clearly wanted to appropriate her research—see Christine Obbo, "Adventures with Fieldnotes," in *Fieldnotes: The Makings of Anthropology*, ed. Roger Sanjek (Ithaca, N.Y.: Cornell University Press, 1990), esp. 290–92, 295–98.

Publications that document the trials of women of color in the academy include *Perspectives on Minority Women in Higher Education*, ed. Lynne Brodie Welch (New York: Praeger, 1992). The essay "Hispanic Women in the U.S. Academic Context," by Sarah Nieves-Squires, is of special interest because of its attention to intragroup diversity as well as cultural and stylistic differences that are also gendered.

A comprehensive anthology that foregrounds the perspectives of "the least institutionally empowered in academe: African American women working as untenured assistant professors, lower-echelon administrators, and artist-in-residence instructors" is *Spirit, Space and Survival: African American Women in (White) Academe*, ed. Joy James and Ruth Farmer (New York: Routledge, 1993). The book's appendix presents an extensive, multidisciplinary bibliography that contains many intriguing citations.

INDEX

ABOUT THE AUTHOR

Lane Ryo Hirabayashi is a professor in the Department of Ethnic Studies and a member of the graduate faculty of the Department of Anthropology at the University of Colorado, Boulder. Among other books, he has published *Inside an American Concentration Camp: Japanese American Resistance at Poston, Arizona* (University of Arizona Press, 1995), which is a companion volume to the present study. Recently Hirabayashi was awarded a major grant from the Civil Liberties Public Education Fund for a study of Japanese American resettlement in Colorado in 1946. In 1998, Hirabayashi joined the International Nikkei Research Project as a participant researcher. Coordinated by the Japanese American National Museum in Los Angeles, this three-year collaborative study, which will involve scholars of many nationalities, will focus on the evolution of Nikkei (overseas Japanese) communities in the Americas.